MEDIEVAL & ENGLISH & THEATRE

VOLUME FORTY-FIVE (2023)

MEDIEVAL & ENGLISH & THEATRE

VOLUME FORTY-FIVE (2023)

Executive Editor: Meg Twycross
General Editors: Sarah Carpenter, Elisabeth Dutton, & Gordon Kipling

D. S. BREWER

Medieval English Theatre is an international refereed journal publishing articles on medieval and early Tudor theatre and pageantry in all its aspects (not confined to England), together with articles and records of modern survivals or equivalents. Most issues are illustrated. Contributions to be considered for future volumes are welcomed: see end of this volume and website for further information:
<www.medievalenglishtheatre.co.uk>

This volume contains material and terminology
that some readers may find distressing

© *Medieval English Theatre* and contributors (2024)

All Rights Reserved. Except as permitted under current legislation, no part of this work may be photocopied, stored in a retrieval system, published, performed in public, adapted, broadcast, transmitted, recorded or reproduced in any form or by any means, without the prior permission of the copyright owner

First published 2024
D. S. Brewer, Cambridge

ISBN 978-1-84384-719-9
ISSN 0143-3784

D. S. Brewer is an imprint of Boydell & Brewer Ltd
PO Box 9, Woodbridge, Suffolk IP12 3DF, UK
and of Boydell & Brewer Inc.
668 Mt Hope Avenue, Rochester, NY 14620–2731
website: www.boydellandbrewer.com

A catalogue record for this title is available from the British Library

The publisher has no responsibility for the continued existence or accuracy of URLs for external or third-party internet websites referred to in this book, and does not guarantee that any content on such websites is, or will remain, accurate or appropriate

MEDIEVAL & ENGLISH & THEATRE

VOLUME FORTY-FIVE (2023)

CONTENTS

Illustrations	vi
Notes on Cover Image and Online Links	viii
Common Abbreviations	ix
Editorial	1

Meg Twycross
    John Blanke's Hat and its Contexts, Part 1: Turbans and
    Islamic Dress at the Court of Henry VIII   3

Sadegh Attari
    Disjointed Unison: Bodily Porousness and Subversion in
    the Croxton *Play of the Sacrament*   68

Mark Chambers
    The Disabled Body *as* Performance: 'Disabled'
    Performers in the Records of Early English Drama   102

Janet Cowen
    From Huy to Primrose Hill: An Early Twentieth-Century
    English Re-Playing of a Fifteenth-Century Liégeois
    Nativity Play   126

Aurélie Blanc
    'More medieval morality play than 21st century': Spectacle
    and its Meaning at the Coronation of King Charles III   153

Reports of Productions

Sarah Carpenter
    The Seven Sages of Scotland: The Scottish Storytelling
    Centre, Edinburgh, Saturday 22 July 2023   185

Editorial Board	194
Submission of Articles	195

ILLUSTRATIONS

Meg Twycross: 'John Blanke's Hat'.

Fig. 1 The second row of trumpeters sounding *A l'hostel*. London: College of Arms MS Westminster Tournament Roll, mb 28, detail. — 6

Fig. 2 Images of 'John Blanke'. (a) Westminster Tournament Roll mb 4 detail (some paint loss); (b) Westminster Tournament Roll mb 28 detail. — 8

Fig. 3 Charlemagne negotiates with the African king Aygolant; Spanish Saracen brings gifts to Charlemagne. Paris: Bibiothèque nationale de France MS français 2813 (*Grandes Chroniques de France*, 1375–1380) fols 115v and 121r. — 14

Fig. 4 The Siege of Constantinople in 1453 by Mehmed II (detail). BNF MS français 9087 ('Guidebooks to the Holy Land' translated Jean Mielot ?1460s) fol. 207v. — 14

Fig. 5 A battle, probably between Sancho Abarca and the Moors at Pamplona. British Library Additional MS 12531, the Genealogy of the Kings of Portugal (1530–1534) fol. 4r, bas de page. — 15

Fig. 6 Two views of a (Mameluke?) Turban. London: BL Cotton MS Julius E IV/3 (The Beauchamp Pageant), fol. 10v, details. — 23

Fig. 7 Mummers in Turkish Costume from the *Freydal* of the Emperor Maximilian I. Vienna: Kunsthistorisches Museum, Kunstkammer inv. No. 5073 fol. 172. — 26

Fig. 8 The King of Tunis in Barbary. Biblioteca Nacional de España RES/285 fol. 15r; *Códice de trajes* ('Book of Costumes'), copy after Christoph von Sternsee (c.1548–1549). — 29

Fig. 9 Turbans in Turkish Mummery, *Freydal*. Vienna: Kunsthistorisches Museum, Kunstkammer inv. No. 5073 fol. 172, detail. — 37

Fig. 10 Janissary; detail from Hans Weigel *Habitus Praecipuorum Populorum* (1577) CXCIII. — 39

ILLUSTRATIONS

Fig. 11	'This is how the Moorish girl looks in her house.' Nuremberg: Germanische Nationalmuseum Hs 22474; Christoph Weiditz *Trachtenbuch*, page 103.	42
Fig. 12	'This is how the Moriscos dance with each other, snapping their fingers as they go.' Nuremberg: Germanisches Nationalmuseum Hs 22474; Christoph Weiditz *Trachtenbuch* page 107, detail.	43
Fig. 13	Egyptian Women: (a) François Desprez *Recueil de la diversité des habits* (1562); (b) Hans Weigel *Habitus præcipuorum populorum* (1577); (c) Braun and Hogenberg *Théâtre des Cités du Monde* (1572).	45
Fig. 14	Heraldic Saracens and *Morians*. British Library MS Harley 2076 fols 144r, 62r, 146v; Additional MS 45132 fols 312v, 47r, details.	52–54
Fig. 15	*Le Roy desarmey*: Henry surrounded by attendants. London: College of Arms MS Westminster Tournament Roll, 1511, membrane 35, detail.	57
Fig. 16	The Earls in *The Procession of Parliament 1512*: Trinity College, Cambridge, shelfmark O.3.59, recto part 10, detail.	58

Mark Chambers: 'The Disabled Body *as* Performance'.

| Fig. 1 | 'Death of the Virgin, funeral procession' (c.1340), detail. Lady Chapel, south clerestory window SIV, panel 4b, York Minster. | 109 |

Janet Cowen: 'From Huy to Primrose Hill'.

| Fig. 1 | The Adoration of the Kings. Original photograph of a scene from the performance of 1924. | 139 |
| Fig. 2 | The Virgin Mary with St Anne, Mary Jacobi, Mary Salome, and Joseph. Original photograph of a scene from the performance of 1924. | 139 |

Full credit details are provided in the captions to the images in the text. The editors, contributors, and publisher are grateful to all the institutions and persons for permission to reproduce the materials in which they hold copyright. Every effort has been made to trace the copyright holders; apologies are offered for any omission, and the publisher will be pleased to add any necessary acknowledgement in subsequent editions.

NOTES

COVER IMAGE

The image on the cover is from Madrid: Biblioteca Nacional de España MS RES/285, *Códice de Trajes* ('Costume Book') c.1548–1549, fol. 1r; online in the Biblioteca Digital Hispánica at <http://bdh-rd.bne.es/viewer.vm?id=0000052132&page=1> #5. It shows a rider in the *juego de cañas* ('game of canes'). He is dressed as a Moor, with turban, scimitar, and the characteristic heart-shaped shield with tassels, the *adarga*. He is riding with very short stirrups, like a jockey. The spear, which is made out of cane, nonetheless has a vicious-looking head.

The manuscript was commissioned by Christoph von Sternsee, captain of Charles V's German imperial guard. The artist is unknown, though Katherine Bond argues for the involvement, possibly as source material, of Jan Cornelisz Vermeyen, who was also in the Emperor's entourage.[1] He produced the cartoons for the tapestries of the 1535 Conquest of Tunis from personal experience.[2] In March 1539 he painted a *juego de cañas* played before the Emperor Charles V and Isabella of Portugal in Toledo: see <https://rkd.nl/en/explore/images/49155>. The jousting figures are reminiscent of this one. The painting is owned by the Stopford Sackville family, and is currently in Drayton Huse, Lowick, Northamptonshire. There is a preparatory sketch in the Louvre: see <https://rkd.nl/en/explore/images/53800>.

The image is reproduced under the conditions of Creative Commons CC-BY 4.[3]

ONLINE LINKS

An active list of all the URLs referred to in the current volume is posted on the METh website at <www.medievalenglishtheatre.co.uk/urlsvol45.html>. This enables the reader to view coloured images and link to video, besides giving access where possible to online texts and articles.

1 Katherine Bond 'Mapping Culture in the Habsburg Empire: Fashioning a Costume Book in the Court of Charles V' *Renaissance Quarterly* 71 (2018) 530–79.
2 See <https://canon.codart.nl/artwork/vermeyen-tapestry-cartoons/>. The cartoons (1546) are in the Kunsthistorisches Museum, Vienna.
3 See note on page <http://bdh-rd.bne.es/viewer.vm?id=0000052132&page=1>.

COMMON ABBREVIATIONS

DMLBS	*A Dictionary of Medieval Latin from British Sources* edited R.E. Latham, D.R. Howlett, and R.K. Ashdowne (British Academy: Oxford, 1975–2013): available online via subscribing libraries or from <http://logeion.uchicago.edu> (search by headword).
EETS	*Early English Text Society*: *OS* Ordinary Series, *ES* Extra Series, *SS* Supplementary Series.
HMC	Historical Manuscripts Commission.
Letters and Papers	*Letters and Papers, Foreign and Domestic, of the Reign of Henry VIII* edited J.S. Brewer, James Gairdner, and R.H. Brodie (London: HMSO by Longman, Green, Longman, Roberts & Green, 1862–1932); online at <https://www.british-history.ac.uk/search/series/letters-papers-hen8>.
MED	*Middle English Dictionary*: online version © 2001, the Regents of the University of Michigan <https://quod.lib.umich.edu/m/middle-english-dictionary/dictionary> available via subscribing libraries.
NRS	National Records of Scotland.
ODNB	*Oxford Dictionary of National Biography*: online version (Oxford UP, 2004–ongoing) at <https://www.oxforddnb.com/> available via subscribing libraries.
OED	*Oxford English Dictionary*: online version © 2019 Oxford University Press <www.oed.com> available via subscribing libraries.
PL	*Patrologia Latina* edited J.-P. Migne, 221 vols (Paris: Migne, then Garnier, 1844–1891). Online at <https://catalog.hathitrust.org/Record/007035196>.
REED	*Records of Early English Drama.*
STS	*Scottish Text Society.*
TNA	Kew: The National Archives.

EDITORIAL

The forty-fifth meeting of *Medieval English Theatre* in 2023 celebrated a return to in-person gathering, after three years of remote conference. The topic of the conference, 'Bodies and Embodiment', warmly hosted by Liv Robinson at the University of Birmingham, seemed particularly apt for the creative and collegial discussion that this enabled, both in and out of the seminar room.

In an opening panel on 'The Body as Signifier', Clare Egan investigated how early seventeenth-century performed libels could be enacted upon the body of the libelled. Two thoughtfully complementary papers followed, on the highly body-focused Croxton *Play of the Sacrament*. Mark Chambers set the view of the disabled body that the play enacts against the surviving record evidence for performers with disabilities, while Sadegh Attari explored how the liveness of performance might affect its dynamic of bodily wholeness and fragmentation. In a panel on 'Embodiment and Spectatorship', Gillian Redfern considered how Garcio's lively relationship with the spectators in the *Mactacio Abel* sets his physical and spiritual flexibility against the stasis of Cain. Then, exploring the so-called 'abstractness' of allegorical plays, Greg Walker demonstrated powerfully how the materiality of the actor's body is the primary agent of the audience's response. The afternoon was devoted to various kinds of 'Creating/Performing the Body' for audiences in the here and now. A video reading of the fifteenth-century *A Disputation Betwix the Body and the Worms*, devised by Meg Twycross, brought out its range of comic and deeply poignant views of mortality. Ivan Cutting reported on a local touring company's performance of medieval plays, not as a 'heritage' endeavour but by lively adaption of the texts to modern preoccupations. This was followed by Jeff Stoyanov's characteristically lively and engaging remote presentation on *Dux Moraud*, and some compelling and thought-provoking extracts from a video version of the fifteenth-century Huy play of *The Pilgrimage of the Life of Man*.

METh 45 opens on an important topic from the previous volume, before expanding on two themes from the conference. In volume 44, Nadia van Pelt explored in depth the documentary evidence for the career of John Blanke. Now Meg Twycross presents the first scholarly investigation of the image of the Tudor trumpeter in the *Westminster Tournament Roll*, questioning recent speculation and uncovering the surprising complexity of the visual representation of Islamic dress at the court of Henry VIII. Two articles arising from papers from the conference then discuss issues of bodily integrity, both beginning from the Croxton *Play of the Sacrament*. Sadegh Attari questions the assumed medieval privileging of the whole over the damaged body and, drawing on Deleuze's concept of *becoming*, proposes how, in performance, the play can move to obliterate the distinction between Jewish and Christian bodies. Mark Chambers considers how recent Disability Studies have taken the play as a model for medieval views of disabled and damaged bodies, before inviting us to consider the scanty but often contrasting evidence of lives lived, and performances informed, by actual disabled performers.

The three final contributions all reflect on twentieth and twenty-first-century performances of medieval material, and its adaptation for later times and sensibilities. Janet Cowen analyses the surviving documentary and visual evidence for a scarcely known 1924 church performance of a fifteenth-century Liégeois Nativity play, translated by the Imagist poet Richard Aldington, which reveals much about early twentieth-century views of medieval drama. It offers a fascinating comparison to the essay in *METh 40* on the recent investigation, translation and performance of the original play as part of the University of Fribourg's Medieval Convent Drama project. The 2023 coronation of King Charles III, the first coronation in England for seventy years, prompted Aurélie Blanc's analysis of the celebration, and reception, of a spectacular ceremony apparently balanced between asserting its medieval origins and demonstrating its modern relevance. The volume closes with a review of a storytelling performance based on a late fifteenth-century version of *The Seven Sages of Rome*, which addressed the problematic material of the original both through the original tales and in modern re-imaginings. This volume displays our continuing commitment both to the rigorous pursuit of evidence to understand early theatre in its own times, and to modern performance as a means of engaging us with that theatre in our own. Our 2024 *METh* meeting on *Dramatic Margins* will doubtless offer new opportunities for both.

JOHN BLANKE'S HAT AND ITS CONTEXTS
Part 1: Turbans and Islamic Dress at the Court of Henry VIII

Meg Twycross

Last year I had the pleasure of acting as editor for Nadia T. van Pelt's ground-breaking article on 'John Blanke's Wages'.[1] This acquainted me with the website of the Project devoted to John Blanke,[2] one of the trumpeters to Henry VII and Henry VIII, and the claims being made on his behalf as 'the first person of African descent in British history for whom we have both an image and a record'.[3] The existence of visual as well as documentary evidence for John Blanke has proved irresistible; it gives him a face, however fictitious, and one apparently sufficiently characterised for a modern viewer to relate to. A name and a handful of appearances in administrative accounts are not nearly so evocative – though his surname and the tag, 'the blacke Trumpet', that often accompanies it are intriguing.

To summarise what we know of him:[4] he first appears in November 1507 in Henry VII's Chamber Books as 'John Blanke the blacke Trumpet'. He is paid 20s a month, half the wages of the elite King's trumpeters, until January 1508/1509, when he appears to have been added to the strength on full wages of 40s a month. On 21 April that year, Henry VII dies, and John Blanke, with the other King's trumpets, is granted mourning livery for the funeral on 9 May 1509; then on 24 June 1509 comes the coronation of Henry VIII, for which nine named 'Kyngs Trompyttes', including John Blanke, are given scarlet livery. Some time around December 1509 he asks, apparently satisfactorily, for his salary arrangements to be regularised: he seems to have dropped back to 20s, possibly in the administrative confusion that always followed the death of one monarch and the accession of the next. On 12–13 February 1510/1511 he appears at the Great Tournament in Westminster, not by name, but as a presumably

---

1 Nadia T. van Pelt 'John Blanke's Wages: No Business Like Show Business' *Medieval English Theatre 44* (2022) 3–35.
2 <https://www.johnblanke.com>.
3 <https://www.johnblanke.com/about-copy.html>.
4 For a comprehensive account of the records, see Nadia van Pelt's article.

identifiable image in a commemorative heraldic painting.[5] On 14 January 1511/1512, not quite a year later, he is given a suit of clothes of violet cloth for his wedding[6] – and that is the last we hear of him. The next time the king's trumpeters are listed by name, in February 1513/1514, his is not among them. His time in the limelight of the English court could have lasted as little as four years, or as long as six.

So far, no one has found out what happened to him. He may have retired, he may have died, he may have moved on to another court, his new wife may have been a wealthy widow and set him up in business: we just don't know. Nor do we yet know where he came from, though there are several more-or-less plausible suggestions.[7] We really know very little about him. The invitation by Michael Ohajuru, the initiator and driving force behind the John Blanke Project, to 'imagine the black Tudor trumpeter' gave his contributors a lot of room to manoeuvre.[8]

It is his image that has captured the imagination. It is recorded, twice, in the College of Arms 'Great Tournament Roll of Westminster',[9] produced to commemorate the lavish tournament celebrating the birth on New Year's Day 1510/1511 of Henry VIII's son and heir. The roll records the second day of jousting: he and five other trumpeters (there were actually 15)[10] appear heralding the joust on membranes 3–4 and blowing

---

5   Sydney Anglo was the first to identify him: see 'The Court Festivals of Henry VII' in *The Bulletin of the John Rylands Library 43* (1960) 42, and *The Great Tournament Roll of Westminster* edited Sydney Anglo (Oxford: Clarendon Press, 1968) 85 note 2.

6   TNA E101/417/6 #50; image online at <http://aalt.law.uh.edu/AALT7/E101/E101no417/E101no417no6/IMG_0161.htm>. Calendared in *Letters and Papers 1* 505 #1025 (14 January 1512); online at <http://www.british-history.ac.uk/letters-papers-hen8/vol1/pp502-510>; also BL Egerton MS 3025 fol. 18r, which records their making, and that they were made of violet *velvet*.

7   See van Pelt 'John Blanke's Wages' 5 note 10 for a list.

8   'So, if John Blanke's image is not true to life, being only a caricature then just as artists and patrons were free to create their own ideas of The Black Magus and St Maurice so artists should be free to portray John Blanke as they might imagine him from his role and his record, while historians were invited to comment on John Blanke's presence and significance'; <https://www.johnblanke.com/about.html>. The subtitle to the Project is now 'Imagine the Black Tudor Trumpeter'; <https://www.johnblanke.com>.

9   London: College of Arms MS Great Tournament Roll of Westminster, mbb 4 and 28.

10 BL Additional MS 21481 (Household Book of Henry VIII for the years 1509–1518) fol. 53r: 'Item to the kinges xv Trumpettes vpon theyr warraunte signed for thir duetyes belongyng to their office of Auncientie appertaignyng for the Justes

A l'hostel to end the day's proceedings on membranes 27–8 (Fig.1). The images are slightly different but clearly drawn on the same model. One possible model might of course have been John himself, though this seems unlikely, for reasons that I will discuss in due course.

He looks rather wistful, insofar as one can look wistful when playing the trumpet: young and vulnerable. Possibly the artist based him on the image of the youngest of the Magi *qui fut moriane* ('who was a Moor')?[11] We could do with a thorough investigation of the sources of the image. The puffed-out cheeks and the fact that in the second version his face is slightly shorter than his colleagues', also make him look youthful.[12] The skin colour he has been given, especially again in the second version, draws attention by contrast to his eyes, though they are in fact constructed in the same way as those of his lighter-skinned colleagues. He is a very attractive and compelling figure onto whom to project one's emotions.

> holden at Westmynster the xij[th] day & xiij[th] day of ffebruary last passed: xxvj li xiij s iiij d'; transcription online at <https://www.tudorchamberbooks.org/edition/folio/LL_BL_AddMS_21481_f0053r.xml>, image online at <https://www.bl.uk/manuscripts/Viewer.aspx?ref=add_ms_21481_fs001r>. £26 3s 4d is 40 marks, which must be a flat fee: it is not easily divided between 15. Fifteen trumpet banners were ordered for the occasion; see BL Additional MS 18826 fol. 16, printed in Anglo *Great Tournament Roll* 137; and TNA E101/417/4 fol. 21r, warrant issued 12 February 1511 in *The Great Wardrobe Accounts of Henry VII and Henry VIII* edited Maria Hayward (London Record Society 47; Woodbridge: Boydell Press for the Society, 2012) 111.
>
> 11 Observation on Philip the Fair's visit to Cologne Cathedral, which holds the relics of the Three Kings; Antoine de Lalaing 'Relation du Premier Voyage de Philippe le Beau en Espagne en 1501' in *Collection des Voyages des Souverains des Pays-Bays: Tome Premier* edited M. Gachard (Bruxelles: F. Hayez, 1876) 332. He is identified as Balthazar. There has been a great deal of activity on the subject of the Black Magus, but Paul H.D. Kaplan *The Rise of the Black Magus in Western Art* (Ann Arbor MI: UMI Research Press, 1985) remains a good introduction to the subject.
>
> 12 The same is true of the trumpeters in the *Retabulo de Santa Auta* used as a cover image on the previous volume of *Medieval English Theatre*; 'Shawm band with sackbut player', detail showing the *Encontro de Santa Úrsula e do Princípe Conan* ('Meeting of Saint Ursula and Prince Conan'), from left panel interior of the *Retábulo de Santa Auta* ('Retable of St Auta') (1522–1525), Museu Nacional de Arte Antiga, Lisbon. For full image see <https://en.m.wikipedia.org/wiki/File:Bottega_di_lisbona,_retablo_di_sant%27auta,_1522-25,_matrimonio_di_s._orsola_e_il_principe_conan_3_musici.jpg>. The trumpeters here look down in concentration as they blow, and are more convincing as players: Blanke and his colleagues look as if they had paused in the act to consider something, or perhaps were just about to start.

FIG. 1: The second row of trumpeters sounding *A l'hostel*.
London: College of Arms MS Westminster Tournament Roll, mb 28 detail.
Reproduced by permission of the Kings, Heralds, and Pursuivants of Arms.

And it is very difficult, as I have discovered myself, not to talk about the image as 'him', as if it were alive, or at least a genuine representation of what he looked – and felt – like. We must keep reminding ourselves that this is a painting, and is subject to all the usual caveats about portraiture at the time; if, again, it was intended as a 'real' portrait. Any emotions we may feel are ours, not the painting's.[13]

Michael Ohajuru asked for imaginative responses to this image, both pictorial and verbal. The difference in the reactions to these responses has been interesting, in that they point up an apparent difference between the way we react to images and the way we react to words. No one could take the pictorial responses to Blanke as being anything but imaginary[14] – though Ohajuru, a trained art historian, had to sound a note of caution when some of his contributors started talking about the image in the Roll itself as if it were a photographic record. Verbal responses are much more difficult to keep under control, especially when they come up with snippets of documentary evidence. All too quickly speculation can harden into historical 'fact'.

John Blanke's 'Turban'

One such conjecture is about his headgear. It is noticeable in the painting that John Blanke is the only one of the six trumpeters to wear something on his head. His fellow trumpeters are bareheaded. The object in question is rather like a modern beret: soft, brimless, slightly padded in appearance (although that might just be his hair), and brown in the first image, green in the second, with a yellow network pattern sketched lightly over it. It has been identified as 'a turban' (FIG. 2 (a) and (b)).[15]

---

13 For example, the downcast eyes of Dürer's 1521[?] drawing of Katherina, the black servant of the Portuguese royal factor João Brandão in Antwerp (see <https://commons.wikimedia.org/wiki/File:Albrecht_D%C3%BCrer_-_The_Negress_Katharina_-_WGA07097.jpg>), have been interpreted both as her response to her enslavement – for example, in <https://blackcentraleurope.com/biographies/albrecht-duerers-katharina-mj-montgomery> – and the properly modest way for a young woman of 20 to direct her gaze; Ulinka Rublack *Dressing Up* (Oxford UP, 2010) 185. In fact, almost none of his female (or indeed male) portraits are looking directly at him, and most of them are looking downward. It is one of the facts of portraiture. The only person looking directly at us is the artist himself, because it is difficult not to do a self-portrait without looking straight in the mirror. Another of the dangers of selective interpretation.

14 Ohajuru had asked for the images to be in black and white; <https://www.johnblanke.com/about.html>.

15 The identification was originally made by Anglo *Great Tournament Roll*: 'All bare-headed except for a negro (in the centre of the second row) who wears a brown turban latticed with yellow' (85); 'the negro in the centre of the second

Fig. 2: Images of 'John Blanke'.
(a) Westminster Tournament Roll mb 4 detail (some paint loss);
(b) Westminster Tournament Roll mb 28 detail.
Reproduced by permission of the Kings, Heralds, and Pursuivants of Arms.

It is a point of faith among most of the website contributors that John Blanke was unique, and so he is in the 1511 Roll because of his skin colour and the shape of his face. He is also marked out from the other five trumpeters by the fact that his head alone is covered. This has become a major point in the discussion of his uniqueness; but more than that, it is assumed that the painter is recording something that he wore in real life, and that this is an indicator of his free-spirited autonomy. The painted image has been given human agency: John Blanke has made a choice. Kate Lowe's blog gives the most detailed version of this view:

> Not only is his skin colour different to that of his 'white' colleagues – a difference about which no choice could have been made either by him or by others – but in addition a major form of difference *that is of his own choosing*[16] – his head-gear – also sets him apart from his fellow trumpeters.[17]

---

row has changed into a turban of green with a linear design in gold' (98). This has been taken up as '[he] alone wears a turban'; <https://www.johnblanke.com/s-i-martin.html>.
16   My italics.
17   See <https://www.johnblanke.com/kate-lowe.html>.

This is significant, it is suggested, because it not only demonstrates private choice, and thus a personality, but must say something about his acceptance into the social fabric of the Tudor court, and thus their toleration of people who might have been considered outsiders (provided, it is suggested, they were assertive enough to demand it). Not only has he 'chosen to wear (insisted on wearing?)' this head covering, but:

> he has been officially sanctioned to do this not in the private sphere but as a salaried member of a royal corps processing publicly at Westminster, the seat of English monarchical power, in celebration of the birth of the heir to the throne, and to top it all the image of him wearing this major marker of difference was recorded twice at the time, and has survived for 500 years.

There is of course no proof of this contention. The painting *may* record both the gesture of choosing his own headgear and the authorities' (declared or tacit) permission for him to do so, but we have no documentary evidence either of his choice or their acquiescence – or how serious a deviance this might have been. Was it a 'major marker of difference'? All we know is that in the painting he is wearing some form of headgear, whereas his five companions are not. It is possible that the painter has recorded something that was a trademark costume of this particular trumpeter; on the other hand, it may merely have been a feature of another painting, possibly of the Black Magus, which had served as his model for the image of an African. But Anglo's identification as 'a turban' has been enthusiastically seized on, because it is also assumed by some to underline a further potential point of difference – religion:

> The multicoloured (brown and yellow/green and gold) patterned cloth of the head-gear is a religious and cultural, rather than a fashion, statement, and must signal that John Blanke was a Muslim, or at least had been raised in a Muslim cultural context.[18]

---

18 <https://www.johnblanke.com/kate-lowe.html>. Nadia van Pelt points out that Kate Lowe, in her chapter on 'The Stereotyping of Black Africans in Renaissance Europe' in *Black Africans in Renaissance Europe* edited T.F. Earle and K.J.P. Lowe (Cambridge UP, 2005) 17–47, does not refer to it as a turban, though she insists on it being 'vital to his cultural identity' (39); Nadia T. van Pelt 'John Blanke's Hat in

One imagines that of the three or four colours mentioned (the yellow was probably meant to indicate gold), it is the green that has attracted attention. There is a general impression today that green is the colour of Islam.[19] It is mentioned in the Qur'an as being the colour of the robes worn in Paradise, and is popularly said (on what authority I do not know, but those who have lived in the Arabian desert will understand why) to have been the Prophet Muhammad's favourite colour.[20] But was this the case at the time?

John Blanke's Headgear in its Sixteenth-Century Context

It is too easy to apply our twenty-first-century assumptions to a sixteenth-century image, especially one that comes without any written explanation. We need to look into Tudor knowledge and understanding of Islamic dress, especially headgear, and most importantly, their attitudes towards it. Was it, and therefore also those who wore it, viewed with toleration, as is being suggested? The standard response, which was to refer to them as 'God's enemies', suggests not: 'hys entent was to make warre on the Moores, beynge Infideles and enemies to Gods law'; 'surely it is agaynste my hart, whiche euer hath desired to fight agaynst Gods enemyes'.[21] With curiosity? With fear? Would they even have recognised what it was? In what follows here, I hope to give answers to some of these questions. Some of them are rather surprising. For the time being we shift away from focusing on the figure of John Blanke, but we shall

    the Westminster Tournament Roll' *Notes and Queries* (December 2021) 387–9 at 388; <https://doi.org/10.1093/notesj/gjab156>.

19 'Tradition is unanimous that the Prophet never wore a green turban, and there is no support for the colour green in law or tradition. But green is the colour of Paradise, and it is also said to have been the Prophet's favourite colour; some say that the angels at Ḥunayn (or also at Badr) had green turbans'; W. Björkman 'Tulband' in *The Encyclopaedia of Islam 10* (Leiden: Brill, new edition 2000) 610; online at Gale eBooks (subscription).

20 Unsurprisingly, there are many references in the Qur'an to Paradise, but the specific one is Surah 76:21: 'they will wear garments of green silk and brocade'; *The Qur'an* translated M.A.S. Abdel Haleem (World's Classics; Oxford UP, 2005, corrected reprint 2016) 401. In Surah 55:76 'They will all sit on green cushions and fine carpets' (355).

21 Edward Hall *The Vnion of the Two Noble and Illustre Famelies of Lancastre and York* (London: Richard Grafton, 1548) 'The triumphant reigne of Kyng Henry the VIII' fol. xj recto (of Ferdinand of Aragon); fol. xij verso (Lord Darcy on being dismissed by Ferdinand from the Moorish expedition).

return to him later with, I hope, a better understanding of where he fits into the picture.

Turbans

To return to the question of colour: the same vague concept about green being a marker of Islam, or at least associated with the Prophet, does seem to have been current in England in the later sixteenth century and early seventeenth century:

> The particular praeference which is giuen to this, or that colour, aboue the rest by seuerall persons, how, or whence doth it come? That there is a national as well as a personal respect cannot be deny'd, and [*some*] colours rather then other are vulgarly [*popularly*] appropriated to special vses, as symbolical to them ... Who dares in TVRKIE weare greene, the colour of MAHOMET, but the SVLTAN him-selfe, or those of his bloud?[22]

As this suggests, it is unlikely, however, that John Blanke, if he were a practising Muslim, would have been wearing a green turban: at the time, in the Ottoman Empire at least, green turbans were reserved for descendants of the Prophet.[23] The quotation above (from 1610) sounds like a slightly distorted version of an observation by Nicolas de Nicolay in *Les navigations, peregrinations et voyages faicts en la Turquie*, his illustrated account of the French embassy that he accompanied to Istanbul in 1551:

---

22 Edmund Bolton (1575?–1633?) *The Elements of Armories* (London: George Eld, 1610) 130–1. Bolton is very interesting on the significance of heraldic colour. 'Those of his blood' is ambiguous: does it refer to relatives of the Sultan or of the Prophet?

23 'In the history of religion the green turban is important, as the well-known badge of the descendants of Muḥammad. The green turban as a badge of the sharīfs is, however, of much later origin ... [*after several centuries of vicissitudes*] In 773/1371–1372 the Mamlūk sultan al-Ashraf Shaʿbān ordered that the turban cloths (al-ʿaṣāʾib ʿalā ʾl-ʿamāʾim) of the ʿAlids should be green, and from 1004/1595–1596 the whole turban became green by order of the Ottoman governor of Egypt, al-Sayyid Muḥammad al-Sharīf. This fashion spread from Egypt to other Muslim countries ... It is now regarded as a law that no non-ʿAlid should wear the green turban'; Björkman 'Tulband' in *The Encyclopaedia of Islam 10*, 610. It may only have become official in 1595–1596, but de Nicolay notices it in Turkey at least forty years earlier (see next note).

PLVSIEVRS se treuuent entre les Turcs, qui se disent (& telz sont maintenus) parens de Mahomet, les vns desquelz portent le Tulbant verd, & les autres seaulememnt le Muzauegia, c'est à dire vn bonnet de dessoubs le Tulbant de couleur verde, & tout le reste du Tulbant blanc. Ilz portent telle couleur par ce qu'ilz disent que leur prophete la portoit en la teste.[24]

There are diuers amongst the Turks, which doe call themselues & for such are reputed, kinsmen of Mahomet, wherof some doe weare a greene Tulbant, and the other a Muzauegia, which is to say, a bonnet whiche they doe weare vnder the Tulbant being of colour green; & al the rest of the Tulbant white. They do weare such colour for that they say their prophet ware the like on his head.[25]

De Nicolay seems to have been the first to transmit this information to the West. He also comments on a whole range of turban-colour conventions for religion and race *à fin que par telle diuersité de couleurs ilz soyent cogneus les vns parmy les autres* ('so that by these different colours they should be distinguished [one group] from another'):[26] they underline the religious toleration (with conditions) of the Ottoman Empire, which was far greater than that of Western Christendom. Nicolay's illustrations are woodcuts, thus in black and white, but another traveller, Lambert de Vos, in his manuscript costume book (1574),[27] provides confirmatory colour illustrations of these from his own experience, including the green ones.

24 Nicolas de Nicolay *Les navigations, peregrinations et voyages faicts en la Turquie* (Antwerp: G. Silvius, 1576) book 3 ch. 20, page 196; online at <https://gallica.bnf.fr/ark:/12148/bpt6k853119.image>. First published in 1567, it attracted immense interest, was translated into several languages, and because of its lavish provision of woodcut illustrations was the major impetus behind the costume-book vogue of the second part of the sixteenth century.

25 *The nauigations, peregrinations and voyages, made into Turkie by Nicholas Nicholay Daulphinois, Lord of Arfeuile, chamberlaine and geographer ordinarie to the King of Fraunce ... translated out of the French by T. Washington the younger* (London: Thomas Dawson, 1585) 108.

26 Nicolas de Nicolay *Les navigations* 279. These include yellow turbans for Jews (247, 279), blue streaked with red and white for Armenians (250), and blue for Christians in Macedonia (279).

27 Lambert de Vos 'Türkisches Kostümbuch' c.1574; Bremen: Staats- und Universitätsbibliothek, ms. Or. 9 fol. 12r, at <https://brema.suub.uni-bremen.de/ms/content/pageview/1616750>.

But otherwise, as de Nicolay suggests, the predominant colour was white,[28] and that is how the West seems to have envisaged it. Looking at turbans in general, their shape as well as their colour, I do not pretend to have conducted an exhaustive statistical survey of Western depictions going back to the 'Saracen' images of the Crusades, but spot checks suggest that in the fourteenth century and early fifteenth century they were shown as simple twisted cloths (the *torse*) tied round the forehead or the base of the helmet (FIG. 3). I am talking here about illustrations to histories, not romances or biblical illustrations, or the *Livres des Merveilles* purporting to record adventurous journeys to the Far East (Marco Polo's Kublai Khan is made to wear some extraordinarily inauthentic headgear);[29] but this is also how they seem to have been worn in pageants, jousts, and entertainments (I will come back to this later). Sometimes the cloth envelops the whole head, but is still tied at the back in the characteristic large knot.

From the mid-fifteenth century headdresses in general become larger, more complicated, and occasionally fantastical for a while – though some of the hats that appear to be fantasies are versions of that worn by the Emperor John VIII Palaeologus in the portrait medal by Pisanello.[30] In FIG. 4, the central figure, presumably Mehmed II, is wearing a Byzantine

---

28 'The commonest colour for the turban is white. The Prophet is said to have been fond of this colour, and it is considered the colour of Paradise. There is not actually a *ḥadīth* telling us that the Prophet's turban was white, but this is probably only because white was the normal colour'; Björkman 'Tulband' in *Encyclopaedia of Islam* 10 609. Maria Pia Pedani cites a tradition that Alaeddin, son of Osman, chose white as the colour for Ottoman turbans, to distinguish them from the headgear of the Byzantines and Turkomen, 'Gentile Bellini e l'oriente (Gentile Bellini and the East)' (Incontri presso la Sala dell'Albergo Scuola Grande di San Marco Venice – 23 June 2016) online at <http://www.levantineheritage.com/pdf/Venetian_Mamluk_mode_and_Gentile_Bellini.pdf>; but the *Encyclopaedia of Islam* says that his proposal was restricted to the wearing of a conical white headdress by the military and the administration.

29 See, for example, BNF MS français 2810 fol. 278; <https://gallica.bnf.fr/ark:/12148/btv1b52000858n/f278>. The manuscript (c.1400–1420) used to belong to Jean de Berri; it is well worth browsing. For a more authentic image of the Khan, see <https://en.wikipedia.org/wiki/Kublai_Khan#/media/File:YuanEmperorAlbumKhubilaiPortrait.jpg>.

30 Portrait medal produced 1438–1442; <https://www.britishmuseum.org/collection/object/C_G3-NapM-9>. In the *Nuremberg Chronicle* (1493), the woodcut of Mehmed II shows him wearing the same Byzantine hat, presumably because he is ruler of Constantinople; Hartmann Schedel and Michael Wolgemut

Fig. 3: (Left) Charlemagne negotiates with the African king Aygolant <https://gallica.bnf.fr/ark:/12148/btv1b84472995/f238.item>; (right) Spanish Saracen brings gifts to Charlemagne <https://gallica.bnf.fr/ark:/12148/btv1b84472995/f249.item>; Paris: BNF MS français 2813 (*Grandes Chroniques de France*, 1375–1380) fols 115v and 121r. Reproduced in compliance with the copyright rules of the Bibliothèque nationale de France.

Fig. 4: The Siege of Constantinople in 1453 by Mehmed II (detail). BNF MS français 9087 ('Guidebooks to the Holy Land' translated Jean Mielot ?1460s) fol. 207v. Commissioned by Philip the Good, Duke of Burgundy, and owned by Emperor Maximilian I. <https://gallica.bnf.fr/ark:/12148/btv1b100215049/f426.item>. Reproduced in compliance with the copyright rules of the Bibliothèque nationale de France.

Fig. 5: A battle, probably between Sancho Abarca and the Moors at Pamplona. BL Additional MS 12531, the Genealogy of the Kings of Portugal (1530–1534) fol. 4r, bas de page. <https://www.bl.uk/catalogues/illuminatedmanuscripts/ILLUMIN.ASP?Size=mid&IllID=28866>
© The British Library Board.

hat with a *torse* round it. He is also lavishly bearded, whereas Mehmed's beard, when he wore one, was very short.

Then, under the influence of eyewitness accounts of the costume of Ottomans, Mamelukes, and Moors, they become genuine reportage. In the magnificent 'Genealogy of the Kings of Portugal' (1530–1534) attributed to Simon Bening and Antonio de Holanda, Flemish artists working for the Portuguese court,[31] the *bas de page* sometimes records battles against the Moors in Spain (Fig. 5). The Moors are marked out *en masse* by their white (and in two cases yellow) turbans, and the Christians by their helmets.[32]

Liber chronicarum (Nuremberg: Anton Koberger, 1493) fol. 256v; image online at <http://daten.digitale-sammlungen.de/bsb00034024/image_586>.

31 London: BL Additional MS 12531. See <https://www.bl.uk/manuscripts/FullDisplay.aspx?ref=Add_MS_12531>.

32 The Moors carry a characteristic heart-shaped shield with tassels, the *adarga*, wear scimitars, and wield what look like cane spears (the shafts are a different colour from those of the Christians). Their faces are swarthy, not black, and they are bearded.

Turks and Moors

At the time of Henry VII and VIII, the wearers of turbans, or at least those who were familiar to the West, were largely classified as *Turks* or *Moors*. Earlier they had been known generically as *Saracens*, which just seems to imply a Muslim, or somebody against whom one would go on Crusade, so possibly domiciled in the Holy Land.

The terms *Turk* and *Moor* seem to be roughly geographically based, with political overtones. *Turks* referred to the Ottoman Empire, which had come sharply into focus for the West with the capture of Constantinople by Mehmed II in 1453. *Moors* came from North Africa and had been finally driven out of Spain with the Conquest of Granada in 1492. Sir Thomas Elyot in his *Dictionary* of 1538 defines them under *Aphrica*: 'one of the thre partis of the world wherof the inhabitantes be at this day called generallye *Moores* or *Morynes*, the countreyes be nowe called *Tunyse*, *Fese* [Fez], *Marocke*'.[33] If this seems rather a restricted view of Africa, the reasons are probably that Elyot's *Dictionary* is a Latin-to-English one, and his description manages to combine the continent with (somewhat inaccurately) the Roman province; that European exploration of the rest of Africa had really only just reached public consciousness; and that the Barbary Coast was the area which inspired the most apprehension in Europe, because of the Corsairs. They were notorious up to the nineteenth century as raiders and slavers; coast dwellers from Djerba to Ireland feared ending up in the slave markets of Tunis, Algiers, and Morocco.[34] Their activities were at their height in the sixteenth century, and King Ferdinand of Aragon's continual appeals to Henry VII and then Henry VIII to join him in expeditions against 'the Moors of Barbaria' are part of this effort to contain and if possible subdue them.[35]

---

33   Sir Thomas Eliot *The Dictionary* (London: Thomas Berthelet, 1538) under *A ante P* (fol. VII verso).

34   The Corsairs were finally neutralised in 1830 with the French capture of Algiers. The raid on Baltimore, County Cork, in 1631 left the town deserted. European nations were continually at war with them, with varying success. The Barbary expedition of 1390 by the Genoese and the French against Mahdia in Tunis is recorded in Froissart's *Chronicles* as a Crusade.

35   In 1506, Katherine of Aragon, then Princess of Wales, appealed to her father-in-law Henry VII to ransom her cook and his family from them, because 'he rescues a certain number of Christian slaves yearly in Africa' – it was a kind of charitable trust; *Calendar of Letters, Despatches, and State Papers: Relating to the Negotiations Between England and Spain, Preserved in the Archives at Simancas*

Despite the tendency to think of all *morians* as dark-skinned, at the time they were distinguished as two types of Moor, 'white mores and black moors'.[36] This was a purely ethnographical description, except when 'Moor' was used in a derogatory sense to denote a Muslim. Leo Africanus (c.1494–c.1554), himself a Moor, was born in Granada, brought up in Fez, educated at the University of al-Qarawiyyin, became a diplomat, was captured by Christian pirates, imprisoned in Rhodes, presented to Pope Leo X, baptised, freed, and employed by the Pope as an encyclopaedic source of information. He was a distinguished geographer, who wrote among other works the *Cosmographia et Geographia de Africa*, an extremely detailed account of the continent, finished in 1526 and published in Italian in 1550. He goes into considerable detail about the possible origins of the five ethnic groups in Africa, the last of which is *gli Africani bianchi and gli Africani ... della terra negra*.[37] This was explained in the introduction to the 1600 English translation as 'the Africans or Moores, properly so called; which last are of two kinds, namely white or tawnie Moores, and Negroes or blacke Moores'.[38] This may explain why Balthasar, the Magus representing Africa, is sometimes painted as a Black African and sometimes as a lighter-skinned Berber blended with Arab.[39]

and Elsewhere: Volume 1 edited G.A. Bergenroth (London: Longman, Green, Longman & Roberts for the Public Record Office, 1862) 382. Several religious orders devoted to the redemption of Christian slaves were established in various countries from the thirteenth century onwards, and it was considered to be among the Corporal Works of Mercy.

36 Andrew Boorde *The fyrst boke of the introduction of knowledge* (London: William Copland, 1562) sig. Miij verso, on 'the Mores whych do dwel in barbary'. He follows it up with a chapter on the Turks. Antoine de Lalaing (see note 11) credits Philip the Handsome with urging Ferdinand and Isabella at Toledo to expel the *blans Mores* from Spain (225).

37 Leo Africanus 'Della Descrittione dell'Africa et delle cose notabili che ivi sono, per Giovan Lioni Africano: Prima Parte' in *Primo Volvme delle Navigationi et Viaggi nel quale si contiene la Descrittione dell'Africa* (Venice: heirs of Lucantonio Giunti, 1550) fol. 2r.

38 *A geographical historie of Africa, written in Arabicke and Italian by Iohn Leo a More, borne in Granada, and brought vp in Barbarie* translated John Pory (London: George Bishop, 1600) 6.

39 The other two Magi should represent Europe and Asia, but artists do not seem to have made much visual distinction between them, possibly because for them the East was the Near East and included Byzantium: the *Tres Riches Heures*' oldest Magus is said to be a portrait of the Emperor Manuel II Palaeologus. But they are

John Blanke would have been considered a Black Moor; though, interestingly, *Moor* or *morian* is not a word used of him in the accounts. Whether this implies that he did not come from North Africa or the Iberian Peninsula, or whether the phrase 'the black trumpet' was felt to be sufficient, we cannot really tell. Henry VII's accounts pay a mysterious *morian* who turns up in May 1499, is 'rewarded' with different sums almost every month, and then disappears after the end of October; and the court of Scotland was famously home to the two 'Moris lasses' and the 'More taubronar' [*tabor player*], his wife and baby, so the word is used in official documents.[40]

This might seem to restrict our investigations to the Iberian Peninsula and North Africa, if it were not that Christian Europe had become fascinated with the costume of the Turks and their turbans. (The very word *turban* is a Turkish loan word.)[41] As de Nicolay's book shows, in the Ottoman world turbans were used as social markers, as well as sectarian ones. They distinguished between ranks in the Sultan's household, and above all in the army. Information about Ottoman costume clearly began to percolate back to Western Christendom well before the publication of travel literature and costume books. One of the side-effects of this, as we shall see, is its appearance in court entertainments such as maskings and disguisings. There is nothing to create awareness of a nation like the possibility that you may have to fight them; but why should one wish to dress up as them? Was it a way of neutralising the threat? Or the thrill of becoming the Other?

not as distinctive, possibly because not as familiar, as the youngest Magus. The Far East was a matter for Marvels.

40 See <https://www.tudorchamberbooks.org/edition/> and search for *moryan/morean*. He first appears on 24 May 1499 being rewarded 5s: TNA E101/414/16 fol.65v, transcription online at <https://www.tudorchamberbooks.org/edition/folio/LL_E101_414_16_f0065v.xml>. He then appears regularly as '*the* morean', which suggests he is the same man, being given various sums, until the 31 October, when he is given 3s 4d, and disappears. A *reward* is an *ex gratia* one-off payment: whatever he did, he was not, like John Blanke, on the payroll. For the 'Moris lasses', the taborer, and two 'More freris' (were they brothers or friars?), see *Accounts of the Lord High Treasurer of Scotland: Vol. 3 A.D. 1506–1507* edited Sir James Balfour Paul (Edinburgh: HMSO, 1901) 113, 108, and Index.

41 *OED* sv *turban*. The word *tulip* comes from the same source: a bed of tulips is like a regiment of colourful turbans.

There was a very live possibility of military confrontation. The Ottoman Turks had taken Constantinople in 1453, and radically altered the balance of power with Christendom. By the time he died in 1481, Mehmed II was master of the Balkans as well as Anatolia, and had revitalised the city of Constantinople as a fitting seat for the *qayṣar-i Rūm*, the successor in his eyes of the Caesars of the Roman Empire. Hungary was the next battleground, and Austria was threatened. The Battle of Mohács (1526) and the Siege of Vienna (1529) were still in the future, but it was clear how things were going. The Emperor Maximilian spent a great deal of effort trying to persuade Henry VII to join in a Crusade against the Turks in Hungary, and was temporarily appeased with a subsidy of £10,000, delivered in 1502.[42] Henry however continued to assure the Pope of his willingness to join in such a Crusade, while simultaneously promising Ferdinand of Aragon that he would engage in one against the Moors in Africa.[43] The old enemy had not vanished with the advent of the new, especially as the new appeared to be taking over the old. From the beginning of his reign, Henry VIII was badgered by his father-in-law, the same Ferdinand of Aragon, to join in an expedition against 'the Moores of Barbaria'. He professed himself eager to go in person and fight 'against the Moors and Infidels, enemies of Christ's faith' but instead, after the Westminster Tournament, sent a force of archers under the command of Lord Darcy. They arrived at Cadiz,[44] but the English soldiers who were allowed onshore got drunk on 'hote wynes' and went on the rampage (*plus ça change*), and Ferdinand diplomatically asked Darcy to leave, since

42   This sum was agreed at the Treaty of Antwerp in 1502. BL Add MS 7099 fol. 77 (1502): 'Item delivered & payd by the kings comaundment to harman rung for and to thuse & behove of the king of the romans in silver £10,000 0s 0d': <https://www.tudorchamberbooks.org/edition/folio/7099_fo_077.xml>. In 1508 he is holding out for a further 100,000 crowns; *Simancas* 461; 23 July 1508, Maximilian to Margaret of Austria.

43   See, for example, *Simancas* 414–15: Greenwich, 15 May 1507, Henry VII to Pope Julius II. He (Henry) 'has been always inclined to shed the blood of the enemies of the Catholic Faith, the Turks and other Infidels, in order to avenge all the injuries and cruelties committed by them on Christians, and to reconquer the Holy Sepulchre'. On 5 October 1507, he was also assuring Ferdinand of Aragon that he was eager 'to make war on the Infidels in Africa, at the bidding of Ferdinand. If, for some reason or other, however, Spain could not now engage in an African war, he would fight against the Turks in Hungary'; *Simancas* 437–8.

44   Hall calls it 'the porte of Caleys in Southspayne'; *Union* 'Henry VIII' (see note 21) fol. xij verso.

because of the threat of war with France, 'he hathe taken an abstinence of warre with the Moores tyll another time'. The expedition was postponed *sine die*; but several young men including Henry Guildford, later to be Henry's Master of the Revels, went on to Ferdinand's court, 'where they were highly entertained' and knighted. We shall see how this might have enhanced their awareness of Moorish culture, and particularly dress, in due course; though as we shall also see, they were by no means the first Englishmen to be entertained at the court of Ferdinand and Isabella.

Reporting contemporary Muslim costume

Encounters between two civilisations, however, even when they are a military threat to each other, are never as black and white as we tend to paint them. There can still be commercial relations – Venice is the obvious example – and person-to-person cultural exchange. Surprisingly to us, the cultural rapprochement came from the Turkish side. Sultan Mehmed II, the conqueror of Constantinople/Istanbul, was interested in European art, especially portraiture (the Ottomans were never prescriptive about not portraying the human form) and its ability to create a lasting memorial of the sitter. In 1461 he attempted to acquire a portrait medallist from Sigismondo Malatesta of Rimini,[45] but the artist chosen, Matteo de' Pasti, was arrested in Crete by the Venetians as a spy and never reached Istanbul. More successful was Costanzo da Ferrara, sent by the King of Naples, who spent several years in Istanbul in the 1470s, and produced the classic portrait medal of Mehmed that became the model for later depictions of the Turk, including Dürer's 'Ottoman Rider' (c.1495), which in its turn was copied and adapted by print artists.[46] Paintings and sketches can only have a limited audience: print

---

45 Portrait medals were an Italian development of the early fifteenth century; Pisanello is usually credited with the invention of the genre, with his 1438 medal of the Byzantine Emperor John VIII Palaeologus. Ironically, Mehmed II, who became the next ruler of Constantinople to be commemorated in a portrait medal, had ousted John VIII's successor.

46 For images, see <https://it.wikipedia.org/wiki/Costanzo_da_Ferrara>; also <https://www.britishmuseum.org/collection/object/C_G3-PolMII-10-D-x>, 'Cast bronze medal of Sultan Muhammad II, made in Italy in 1481'; Albrecht Dürer 'Ottoman Rider', c.1495, ink and watercolour on paper, 30 cm × 21 cm, Albertina, Vienna, Graphische Sammlung, no. 3196, D 171; <https://sammlungenonline.albertina.at/#/query/8b63243f-8837-4f67-b5a2-60b6dac4cddd>. On Dürer's use of Costanzo's work, see the Open University's programme on the art of

reaches a mass one. So, though this is less familiar to us, do medals: once the die has been created, it can be used to make multiple casts (copies). This one was highly influential.

Then, in August 1479, Mehmed negotiated with the Republic of Venice, with whom, after a long and draining struggle, the Ottomans had resumed diplomatic relations, to send him *unum sculptorem et funditorem [a]eris* ('a[nother] sculptor and bronze founder').[47] They sent Gentile Bellini: the result, besides a slightly less distinguished medal,[48] was the famous portrait of Mehmed II now in the National Gallery.[49] The credit for the well-known handful of sketches of Turks and their costumes is still being disputed between Bellini and Costanzo:[50] they bring the models even more vividly before our eyes than do Holbein's drawings of the courtiers of Henry VIII. They had only a limited audience, but they give us a point of reference.

The other Islamic nation that attracted the attention of Venetian painters were the Mamelukes of Egypt. Bellini and his more famous brother Giovanni created a vast painting on the subject of 'St Mark preaching in Alexandria', which shows a variety of headgear, including the

---

Renaissance Venice at <https://www.open.edu/openlearn/history-the-arts/visual-art/art-renaissance-venice/content-section-1.4>. On the widespread dissemination of the portrait medals of Mehmed II, see Charlotte Colding Smith *Images of Islam 1453–1600* (London and New York: Routledge, pb 2018) 35–6.

47   The clearest exposition of Mehmed's employment of Italian artists is in the Open University's programme. On his medals, see Julian Raby 'Pride and Prejudice: Mehmed the Conqueror and the Italian Portrait Medal' in *Studies in the History of Art 21* (Symposium Papers 8: Italian Medals, edited J. Graham Pollard, 1987) 171–94; <https://www.jstor.org/stable/42620181>; on Mehmed as patron of western artists, see Raby's 'A Sultan of Paradox: Mehmed the Conqueror as a Patron of the Arts' *Oxford Art Journal 5:1* (1982) 3–8; <https://www.jstor.org/stable/1360098>.

48   See <https://collections.vam.ac.uk/item/O142648/mehmed-ii-medal-bellini-gentile/> for image and commentary; also BM <https://www.britishmuseum.org/collection/object/C_1883-0303-1>.

49   See <https://www.nationalgallery.org.uk/paintings/gentile-bellini-the-sultan-mehmet-ii>.

50   For example, the seated woman <https://www.britishmuseum.org/collection/object/P_Pp-1-20>; the Janissary <https://www.britishmuseum.org/collection/object/P_Pp-1-19>; two sketches of Turkish men <https://sammlung.staedelmuseum.de/en/person/bellini-gentile>; the man in a turban from the Louvre <https://commons.wikimedia.org/wiki/File:Standing_Ottoman.png>.

tall, red, hairy sugarloaf, the *zamṭ*, worn by the military, and, interestingly, a whole bevy of women.[51] Giovanni Mansueti and Vittore Carpaccio, both pupils of the Bellinis, specialised in large-scale paintings of the lives of saints in which Ottoman and Mameluke costume stood in for that of the biblical Jews or, in the case of St George, the princess's Libyan relations. Again, their mass-audience influence was probably limited, but they were seen by other artists, and the motifs were passed on.

The Mamelukes of Egypt had another and probably more grassroots claim to European interest. Up to 1517, when the Ottomans conquered it, they were the rulers of Palestine and thus of Jerusalem. Pilgrims might expect to be escorted from Jaffa to Jerusalem, voluntarily or not, by armed Mamelukes. More important visitors, such as Richard Beauchamp Earl of Warwick, were given special treatment. He was greeted and entertained by the Governor of Jerusalem himself. The illustrations to his 'Pageant' – created in the 1480s or 1490s, though the pilgrimage took place in 1408–1409 – shows his Mameluke companions wearing a three-tier conical turban, intricately wrapped, with a tassel (the end of the turban cloth or the top of the cap, though it looks like a piece of material) sticking out of the top (FIG. 6). The rear view shows two long ends hanging out from under the turban.[52] This looks as if it might be a genuine recollection or at least a report from a returned pilgrim. The Governor himself wears a hat with a curly brim that looks like a Marvel of the east.

However, probably the most influential source of costume information for armchair travellers was a pilgrimage handbook published in Mainz in in 1486. Pilgrims, including English pilgrims,[53] continued to journey to

---

51   See <https://en.wikipedia.org/wiki/St._Mark_Preaching_in_Alexandria#/media/File:Gentile_e_giovanni_bellini,_predica_di_san_marco_in_alessandria_01.jpg>. Maria Pia Pedani 'Gentile Bellini e l'oriente (Gentile Bellini and the East)' (see note 28) discusses it and identifies the different types of headgear.

52   London: BL Cotton MS Julius E IV/3, fol. 10v, though they also appear on fol. 9v. For the 'Pageant', see *The Beauchamp Pageant* edited Alexandra Sinclair (Donington: Paul Watkins for the Richard III and Yorkist History Trust, 2003). For the ends of the turban and the significance of the way they are arranged, see *Encyclopaedia of Islam* sv *Turban*, under *'Aḏhaba*.

53   For example, Sir Richard Guildford, father of Edward Guildford, Master of the Horse, who appears in the Tournament Roll, died in Jerusalem on 6 September 1506. His chaplain published an account, *The Pylgrymage of Sir Richard Guylforde to the Holy Land* (London: Richard Pynson, 1511) edited by Henry Ellis Camden

FIG. 6: Two views of a (Mameluke?) Turban.
London: BL Cotton MS Julius E IV/3 (The Beauchamp Pageant), fol. 10v, details.
© The British Library Board.

the Holy Land both before and after the Ottomans conquered it in 1517. Handbooks were written to familiarise would-be travellers with what they might expect to see and pay. Bernhard von Breydenbach capitalised on the new print technology by illustrating his contribution to Jerusalem travel literature with woodcuts by his travelling companion the Flemish artist Erhard Reuwich. These showed, among other things, the dress of the Saracens, Jews, Syrians, Arabs, and Abyssinians. His *Peregrinatio* was immensely popular, was translated into several languages, and is generally considered to be the genesis of the costume books that proliferated in the sixteenth century.[54]

These were an offshoot of the diplomatic relations between the Ottoman Empire and the West. Bellini and his compatriots were only

---

Society (1851). Since Sir Richard was seriously ill, they hired camels and an escort of Mamelukes to get him to Jerusalem.

54 Bernhard von Breydenbach *Peregrinatio in terram sanctam* (Mainz: Peter Schöffer, 1486); online at <https://www.digitale-sammlungen.de/en/view/bsb00051697>. The account by Felix Faber, who was on the same pilgrimage, is much more detailed, and gives lively accounts of their interaction with the locals: *Fratris Felicis Fabri Evagatorium in Terre Sancte, Arabie et Egypti Peregrinationem* edited Conrad Dietrich Hassler (Stuttgart: Literary Society of Stuttgart, 1843).

the beginning. Visitors were fascinated by the costume of Istanbul and the Ottoman court, and especially the range, variety, and protocol of its turbans.[55] However, the spate of costume books and albums portraying Ottoman dress, with occasional nods in the direction of other costumes of the world, did not start until after our period, probably kick-started by Nicolas de Nicolay's *Navigations*,[56] so they cannot have been direct sources of information for the court of Henry VIII. They would have had to rely on Breydenbach, anti-Turk propagandist woodcuts, and works by artists such as Dürer[57] – and of course personal experience. We, however, can use the costume books as points of reference when checking the accuracy or otherwise of earlier Western renderings.

One possibly unexpected area that shows an interest in Ottoman costume is the *mummery* or disguising. Our earliest visual evidence comes from the *Freydal* of the Emperor Maximilian.[58] This is going to reappear in my argument later on, so I shall explain it briefly here. The *Freydal* was part of the Emperor Maximilian's campaign to memorialise himself visually – precisely what the Sultan Mehmed II was eager to do, though not in a fictional mode. It is a sequence of paintings commemorating his tournaments and masked costumed dances, which he calls *mummereien*.[59] It purports to be the record of the 64 sessions of jousting and dancing mounted by the prince Freydal to impress the young queen from a foreign land whom he is courting: a transparent account, if romanticised, of Maximilian and Mary of Burgundy. There is a parallel romance about his journey to her court to woo her in *Theuerdanck*, and an allegorical autobiography in the *Weisskunig* (the 'White/Wise King'), which devotes a chapter to the young king's love of and skill in

---

55 For an accessible illustrated history of costume, see Betül İpşirli Argıt 'Clothing and Fashion in Istanbul (1453–1923)' on the website *History of Istanbul*; <https://istanbultarihi.ist/485-clothing-and-fashion-in-istanbul-14531923>. On the variety and names of turbans, see *Encyclopaedia of Islam* sv *Turban*, and Pedani 'Gentile Bellini e l'oriente', who gives illustrations.

56 Not published until 1574, although the embassy he accompanied was in 1551.

57 See Colding Smith *Images of Islam* chapter 5.

58 Vienna: Kunsthistorisches Museum, Codex Ms. 2831. Facsimile edited by Stefan Krause *Freydal: Medieval Games: the Book of Tournaments of Emperor Maximilian I* (Cologne: Taschen, 2019). See <https://en.wikipedia.org/wiki/Freydal_tournament_book>, which gives a full set of images, from the facsimile, of each illustration at the end.

59 The word can be spelt with a single 'm' or double 'mm' in the middle.

arranging *panggeten/vnd Mumereyen* ('shows and mummeries').[60] These were all intended to be printed and illustrated with woodcuts, to get the maximum publicity exposure; in fact, only the *Theuerdanck* (1515) was printed during Maximilian's lifetime, and the *Weisskunig* had to wait till 1526, after his death in 1519. The *Freydal* remained unpublished until modern times.

Though *Freydal* purports to record events that would have taken place in 1477, Maximilian did not start to plan it until 1502, and the illustrations were executed between 1512 and 1515. They are thus exactly contemporary with the first years of Henry's reign and the Tournament Roll. There is no reason to believe that the *mummereien* did not take place – the one thing we do have about them is the names of some of the people who took part – but not all in 1477.[61] The costumes of the audience are of the early 1500s, and it is highly unlikely that anyone except a fictional hero would have the time, let alone the stamina, to joust and dance for 256 days without a break.

They are the earliest records that we have of the costume of what Henry's court would have called *disguisings*, and they present a dazzling range of what one could dress up as: giants, women, miners, huntsmen, merchants, pilgrims, landsknechts [*mercenaries*], morris dancers, old-fashioned Burgundians, Venetians, Hungarians with bird's faces – and Turks (FIG. 7). The Turks' caps are fluted in the same way as in Bellini's portrait of Mehmed II, though the turban is wrapped rather less elaborately, is much less tall, and has conspicuously been plaited.[62] This could be a rather careless reading of Bellini's portrait medal (one would think Costanzo's was too sharp to be misinterpreted), but if so, the cap under it has been adapted to include a large turn-down to accommodate the wearing of a mask. The mask-faces are exaggeratedly ferocious to emphasise the Turkish threat. The hanging sleeves appear on the obverse of Bellini's medal, but the rest of the costume looks much more like stock Hungarian.

60 For an online facsimile of *Theuerdanck*, see <https://www.digitale-sammlungen.de/en/view/bsb00013106?page=,1>; for *Weisskunig*, see <https://digi.ub.uni-heidelberg.de/diglit/maximilian1775/0001/image,info>, mumming image PLATE 30 at #80a; <https://archive.org/details/derweisskunigein00trei/mode/2up>.

61 One (#51, the Hungarians with bird masks) has been identified as being on the same theme as a recorded mumming in 1492. There is much more work to be done on them.

62 The turbans of the Barbary Moors in Sternsee's *Codice de trajes* (see note 66) are plaited in the same way: see <http://bdh-rd.bne.es/viewer.vm?id=0000052132&page=1> #19 and #20 (fols 14v–16r).

FIG. 7: Mummers in Turkish Costume from the *Freydal* of the Emperor Maximilian I.
Vienna: Kunsthistorisches Museum, Kunstkammer inv. No. 5073 fol. 172.
© KHM-Museumsverband.
Online at <https://en.wikipedia.org/wiki/Freydal_tournament_book#/media/File:Freydal_fol.172_(Taschen).jpg>.

Though the Turks remain the most popular element in later costume books, we also know quite a lot about the everyday costume of the Spanish Moors, and from an earlier period. The *Trachtenbuch* ('Costume Book') of Christoph Weiditz (also a medal-maker) is largely an illustrated record of the costumes he saw in his journey through Spain, possibly in

JOHN BLANKE'S HAT AND ITS CONTEXTS

1528–1529 in the entourage of the Emperor Charles V, with additions.[63] They suggest that he sees the Moors as just part of the landscape. They had been subdued and, in theory, Christianised. The images that he presents are of domestic and agricultural scenes, mixed in quite naturally with other scenes of everyday life. We see how the *moriscos* dress in Granada, in the house and in the street; a black slave with a leg chain carrying a wineskin; white galley slaves carrying water barrels to their ships, and black galley slaves in Barcelona filling them (together with an apparently completely random drawing of a farthingale standing up by itself); the way the *moriscos* dance, snapping their fingers; a black drummer in the entourage of the Emperor (dressed in European attire but with large earrings). The text consists entirely of captions. He never published it, but it was seen and apparently used by others.[64]

Another very useful collection of Spanish costume drawings was also made for (probably not by) a member of Charles V's entourage.[65] Christoph von Sternsee became the captain of Charles V's German imperial guard. His costume album (c.1548–1549) is about twenty years later than Weiditz. It also starts off with Spain. It covers some of the same topics as Weiditz, whom he may have met in Augsburg, and seems to have reworked some of Weiditz's drawings. In addition, in 1535 Sternsee was part of the expedition that won back Tunis from the

---

63 Nuremberg, Germanisches Nationalmuseum HS 22474. Facsimile online at <https://dlib.gnm.de/item/Hs22474/9>. It is mainly famous for his drawings of the newly discovered inhabitants of the Americas, but it is also an invaluable source for the dress of the Moorish inhabitants of Spain, many of whom are of African descent, from the well-off ladies of Granada to the slaves in Castile. For a printed version, see Christoph Weiditz *Authentic Everyday Dress of the Renaissance: All 154 Plates from the 'Trachtenbuch'* edited Theodor Hampe (New York: Dover, 1994, reprint of de Gruyter edition of 1917).

64 For example, in Braun and Hogenberg's city maps of Spain. Katherine Bond argues for its wider use; 'Mapping Culture in the Habsburg Empire: Fashioning a Costume Book in the Court of Charles V' *Renaissance Quarterly* 71 (2018) 530–79, at 542–4.

65 Bond 'Mapping Culture' argues persuasively for the involvement of Jan Corneliszoon Vermeyen. There are two manuscripts of Sternsee's album. The one in in the Museo Stibbert in Florence is not online; I have used Madrid: Biblioteca Nacional de España MS RES/285, online at <http://bdh-rd.bne.es/viewer.vm?id=0000052132&page=1>. Bond thinks that it is a copy of the Stibbert MS. It lacks some of that MS's material, but also has material that Stibbert has not. It is catalogued as the *Codice de Trajes* ('Costume Book').

Ottomans,[66] and it includes lively pictures of the inhabitants of *Barbaria* (FIG. 8). Neither of these albums, obviously, were available to Henry VIII and his court, but they provide excellent illustrative material on the appearance of Moorish dress twenty or so years later. It may not actually have changed that much.

Contemporaries, then, seem to have had a varied selection of sources for their knowledge of the kind of dress for which John Blanke's headgear has been deemed to be a marker. It ranges from paintings and woodcuts and portrait medals to actual experience. We can use this, and slightly later records to which they could not have had access, as evidence against which to check the accuracy of their knowledge and understanding. But 'contemporaries' is a very general term: we must look more specifically at the court of Henry VIII at the time when the Tournament Roll was painted.

What did the court of Henry VIII know about Islamic dress?

As we have seen, there were sufficient images of what purported to be turbans, especially if we count all the biblical scenes – in printed books, manuscripts, stained glass, tapestry – in which they appear, apparently indiscriminately, on the heads of Jews and Romans. The next question is, 'Would Henry VIII and his court have recognised a genuine turban if Blanke had been wearing one?' Would they have known that it was a sartorial statement of faith (if it was)?

It would have been very strange, and the English court would have been very insular, if they had not. It should be unnecessary to underline the fact that Henry was related by marriage to, and in constant diplomatic touch with, the ruling houses of both Spain and the Hapsburgs, who were facing the Muslim threat in the Mediterranean and in Eastern Europe, respectively. He was married to the daughter of Ferdinand and Isabella, who in 1492, the year after he was born, had completed the *Reconquista* by driving the Moors out of Granada. His new wife had two Moorish female 'slaves', one of whom, Catalina de Motril, was called for in 1531 as

---

66 Katherine Bond points out how in Jan Cornelis Vermeyen's cartoons for the tapestries of the *Conquest of Tunis* (1546–1550), his portrayal of distinctive turbans and hats 'makes it possible to follow the battle narrative'; 'Mapping Culture' 564-6.

FIG. 8: The King of Tunis in Barbary; Biblioteca Nacional de España RES/285 fol. 15r *Códice de trajes* ('Book of Costumes'), copy after Christoph von Sternsee (c.1548–1549). Bibliotheca Digital Hispànica: image from the collections of the BNE. Online at <http://bdh-rd.bne.es/viewer.vm?lang=en&id=0000052132&page=1> #19. The attendant leading the King's horse wears a parti-coloured robe of red-and-white and black-and-white checks.

a witness in the royal divorce case.[67] His sister-in-law Juana, daughter of Ferdinand and Isabella, was married to the Hapsburg heir Philip the Handsome who was briefly King of Castille, and whose son became the Emperor Charles V.

Philip had made two extensive tours of Spain, one in 1501 when he married Juana and became heir presumptive to the Kingdoms of Castille and Aragon, and one on the death of Isabella *la catolica* when he became King of Castille *jure uxoris*. Henry had met Philip in person: in January 1506 he and Juana were shipwrecked on the South Coast on the way to Spain, and Henry, then Prince of Wales, aged 14, was delegated to conduct him to Windsor. When Philip toured Spain on his previous visit there with Juana in 1501, he had even been entertained with what sounds like an early version of *moros y cristianos*, in which he took a (possibly unexpected) part – dressed as a Moor. On Thursday 24 June, he, King Ferdinand, and their suite rode out a quarter of a league from Toledo. They:

> *estoient habillés à la morisque, bien gorgiasement. Ilz avoient sayons de velours cramoisy et velour bleu, tous broudés à la morisque. Les bas de leurs manches estoient de satin cramoisy, et dessus cela ung grandt chaimetaire, aussi un manteau d'escarlate, et sur leurs testes estoient torquiés.*[68]

> were dressed in Moorish fashion, very splendidly. They had gowns of red velvet and blue velvet, all embroidered in Moorish style. The bottoms [*cuffs?*] of their sleeves were of crimson satin, and over

---

67 See Lauren Johnson, *ODNB* sv *Catalina of Motril*. Very little is known about her except that she returned to Spain, married a crossbow maker called Oviedo, and had two daughters. She was sought as a witness in the divorce proceedings as she had been a chamberwoman for Catherine during the weddings with both Arthur and Henry. She did not testify and may have been dead already when she was sought. She and her companion are presumably the 'Two slaves to attend on the maids of honour' mentioned as being in the entourage of Katherine in October 1500 as remaining with her in England; *Simancas 1* 246. We do not actually know if she was a Black Moor or a White Moor.

68 Antoine de Lalaing 'Relation du Premier Voyage de Philippe le Beau en Espagne en 1501' and Anonymous 'Relation de Deuxième Voyage de Philippe le Beau en 1506' in *Collection des Voyages des Souverains des Pays-Bays* edited Gachard 185–6. This one occasion has been expanded by subsequent historians into a passion for Moorish dress, which does not seem to be borne out by what Lalaing says elsewhere.

that a great scimitar, also a cloak of scarlet,[69] and on their heads there were turbans/torses.

They were encountered by the Duke of Béjar with around 400 horses, who attacked them with canes.[70] *Et dist le roy à Monsigneur que en ceste fachon font les More escarmouches contre les crestiens* ('And the King [Ferdinand] told his Lordship [Philip] that this was how the Moors fought skirmishes against the Christians'). Philip, a considerable athlete, was greatly taken by the *juego de cañas* ('the game of canes') and threw himself into learning and practising the technique. One wonders if he told the young Henry about this encounter. We are so fixated on following the paper trail of surviving books and manuscripts that we forget word of mouth and personal experience. The *juego de cañas* appears to have been an entertainment regularly laid on for foreign ambassadors: Roger Machado, Richmond Herald, reports one when he accompanied the English ambassadors to the court of Ferdinand and Isabella in 1489, to negotiate the marriage of the three-year-old Catherine of Aragon with the two-year-old Prince Arthur. About 100 mounted knights and noblemen *escarmucherent et courrirent aveques cannes à la mode comme ilz se combatent aveques les Sarasins* ('skirmished and ran with canes in the way in which they fought with the Saracens').[71] The great scimitars are going to appear again, and so, disguised as 'javelins', are the canes.

It should not be necessary to point out that this was an age when people were alive to and fascinated by the differences in costume

69 Presumably the fabric not the colour.

70 This is not as innocuous as it sounds. The canes were fitted with vicious spear heads: see the drawing of a rider in Sternsee's *Codice de trajes* <http://bdh-rd.bne.es/viewer.vm?id=0000052132&page=1> #5 (our cover image). On the other hand, the painting of a *juego de cañas* in 1539 in Toledo by Jan Cornelisz Vermeyen shows both long ones with spear heads being brandished by what appear to be Moorish warriors, and much shorter headless canes being hurled by most of the participants in the game itself (also dressed as Moors). One hopes that the melée was not as random as it appears in the painting: see <https://rkd.nl/en/explore/images/49155>. The *juego de cañas* was imported, briefly, into England by Philip II of Spain in 1554.

71 'Journals of Roger Machado: Embassy to Spain and Portugal' in *Historia Regis Henrici Septimi, a Bernardo Andrea Tholosate Conscripta; necnon alia quædam ad eundem regem spectantia* edited James Gairdner (Rolls Series; London: Longman and others, 1858) 157–99, at 181. Unfortunately, Gairdner translates *courrirent aveques cannes* as 'ran with dogs'.

between nation and nation, and even city and city.[72] Even élite costume differed between countries. Queens and duchesses arrived to be married in the fashion of their own country and then changed to that of their new to show they had also changed (or at least extended) their allegiance. Catherine of Aragon and her entourage excited great interest in 1501 with 'the straunge dyversitie of rayement of the countreth of Hispayne', which included the later-to-be wildly popular farthingale.[73] As we have just seen, Philip on his visit to Toledo joined his father-in-law in wearing Moorish costume: the chronicler also notes when he is wearing his own Burgundian costume, and when he is wearing Castilian dress in compliment to his hosts and what was expected to be his new kingdom. Earlier, Machado notes carefully when *los reyes catolicos* are dressed according to the fashion of their own country, and when the Infante is wearing a French hat. Were there diplomatic nuances to be gleaned from that?

This interest extended to dressing up in foreign national costume in mummings and disguisings.[74] Possibly this began with an interest in national dances and experimenting with wearing suitable dress for each type.[75] When the dance was masked (as we have seen in the *Freydal*), it added a whole further dimension. The aim was to present oneself as

---

72 See Rublack *Dressing Up* chapter 4, 'Nationhood' (see note 13). Clearly cashing in on this interest, one of the earliest printed costume books (1567), by François Desprez, was entitled *Recueil de la diversite des habits* ('Collection of the variety of costumes'), and most others stress this variety in their titles.

73 *The Receyt of the Lady Kateryne* edited Gordon Kipling EETS OS 296 (1990) 43. The chronicler describes the farthingales as 'beneth her wastes certayn rownde hopys beryng owte ther gownes from ther bodies after their countray maner'. For her entry into London, he is mainly interested in the hats worn by the Princess and her ladies, and the fact that the Spanish ladies ride side-saddle 'upon the wrong side of the mule', so their backs are to the accompanying English ladies (32–3). According to the *Receyt*, the apparel of the last contingent of Spanish ladies 'was busteous and marvelous', and he adds rudely 'they were not the fairest women of the company' (33). Thomas More is said to have been very uncomplimentary about the Spanish ladies' appearance and stature.

74 Stella Mary Newton *Renaissance Theatre Costume and the Sense of the Historic Past* (London: Rapp & Whiting, 1973) remains the most thorough discussion of this: see 175–92 for the *Freydal*.

75 This happened particularly on diplomatic visits and when a foreign royal bride arrived.

someone other than oneself – what better way than pretending to come from an alien country?

Dressing up as Turks and Moors: the Disguising of 1510

Henry was an enthusiastic dancer and, it appears, very much part of this trend. Coincidentally, this enables us to assess the depth of his court's knowledge of Muslim costume, from both major areas, Turkish and Moorish. In the first year of his reign, on 'Shroue Sunday [1510]',[76] just a year before the tournament, 'the kyng prepared a goodly banket, in the Parliament Chambre at Westminster, for all the Ambassadours, whiche, then wer here, out of diuerse realms and countreis'.[77] He staged two disguisings, in which he and his circle, male and female, were dressed up in the costume of various nations. Conspicuous were a pair of Turks (the King himself and his dancing partner Henry Bourchier Earl of Essex, who had organised the show),[78] in the first disguising, with Moors as torchbearers; and in the second, two ladies dressed as Moors; and we not only have the description of the event and its lavish costuming from Hall,[79] we also have the bread-and-butter Revels accounts of Richard

---

76 The date of this entertainment is uncertain. Hall says it was Shrove Sunday (Quinquagesima Sunday, which sounds logical, as it was just before the beginning of Lent), which would have been 10 February 1509/1510; Hall *Union* 'Henry VIII' (see note 21) fol. vj verso. Gibson's accounts however call it 'The disguising finished in the parliament chamber at Westminster last day of Feb. 1 Hen. VIII', which would be 28 February 1510; TNA E36/217 fol. 14r, calendared in *Letters and Papers 2* 1490–1492.

77 Hall *Union* 'Henry VIII' fol. vj verso. The uncertainty about the date makes it difficult to say exactly which ambassadors could have been there. A number had arrived to congratulate Henry on his accession to the throne.

78 It is marginally possible that the idea of a pair of Turkish dancers came from the Earl of Essex, Henry Bourchier, whose heraldic crest is one of those enigmatic fantasy heads later bundled under the all-purpose term, 'a Saracen's head'. However, the colour of its face varies from red to black to white, and its headgear is nothing like that described by Hall and Gibson, being a floppy pointed cap with a pompom (or possibly a bell) at the apex, rising out of a ducal coronet: see, for example, the Garter plates of the Bourchiers in W.H. St John Hope's *The Stall Plates of the Knights of the Order of the Garter, 1348–1485* (Westminster: Constable, 1901) XIV, XXIX, LXI, and LXIII.

79 Hall *Union* 'Henry VIII' fol. vj verso; the whole account covers fols vi verso–vii recto. Hall would only have been 12 at the time, so it seems unlikely, though just possible, to be a personal recollection. On the other hand, he adds details that

Gibson, Yeoman of the Great Wardrobe, for the occasion.[80] We thus know not only about the general effect, but also the details of the costumes.

They are remarkably authentic as far as we call tell from Gibson's accounts. Who was responsible? Gibson tells us that the disguising was 'made by the devyse of the erll of essex',[81] Henry Bourchier, the King's dancing partner. There is nothing in his biography that suggests a personal knowledge of Turkey or Moorish Spain. Another possibility is 'mastere harry Wentworth then master of the Revyllys', but apart from the fact that he was a Gentleman Usher I can find almost nothing about him save that he was responsible for 'the making of a disguysing for a moryce' in 1507.[82] But almost any one of the participants might have weighed in with information and suggestions, and the ladies seem to have been influential in deciding details of their own costumes.

It seems likely that there was some kind of political statement being made, given that the entertainment was for 'the ambassadors', but apart from a general willingness to show awareness of the Turk and Moor, and possibly to take arms against them as enthusiastically promised, on the whole it merely suggests to me the pleasure of becoming the Other, which was the whole ethos of mummings and disguisings. The original intention was to present an image as far from your normal self as possible, so that you would not be recognised; other more complex pleasures, of release from everyday norms and constraints, and inhabiting a costume that felt different and gave you a new sense of your own physicality, followed.[83]

---

    cannot be deduced from Gibson's accounts. For example, Gibson does not account for the making of the Russian costumes, though the 'ij hansys' who needed hats, cloaks, and cotes may have referred to the dancers dressed 'after the fashion of Prusia or Spruce'. Perhaps the Russian costumes were already in the King's store.

80   TNA E36/217 fols 14–24. Calendared under 'Revels', in *Letters and Papers*, Volume 2, 1515–1518 1490–1492; online at <http://www.british-history.ac.uk/letters-papers-hen8/vol2/pp1490-1518>, but transcribed here from the original manuscript. For Gibson, see <https://www.historyofparliamentonline.org/volume/1509-1558/member/gibson-richard-1480-1534>.

81   TNA E/36/217 page 15.

82   TNA E36/214 f113v; see <https://www.tudorchamberbooks.org/edition/folio/E36_214_fo_113v.xml>.

83   One should remember that Henry and his court had been trained to dance almost as soon as they could walk, and that they were considerable athletes in all the martial arts, which involved wearing different types of armour and wielding

According to Hall, the King did not take his seat:

> but walked from place to place, makyng chere to the Quene, and the straungers: Sodainly the kyng was gone. And shortly after, his grace with the Erle of Essex, came in appareled after Turkey fashion, in long robes of Bawdkin, powdered with gold, hattes on their heddes of Crimosyn Ueluet, with greate rolles of Gold, girded with two swordes,[84] called Cimiteries [*scimitars*], hangyng by greate bawderikes of gold.[85]

The second couple were costumed 'after the fashion of Russia or Ruslande', and the third 'after the fashion of Prusia or Spruce'. The 'torchebearers were appareyled in Crymosyn satyne and grene, lyke Moreskoes, theyr faces blacke: And the kyng brought in a mommerye'.[86]

This was only the first part of the entertainment. After supper had been cleared away and the dancing commenced, the King again vanished, 'with certayn other persons', and shortly afterwards a drum and a fife led in a company of masked torch bearers,[87] then 'a certayne number of gentlemen, whereof the king was one', also masked, in short garments (Gibson specifies that these are Almain garments) powdered with castles and sheaves of arrows, the emblems of Castile,[88] and wearing feathered damask bonnets; then six ladies, the last pair of whom:

different weapons. They must have been aware of how different forms of dress affected their movement and balance.

84 This is ambiguous, but Gibson's accounts show that they had one scimitar each.
85 Hall *Union* 'Henry VIII' fol. vj verso.
86 'The King brought in a mommerye' seems to mean that the mummers brought in dice to play with the ladies and guests, not that there was a separate mumming: 'After that the Quene, the lordes and ladyes, such as would had played, the sayd mommers departed, and put of thesame apparel, & sone after entred into the Chamber, in their vsuel apparell.'
87 Hall seems to have got these confused: he says the torchbearers were 'apparayled in blew Damaske pur[f]eled with Ames grey' with matching hoods. According to Gibson, there were 'iiij genttyllmen that bare torchys' with new yellow velvet bonnets and garments (not described) from stock (page 17). There was only one person, the Lord Hastings, dressed in plunkytt [grey blue] damask (page 17) trimmed with gray [badger] fur (page 20).
88 Antoine de Lalaing describes the sheaf of arrows in his 'Relation' as an emblem used by Queen Isabella; Gachard *Collection des Voyages* 221 (see note 11).

were in kyrtels[89] of Crymosyne and purpul satyn,[90] enbroudered with a vynet of Pomegranetes of golde, all the garmentes cut compasse wyse [*on the cross*], hauing but demy sleues, and naked doune from the elbowes, and ouer their garmentes were vochettes[91] of pleasantes, rouled with Crymsyne veluet, and set with letters of golde lyke Carectes, their heades rouled in pleasauntes and typpets lyke the Egipcians, enbroudered with golde. Their faces, neckes, armes & handes, couered in fyne pleasaunce blacke: Some call it Lumberdynes, which is marueylous thine, so that thesame ladies semed to be nygrost or blacke Mores.

More dancing followed, then 'they departed euery one to hys lodgyng'.[92]

Gibson accounts for the costuming according to the type of material used, from whom it was bought, and how much it cost, and then breaks it down into yardage used for each type of costume, so that one must build up the individual sets of garments from their component parts. We are primarily interested in headgear, for male Turkish dancers and Moorish torchbearers from the first entertainment, and for female Moors from the second, but it is worth looking at the whole ensemble because it gives an excellent idea of precisely how accurate, in some cases unexpectedly so, the Islamic costuming was. Note that Turks and Moors seem to be mixed indiscriminately – the Turks are accompanied by Moorish torchbearers. This was a perfectly normal admixture in the Ottoman court; but it is unlikely that the devisor was thinking of that. His three dancing couples were dressed as Turks, Russians, and Prussians, all with interestingly different national costume: the torchbearers are merely a suitably exotic addition. The same goes for the Moorish ladies: they are the last couple in a set of six. The first two couples match each other, but their costumes are not identified either by Hall or Gibson as being from anywhere in particular. Hall gives some details, but all he says is that their head-dresses are 'straunge … to beholde'. It seems that the foreignness is mainly there because of its 'strangeness'.

89   'Initially a sleeved, long garment worn under a gown'; Maria Hayward *Dress at the Court of King Henry VIII* (Leeds: Maney, 2007) 434.
90   Gibson says they were crimson satin and blue satin (page 16).
91   So, in the printed edition of Hall *Union* 'Henry VIII' fol. vij recto: but Gibson calls them '2 rochets of sypers'.
92   Hall *Union* 'Henry VIII' fol. vij recto.

FIG. 9: Turbans in Turkish Mummery, *Freydal*: detail.
Vienna: Kunsthistorisches Museum, Kunstkammer inv. No. 5073 fol. 172.
© KHM-Museumsverband.

While we cannot really look at the headgear without looking at the entire ensemble, I will start each section with it. Taking the Turkish headgear first, it seems to have consisted of 'ij Turkey cappys to euery capp iij quarterys' of a yard of 'Crymsyn velluytt of geen [*Genoa*]'. These were then provided with 'Rowllys' of 'Sypers kerchers' [*cypress kerchiefs*], using 1½ kerchiefs per cap.[93] *Sypers* or 'cypress' was a fine transparent gauze originally from Cyprus',[94] and Gibson uses a lot of it in this disguising,[95] 'for hedys for fruntlettys for smok slevys & oothere nessesares' as well as for two overgarments for the Moorish ladies. He does not say what colour it was, but the list of garments it is used for suggests that it was white. If so, it sounds as if the Turks were costumed like those in the *Freydal mummery* (FIG. 9), with the gauzy kerchiefs

---

93 TNA E36/217 page 15 [ink number] for caps; page 19 for:
   sypers kercheffys ...
   Item for the ij turkys apparellys for Rowllys to the bonyttys of
   Crymsyn velluytt to euery bonytt j peece & dimidium _____ iij pecys.
The tailor was paid 'for makyng of ij turkys Robys ij bonyttys of turkey facyon'; page 24.

94 *OED* sv *cypress* n. 1c.

95 'Item Resevyd of sperys [*sic*] of small syse xxi pecys.' Annoyingly, I do not know what 'small size' is.

plaited or twisted into a *torse* round the base of the caps. Hall's 'greate rolles of Gold' sounds like a mistaken memory (of his or of his informant), or perhaps it refers to the embroidery that seems to have been lavished on all the costumes.[96]

This makes sense, because not only do the caps provide cover for the edges of the masks (oddly enough, masks are not cited in the accounts,[97] but the mention of a *mummery* suggests them), they form a useful base for the turbans. The stupendous turbans of the genuine Turks recorded visually two decades later are wrapped round and secured to extremely tall sugarloaf caps, the crowns of which project out of the top of the turban.[98] The caps worn by the *Freydal* Turks, red and fluted, look identical with that worn by Sultan Mehmed II in the portrait by Gentile Bellini.[99]

Just to complete the image of the costume, the two 'turkys Robys' were made of 'whytte Collyn baudkyn', white baudekin from Cologne. *Baudekin* is 'A rich embroidered fabric, originally made with warp of gold thread and woof of silk; later, with wider application, rich brocade, rich shot silk',[100] which might explain why Hall's informant remembers them as 'powdered with gold'. There is a lot more texture in these costumes then one might at first expect. Even the 'Turkey cappys' are made of Genoa velvet, 'originally a silk brocade velvet with a satin ground'.[101]

The ensemble was completed by 'ij turkey knyffys' bought directly from the cutler, which cost 13s 4d each. Judging from the *Freydal*, a Turk

96 Gibson does not refer to gold baldricks for the scimitars either. Perhaps they came from stock.
97 Detailed wardrobe accounts for the Revels from the reign of Henry VII do not survive. They are mentioned in the *King's Book of Payments* but under the blanket term 'paid to XXX for þe disguising'; for example, in 1496 <https://www.tudorchamberbooks.org/edition/folio/E101_414_6_fo_018r.xml>. Henry inherited his father's masking gear: there may well have been a stock of masks of which the Turks were part. Hall says specifically that the second contingent were masked: 'all with visers.'
98 See, for example, the 1526 woodcut by Jan Swart van Groningen: <https://www.britishmuseum.org/collection/object/P_1904-0519-13>.
99 National Gallery website, <https://en.wikipedia.org/wiki/Mehmed_II#/media/File:Gentile_Bellini_003.jpg>.
100 *OED* sv *baudekin/baudkin*, n.
101 A contemporary example in the Los Angeles County Museums is described as 'Silk cut and metallic uncut velvet on silk satin ground'; online, with image, at <https://collections.lacma.org/node/228788>.

FIG. 10: Janissary; detail from Hans Weigel *Habitus Praecipuorum Populorum* (1577) CXCIII; <https://gallica.bnf.fr/ark:/12148/btv1b71000o4s/f201>. Reproduced in compliance with the copyright rules of the Bibliothèque nationale de France.

is not a Turk without a scimitar – but judging from Philip's costume in Toledo, neither was a Moor. They seem to have been desirable collectors' items at the time: in July 1508 James IV of Scotland had acquired 'ane crukit baslar [*baselard*] of the Turk fasoun with hilt, pomelt, and chaip all gilt' for £4.[102]

Hall's *Moresko* (Moorish) torchbearers turn out from Gibson's accounts to have been two in number. They were dressed in particoloured satin garments 'kutt Compas wyse' (on the cross), half crimson, half green,[103] and lined with blue sarcenet (a thinner silk much used for trimmings and linings). On their heads they wore 'hanggyng koyffys' of yellow sarcenet decorated with crimson velvet letters. A 'hanging coif' suggests a cap with a tail: perhaps they were trying to emulate the Janissary's distinctive headdress, the *börk*, shown here from Weigel (1577) (FIG. 10).[104] To begin with this seems to have tapered to a point

---

102 *Accounts of the Lord High Treasurer of Scotland Volume 4 AD 1507–1513* edited J. Balfour Paul (Edinburgh: HMSO, 1902) 25. £4 Scots was probably equivalent to about £1 English at the time (see 'Scots Currency Converter' on the Scottish Archive Network <https://www.scan.org.uk/researchrtools/scots_currency.htm>).

103 Were the red and blue velvet Morisco garments worn by Ferdinand and Philip also half and half? The wording is ambiguous.

104 Hans Weigel *Habitus Praecipuorum Populorum ... Trachtenbuch* (Nuremberg: printed Weigel, 1577). Detail from <https://gallica.bnf.fr/ark:/12148/btv1b71000o4s/f201.item.r=Hans%20Weigel>.

that only curved over at the very end, as seen in the drawing by Gentile Bellini and in Breydenbach's Janissary woodcut;[105] later it seems to have developed a squared-off end that hangs more convincingly.

These *Morians,* however, were not Turks, but Moors (North Africans), 'their faces black'. They carried 'Javyllyns ... fetherd and heddyd with brod hedys the pece iiijs wheche evsyd & wron [*worn*] by the ij moryns'.[106] These sound intriguingly like the spears used in the *juego de cañas*, especially since Gibson also uses 9 inches of blue Genoese velvet 'for Javellyns garnyshyng'.[107] This could be a fringe or a tassel round the base of the head, or perhaps a pennant, both of which appear in costume-book paintings of riders in the *juego de cañas* (see our cover image) and in images of *Mauri praeliantes*.[108] Who carried the four 'Targettys of past payntyd & betyn by paynterys Crauft with fyne golld' is up to discussion, since there were only two *morian* torchbearers.

The two 'Morians' ladies from the second part of the entertainment are especially interesting because they wore what sounds like a good attempt at a flowing Moorish garment as illustrated by in the *Trachtenbuch* of Christoph Weiditz (FIGS 11 and 12). The *morian* ladies' main garment was (again) divided vertically into two colours, half blue satin, half crimson satin; there were six yards of each, so, however narrow the satin was, it sounds quite ample. Gibson merely says they were 'of mvrreyns facyon' (in Moorish style); Hall or his informant remembers them as 'cut compasse wyse [*on the cross*], hauing but demy sleues, and naked doune from the elbowes'. This cut would make them flare out from the shoulders towards the hem. The Tudor court was fond of half-and-half garments, which could be exploited effectively in the dance,[109] but Weiditz seems to suggest that half-and-half colours were

---

105 See also Lambert de Vos '*Türkisches Kostümbuch*' (note 27) fol. 12r, at <https://brema.suub.uni-bremen.de/ms/content/pageview/1616790> and 13r at <https://brema.suub.uni-bremen.de/ms/content/pageview/1616792>. The officers seem to wear the pointed version: fols 9, 10, and 11r.
106 TNA E36/217 page 20.
107 TNA E36/217 page 15.
108 '*Türkisches Kostümbuch*' *Mauri præliantes*: <https://brema.suub.uni-bremen.de/ms/content/pageview/1616942>, which shows a tassel round the base of the spearhead. De Vos paints one Black Moor and one White Moor, with apparently a ginger beard. It does not look as if it is due to henna.
109 Meg Twycross and Sarah Carpenter *Masks and Masking in Medieval and Early Tudor England* (Aldershot: Ashgate, 2002) 135.

also a feature of Moorish costumes. This was apparently not only in Spain: both the King of Tunis' attendant and the Berber man of the *Codice de trajes* are shown wearing what looks like a gingham garment of black-and-white and red-and-white check.[110]

The ladies' outfit was decorated with 'kutt werkys' in yellow satin. Over that they wore an 'upper garment' of (probably white) cypress (Hall calls it 'pleasantes'); these are described in the tailor's account as 'ij Rochettys of syperus'.[111] Nowadays a *rochet* is a loose white smock-like ecclesiastical garment that goes over the cassock;[112] it is made of very fine linen. In medieval and Tudor times, the word *rochet* was used of any loose outer garment or smock and could be male or female. It sounds as if the costumier was aiming for a loose white transparent garment worn intriguingly over the parti-coloured main garment.[113] The one thing the ladies were not wearing are the baggy trousers that feature in the Weiditz drawings. Presumably their 'kyrtels' came down to the ground. It is hard not to imagine that this was a costume that had been described to Gibson or his informant from life, and it is very far from our image of how a Tudor lady would normally look, with tight, almost rigid, bodice and sleeves. It must have felt very strange to them, like dancing in one's smock.

The most striking thing about them, and the most commented on from Hall onwards, is of course how they disguised themselves as 'nygrost or blacke Mores'. Instead of using paint, which might have been messy to put on and difficult to remove, their visible flesh, 'faces, neckes, armes &

---

110 Madrid: Biblioteca Nacional de España MS Res/285 fols 14v and 15v; *Códice de trajes* ('Book of Costumes') copy after Christoph von Sternsee (c.1548–1549). Online at Bibliotheca Digital Hispànica <http://bdh-rd.bne.es/viewer.vm?id=0000052132&page=1> #19 and #20.

111 TNA E36/217 page 24. The edition of Hall calls them *vochettes*, but this seems to be a typo which entered in the printing process.

112 The Roman Catholic version is short, ends at the knee, and often has a deep hem of lace. The Anglican is more traditional, and comes down to the feet, without lace, much like an alb, but usually with gathered sleeves and worn outside the main garments instead of, like the alb, under them.

113 Weiditz shows the outdoors garb of the Moorish women of Granada as a full, pleated, gauze mantle that comes up over the head and conceals everything but the eyes: *Trachtenbuch* 97: *Allso gandt die morysgen weiber für sich an Zuesechen auf der gassen In granada* ('This is the way the Moorish women look when they go into the streets in Granada'); online at <https://dlib.gnm.de/item/Hs22474/247>.

FIG. 11: *Allso gend die moristgen Junckfrau In Irem Hauss* ('This is how the Moorish girl looks in her house'). Nuremberg: Germanisches Nationalmuseum Hs 22474; Christoph Weiditz *Trachtenbuch*, page 103. Germanisches National Museum Digitale Bibliothek, CC Licence 1. <https://dlib.gnm.de/item/Hs22474/262>.

FIG. 12: *Allso dantzen die morystgen mit ain ander schnölle mit den Fingern dar zue* ('This is how the Moriscos dance with each other, snapping their fingers as they go').
Nuremberg: Germanisches Nationalmuseum Hs 22474;
Christoph Weiditz *Trachtenbuch* page 107 (detail).
Germanisches National Museum Digitale Bibliothek, CC Licence 1.
<https://dlib.gnm.de/item/Hs22474/272>.

handes' was wrapped in black gauze, *lvmbardyns*.[114] Hall identifies it as 'fyne pleasaunce blacke ... which is marueylous thine'. Gibson used seven pieces of *lumbardyns* on the two ladies and the two *mvrreyn* torchbearers, and for once gives the measurements: each piece was 2½ yards long by 12 inches wide.[115] The pre-performance wrapping must have looked like an elaborate form of mummification, but presumably both men and women were able to breathe through the gauze.[116]

Hall says that their heads were 'rouled in pleasauntes and typpets lyke the Egipcians, enbrouderd with golde'. This identification with the Egyptians is his addition – Gibson merely says 'Item for ther hedys & Rowllys to euery of the apparll' – and may be made in hindsight; his *Chronicle* was not published till 1548. The earliest image of an Egyptian woman that I know of (FIG. 13 (a)) comes from François Desprez's *Recueil de la diversité des habits* (Paris, 1562, but said by the author to be based on earlier sketches of the 1540s).[117] It shows a woman in an improbably large cartwheel turban – improbably large because her head seems improbably small in proportion to her body – with free-flowing hair. The next image (FIG. 13 (b)) is from Hans Weigel's 1577 *Trachtenbuch*, and shows a much more restrained form of headgear, though the roll is

---

114 Strangely, there is no entry for this in *OED*.

115 TNA E36/217 page 18:
Item Reseuyd vij pecys of lvmbardyns spent & imployd vppon the ij ladys moryns in [*and*?] men yn lyke manere the lenght of the pece ij yardys & hallf _____
Summa spent of lvmbardyns vij pecys
lenght xvij yardys dimidium the breed xij ynchys.

116 In James IV's famous Tournament of the Wild Knight and the Black Lady, in 1507 the Lady was given 'ane pair of blak sleffis and gluffis to hir of blak seymys leder' *Treasurer's Accounts 3* 259 (*DOST* suggests that *seymys* is a variant of *chamois*); *Treasurer's Accounts 4* 64. This suggests that she was not actually the 'Black Moir' of Dunbar's poem, but a court lady dressed up as one. The two 'Moor lasses' appear regularly in accounts but were presumably of far too low a social status to preside over a tournament.

117 François Desprez's *Recueil de la diversité des habits* (Paris: Nicholas Breton, 1562) dedication to Henry de Bourbon, sigs a ij verso – a iij recto: *ayant suiuy quelque dessein[s] du defunct Roberual, capitaine pour Le Roy, et d'vn certain Portugoys ayant frequenté plusieurs & diuers pays*. (Roberval was sent in 1542 by Francis I to colonise what is now Canada.) See detail in FIG. 13 (a) from the BNF département Réserve des livres rares, RES-G-2671, online at <https://gallica.bnf.fr/ark:/12148/bpt6k87071655.r=Francois%20Desprez?rk=42918;4>.

FIG. 13: Egyptian Women

All images from the
Bibliothèque nationale de France,
and used in compliance
with their copyright rules.
URLs are in the footnotes to the text.

(a) François Desprez
Recueil de la diversité des habits
(Paris: Nicholas Breton, 1562)
fol. 54r: *L'Egyptienne* (detail)

(b) Hans Weigel
Habitus præcipuorum populorum
(Nuremberg: Weigel, 1577)
PLATE CCXVIII: Woman of Cairo

(c) Georg Braun and
Frans Hogenberg
Théâtre des cités du monde,
Vol.1 (1645, published from
original plates of 1572 edition)
detail from *Cairus qui olim*
Babylon: Ægypti maxima Urbs

still the main feature.[118] She appears to be bare-faced; but the caption to Braun and Hogenberg's map of Cairo (FIG. 13 (c)), which appeared two years earlier but seems to have used the same model, stresses that they are wearing veils: *Sic vestiuntur nobiles foeminæ, cum aureo ornamento in capite, Et byssino panno ornatæ, facie cooperta, qua videre, sed videri non possunt* ('This is how the noblewomen are dressed, with gold ornaments on their heads, and adorned with very fine material,[119] with their faces covered, by which means they can see but not be seen').[120]

François Belleforest, who reproduces the same map in his *Cosmographie Universelle*, which came out the same year, not only renders this in French,[121] but discusses the women's attire in more detail in his main text:

> *Les femmes vont aussi richement vestues, & portent de magnifiques joyaux avec des chapeaux, ou guirlandes sur le front, & des coliers, & iaserans* [linked chain necklaces] *bien & richement atournez, & sur la teste des escoffions* [padded rolls] *de grand pris, & faits en pointe, & hautes de demy pied leur robes longues & diuerses couleurs auec les manches estroites, & le font passementé, & ouuré de tresbelles, & subtils recamures* [raised embroidery on brocade], *ayants la face couuerte de certains voiles faits de poil tissu qui sont noirs, par lesquels ells voyent les hommes, sans qu'on les puisse voir.*[122]

---

118 Hans Weigel *Habitus praecipuorum* Plate CCXVIII. The image in FIG. 13(b) is from BNF *département Arsenal*, ARS EST-1277, online at <https://gallica.bnf.fr/ark:/12148/btv1b7100004s.r=Hans%20Weigel?rk=150215;2>.

119 *Byssus*, a very fine woven linen, later also silk and other materials.

120 Georg Braun and Franz Hogenberg *Civitates Orbis terrarum* (Cologne: Theodor Graminaeus, 1572) #55. This was the first of six volumes, but each has a different name; online at <https://archive.org/details/civitatesorbiste00brau/page/n249/mode/2up>. The image in FIG. 13 is from the 1645 edition but uses the original 1572 plates; it is, however, numbered #56. The detail is taken from the BNF *département Cartes et plans*, GE DD-1605 (56), online at <https://gallica.bnf.fr/ark:/12148/btv1b53178893h/f1.item>.

121 *Ainsi sont vestues les Dames de grande maison, ayans vn ornement doré sur la teste et estans vestues de soye & fin lin, portans sa face couuerte d'vn voile par lequel elles peuuent voir, sans qu'on les apperçoit*; Braun and Hogenberg *La cosmographie vniuerselle de tout le monde: Vol. 2* (Paris: Michel Sonnius, 1575) map placed after col. 1999.

122 *La cosmographie vniuerselle 2* col. 2004.

The women are also richly dressed, and wear magnificent jewellery, with hats or garlands on their foreheads, and collars and chain necklaces well and richly decked out, and on their heads very costly padded rolls, made with embroidery [?] and half a foot high; their garments long and varicoloured with narrow sleeves, and they ornament them with passementerie and complex raised embroidery; their faces are covered with certain veils made of camlet [?] which are black, through which they can see men, but without themselves being seen.

Belleforest did not think much of the morals of the Egyptian women, who were overly well dressed, paid little attention to domestic tasks, and gadded about too much, which led to frequent divorces. He also deduces that they wear the veils, not for modesty's sake, but to be able to look at men.

The 'Lumberdynes, which is marueylous thine' may have been intended primarily as a way of indicating skin colour without having to resort to paint, but it incidentally also manages to reproduce the original purpose and effect of the Cairene ladies' veils as reported by Belleforest and Braun and Hogenberg: to see without being seen.[123] It is not far from the netted masks worn by most of the *Freydal* dancers.[124] These look as if they ought to be perfectly transparent to the viewer, but experiment has shown that they are extremely effective at disguising the wearer.

The description of the *morian* ladies' headgear in the accounts, 'sypers kercheffys ... for ther hedys & Rowllys to euery of the apparll', could equally well apply to the kind of attire worn by Weiditz' Moorish girl: a kerchief draped over the head and held in place by a roll with ornamental toggles. The general effect is the same as that of the Cairene

---

123 Note that the Cairene ladies are wearing full-face veils, not a niqāb with an eye-opening.

124 See <https://en.wikipedia.org/wiki/Freydal_tournament_book> ##4, 8, 12, 16 and throughout. They are the rule rather than the exception: only #92 (Hungarians with bird masks), #164 (the curious Punch-like figures), #172 (the Turks), #195 (giants), and #203 (Hungarians with birds' faces again) have full-face masks. Mummers with netted masks also appear in a small scene of *mummerey* on the Triumphal Arch, and the Triumphal Procession includes a company of ten mummers with netted masks in costume marching with torches preceded by one on a horse; *The Triumph of Maximilian I: Woodcuts by Hans Burgkmair and others* edited Stanley Appelbaum (New York: Dover, 1964) 31.

ladies' headwear, save that the roll is on the outside rather than under the kerchief.

Belleforest's description picks out the features for which Ottoman garments seem to have been valued: richness of fabric, use of contrasting colours, and elaborate relief embroidery. These are precisely those that Gibson attempts to reproduce, even the embroidery: 'It*e*m bought d*i*m*i*d*i*um a pow*n*de of [*latten*] wyer by me Rychard gybson the wheche was spent for the imbossyng of the lad*ys* atyer*e*', together with the 'clos sylk' for 'Corsyng [*couching*?] of golld of damask'.[125] Henry VIII occasionally adopted the Turkish style not just for applied decoration, but in everyday garments. As he got older, he seems to have found the kaftan style of overgarment comfortable; he appears in one in two versions of a 1542 portrait.[126]

It would be rash to claim that these costumes show that the early Henrician court had first-hand knowledge of Moorish costume, but possibly only second-hand documentary knowledge of Turkish costume, but it is a possibility. They certainly appear to have had a far more detailed knowledge of the costume both of Turkey and Moorish Spain than one might have expected. Gibson does not give details of the cut, but just says that the garments are 'of Turkey fashion' or 'of Morians fashion'. Either he knew what this was already, or someone had told him. Hall can also confidently refer to the costume of Egyptian women, but that is possibly by hindsight more than thirty years later.

Despite what one might expect, Turks and Moors did not continue to feature largely in Henry's disguisings. (*Morescos* as dances, our *morris*, are a different matter with a different costume.) This is largely because these move on from fairly piecemeal devices, as in 1510, to elaborate themed productions, usually with a romantic content, or actual plays. Some Turkey bonnets turn up in Gibson's accounts on New Year's Eve

---

125 TNA E36/217 page 20.
126 On Turkish fashion in the English court, see Hayward *Dress at the Court of King Henry VIII* 16–17; see also 100 and 226. The Portrait Gallery version after a painting of c.1542 (NPG 486) is reproduced as PLATE 1D on page 15, and can be seen online at <https://www.npg.org.uk/collections/search/person/mp02145/king-henry-viii>. Another portrait showing Henry in a red velvet version and apparently dating from 1542, sold at Sotheby's on 8 July 2015, is at <https://www.sothebys.com/en/auctions/ecatalogue/2015/old-master-british-paintings-evening-sale-l15033/lot.7.html>.

1519,[127] but Hall does not mention the occasion, being preoccupied with the arrangements for the Field of the Cloth of Gold. At the Field, one of the masquerades featured the Nine Worthies: Hector, Alexander, and Julius Caesar, the Classical Worthies, were dressed:

> in Turkay Iubbes [*long garments*] of green cloth of gold wrought like Chamlet very richly, & on their heads bonnetes of Turkay fashion, of cloth of golde of Tyssue, and cloth of siluer rolled in Cypres, kercheffes after the Paynyns fashion, and girdles of cloth of golde with pendantes of the same cut in great flames, and every one buskins of grene damaske.[128]

This is standard apparel in images of the Nine Worthies. The Egyptian ladies make a reappearance on 7 March 10 Henry VIII (1519), but wearing a hybrid costume, black velvet with white slashes, and in Spanish farthingales 'with hoopes from the wast douneward', and apparently only their heads 'tired like to the Egipcians very richely'.[129] 'Strangeness' rather than authenticity appears to be the watchword here.

The heraldic turban

However, there was another, traditional, way of representing a Muslim turban that would probably have occurred first to a heraldic artist, especially in the context of a tournament.

It takes us back at least two centuries, when 'Saracen's heads' started appearing as crests to go on top of helmets. These appear earliest, and in three dimensions, in alabaster tomb effigies, though one must be careful here, as not all the fantasy heads that ended up being classified under the blanket term 'Saracen' were necessarily originally intended to be that. They are not as exaggerated or as varied as the later Turkish turbans, however. What they have in common is a twisted cloth, a minimal

---

127 'Revels: Miscellaneous 1519' in *Letters and Papers 3, 1519–1523* 1552, at British History Online <http://www.british-history.ac.uk/letters-papers-hen8/vol3/pp1548-1559>. I have not seen the original MS.

128 Hall *Union* 'Henry VIII' fol. lxxxiij. Gibson's accounts for this are damaged, but include '3 Turkey bonnets'; 'Revels: Miscellaneous 1519' in *Letters and Papers 3, 1519–1523* 1554; at British History Online <http://www.british-history.ac.uk/letters-papers-hen8/vol3/pp1548-1559>.

129 Hall *Union* 'Henry VIII' fol. lxvij verso. There appear to be no surviving accounts from Gibson for this.

turban, wrapped round the forehead, usually over bare heads, though occasionally over caps. They match the earlier method of showing Saracen costume in manuscripts, presumably because the earliest date from the same time. This motif must have been reinforced by the heraldic use of the twisted cloth or *torse* to cover the join between the crest and the helmet proper.[130]

It also seems to have been the stock way of dressing up as a Saracen. Froissart describes the gifts given to Queen Isabeau and the new young Duchess of Touraine, Valentina Visconti, during the celebrations for Isabeau's 1389 Entry into Paris:

> *Le tiers present samblablement fut apporté en la chambre de la ducesse de Thouraine par deux hommesistorys en forme de moriannes, noircis les viaires et bien richement vestus, toilles blanches envelloppés parmi leur chief si comme se ce fussent Sarsins ou Tartres.*[131]

> The thirde present in lykewise was brought in to the duches of Thourayns chambre by two men / fygured in the fourme of two blacke Moores richely apparelled / with white towelles about their heedes lyke sarazins.[132]

At the jousts to mark the wedding of Katherine of Aragon and Prince Arthur in 1500, 'Sir Nycholas Vaux ... was apparaylid afftir the Guyse of a Turk or Sarasyn wyth a white Rolle of ffyne lynyn cloth abowth his hede the endys hangyng pendaunt wyse'.[133]

There are even a couple of Saracen maidens on the tomb effigies: one, the crest of Sir Fulk Pembridge (d.1409) in St Bartholemew's Church, Tong, Shropshire, wears a cap with the torse twisted round the base,

---

130 Thomas Woodcock and John Martin Robinson *The Oxford Guide to Heraldry* (Oxford UP, 1988) 87–8.

131 Jean Froissart *Chronicles* Book 4: from BL Harley 4379–4380 fols 9v–10r, at <https://www.dhi.ac.uk/onlinefroissart/index.jsp>.

132 John Bourchier, Lord Berners *Here begynneth the thirde and fourthe boke of sir Iohn Froissart of the cronycles of Englande, Fraunce, Spaygne, Portyngale, Scotlande, Bretayne, Flaunders, and other places adioynyng translated out of Frenche ...* (London: Richard Pynson, 1525) fol. clxxiiij verso.

133 *The Great Chronicle of London* edited A.H. Thomas and I.D. Thornley (London: Corporation of London, 1938; facsimile edition Gloucester: Alan Sutton, 1983) 314.

and a long plait;[134] the other in Abergavenny, which became the Herbert family crest,[135] could be the sartorial twin of Weiditz' Moresca.

We can be pretty sure how a heraldic artist from the workshop that produced the Westminster Tournament Roll would have drawn a Moor in a turban if he were asked to do it in the abstract, so to speak, because we have actual examples. At the beginning of the sixteenth century in England, when possession of armorial bearings was seen as a certificate of gentry status, demands for grants and confirmations skyrocketed. This was accompanied by a parallel demand for crests[136] (just as crests were beginning to be replaced on tournament helmets by panaches of feathers), and heralds start to record them in their notebooks. Because they were difficult to blazon (describe in words), the heralds often add little sketches. Besides these, there are some elaborate drawings of banners, which record the crest as if it were a badge; these come especially from the workshop of Garter Wriothesley, which is also thought to have produced the Roll. The combination of collected descriptions and these sketchbooks means that we know what, to a heraldic artist of the time, a *morian* was supposed to look like.

The 1530 *Alphabet of arms* of Thomas Wall,[137] Windsor Herald (Garter 1534–1536), finishes with a section on crests, which gives a fine

134 See <https://www.twentytrees.co.uk/History/England/Place/St-Bartholemews-Church-Tong.html?6k9xj7DB>; the only image I have found which shows the crest in full.

135 St Mary's Priory, Abergavenny, tomb of Sir William ap Thomas of Ewyas (d.1445). It is virtually impossible to find a photograph of the crest, because of the canopy, but there is one at <https://tracyburton.co.uk/weekly-photo-challenge-inside/>, though she interprets it as 'the figure of a small child'. Thomas Wall 'Book of Crests 1' (see note 138) 184:

> #114. HERBERD beryth to his crest a woman morions hede with long here a button in the ende sable a wreth a bout her hede gold and geules standyng in a lyke wreeth manteled asur lyned silver.

See also BL Add. MS 45132 fol. 26v, showing the Herbert *moresca* on a banner.

136 I use the term correctly here, of the object placed on top of the helmet: web searches are bedevilled by the modern assumption that *crest* means 'coat of arms'.

137 London: Society of Antiquaries SAL/MS/679/1: see description in TNA catalogue under <https://discovery.nationalarchives.gov.uk/details/r/5befa1a5-89fb-44cd-b47d-07baea9337dd>. This section was published by Oswald Barron as 'Thomas Wall's Book of Crests' in two parts in *The Ancestor 11* (October 1904) 178–90 and 12 (January 1905) 63–98. The are 649 crests in all, some repeated. A fair number

selection of verbal descriptions of the relevant headgear. They are divided between *morians* and *sarazins* – Turks do not yet seem to have entered the heraldic vocabulary. In many cases we can match them with contemporary illustrations. Here are some examples:

> 69. COTYNGHAM beryth to his crest a sarazins hede silver with a towail bout hit in a wreth silver and sable manteled sable lyned silver. (*1*: 182). The notes suggest that the *towail*, rather than the head, is argent: the face is said to be pro[*per*]. The 'wreath' or torse is marked as argent and sable.

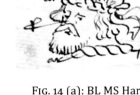

FIG. 14 (a): BL MS Harley 2076 fol. 144r detail.

> 140. CONWEY beryth to his crest a morions hede with a towell about hit in a wreeth gold and sable manteled sable d. ar. (*1*: 188)

FIG. 14 (b): BL MS Harley 2076 fol. 62r detail.

Some are more elaborate.[138] This could be a pageant *morian*, complete with javelin:

---

are London merchants, and country gentlemen, which shows the nature of the market.

138 For an example of another elaborately costumed *morian*, see Wall 'Book Of Crests' 2 66:

> 276. CHAMPENEY OF DEVON SQUYER beryth to his crest a demy moryan from the wast upward clothed w' strayt s[l]eves gold gyrther geules holdyng a ring in his hande and oone hangyng by his ere gold in eche a ruby havyng a copped towell about his hed and hangyng downe silver in a wreth b. ar. the mantel silver replenyshed with roses geules budded gold doubled geules.

481. CULCHET[139] OF CHESCHIRE beryth to his crest a morian standing naked sable holdyng before hym a target lyke a lyons face asure an annelette [ring] in the mouth gold casting a darte above his hede geules the hede fethers and a towell a bout his hede and hangyng downe silver standing in a wreth gold and asur manteled geules lynyd silver. (2: 81)

FIG. 14 (c): BL MS Harley 2076 fol. 146v detail.

Not described in Wall, but a respected member of Henry's court (he was one of the 'sad and ancient knights' put into the King's chamber at the expulsion of the minions, and also one of the 'ancient persons' in the disguising at New Hall in September 1519), was Sir Richard Weston. His crest was 'on a wreath Argent and Sable a Sar'cen's head affronté, with a band round the neck Or, couped at the neck proper, wreathed about the temples Argent and Assure'.[140]

FIG. 14 (d): BL: Add MS 45132 fol. 312v detail.

It looks as if there was a clear distinction between a saracen and a *morian*: the saracen is usually bearded, whereas the *morian*/Moor is cleanshaven, shorthaired, and looks like the generic image of a Black African. Wall does not describe the crest of John Mordaunt, which was

---

139 'CULCHETH, crest in Harl. MS. 5846, fo. 26b a mooryan standing naked, sa., holding a target like a lion's face az., etc., and Stowe MS. 692, fo. 30b as Calcheth'; *Grantees of Arms ... to the end of the Seventeenth Century* edited W.H. Rylands *Harleian Society 66* (1915) 68.

140 On the 1519 disguising, see Hall *Union* 'Henry VIII'. Blazon from *Banners Standards and Badges from a Tudor Manuscript in the College of Arms* with an introduction by Lord Howard De Walden (London: the De Walden Library, 1904) 245.

confirmed by Wriothesley (Garter) and Benolt (Clarenceux) in 1512/1513,[141] but it appears in the Harleian Society *Visitation of Bedfordshire*[142] as:

> Crest. – On a wreath or and azure a Blackamoor's head affrontee, couped at the shoulders, vested sable, bordered or, banded with a wreath round the temples or and gules, and ribbons of the same.

Here it is from the banner in Add MS 45132 fol. 47r. Its mouth is open, but nothing like as dramatically as it appears in Mordaunt's tomb, where it appears to be screaming, though whether in agony or in menace we cannot tell.[143]

FIG. 14 (e): BL Add MS 45132 fol. 47r.

Wall's description, heraldically without punctuation, includes both the headgear of the figure and the torse out of which it rises. 'In a wreath' refers to the torse. The headgear is usually described as a *towell*. Lord Berners translates Froissart's *toilles blanches enveloppés parmi leur chief* as 'with white towelles about their heedes'.[144] The word *turban* did not enter English until the 1580s, and then was fairly clearly considered an exotic loanword, with a variety of

---

141 *Grantees of Arms* 175.

142 *The Visitations of Bedfordshire Annis Domini 1566, 1582, and 1634* edited Frederic Augustus Blaydes *Harleian Society 21* (1884) 41. As the title suggests, this is a nineteenth-century composite work mainly interested in genealogy, so one cannot tell whether this is a quotation or not. The crest here is said to be from BL Additional MS 37147. It was confirmed on 29 February 1512–1513, by Thomas Wriothesley and Benolt: see *Grantees* sv *Mordaunt, John, of Turvey, Bedf[ordshire]*.

143 In All Saints', Turvey, Bedfordshire: see <https://www.nationalchurchestrust.org/church/all-saints-turvey#lg=1&slide=0>. One of a small group popularly known as 'the strangled saracen', because of their protruding tongues: a classic one is the monument to John Strelley (d.1502) at All Saints', Strelley, Notts.; see <https://www.twentytrees.co.uk/History/England/Place/All_Saints_Church_Strelley__Nottinghamshire.html>. Again, one cannot tell whether this is what it is meant to be, or if it is a menacing gesture. A lot of the heraldic descriptions of the crest include 'langued gules', which implies a red tongue.

144 Berners *Boke of Sir Iohn Froissart* (see note 133).

spellings.[145] A *towel* was usually made of linen, and could be long and narrow, suitable for wrapping round one's head or using as a sash.[146] The *OED* cites Chaucer's Hate in the *Romaunt of the Rose*, whose head was wrapped 'Ful grymly with a greet towayle' (lines 160–1), and that is how the illustration in Harley 4425, produced about 1490–1500, shows her.[147]

Heraldic artists thus had a very firm, even stereotypical, impression of what a Moor would have worn on his or her head. The recent suggestion about the image of John Blanke that:

> In the roll the head-gear is not shown as a piece of folded and twisted cloth (which is what a turban is) but as a hat; that is, the illuminator seems to have focused on the decorative traits of colour and pattern instead of representing how the cloth was wound around the head. This prioritising is in line with the function of the roll as an heraldic record of an event, where an accurate representation of style takes second place to an accurate representation of heraldic features[148]

just does not hold water. John Blanke's headgear is nothing like a turban (or *towel*) as a heraldic artist would be trained to draw it.

The conventions of heraldic painting

Here we need to ask what exactly we might expect from a heraldic artist as a visual record of an event.[149] The first thing that everyone points out

---

145 See *OED* sv turban. The earliest quotation (dated 1561) clearly refers to the cap round which the turban is built, not the cloth itself. In some heraldic manuscripts it is called a *turbot*, which creates an interesting image.

146 See *OED* sv towel n. 2b.

147 BL Harley MS 4425 fol. 8r: the French reads. *Et sa teste entortillee | Tres ordement dune touaille | Qui moult estoit dorrible taille* (fol. 8v). The artist has also decided to show Daungier, whose costume is not described, as a bearded Turk with vast white turban and the obligatory scimitar to back up his club. It was clearly the best way of conveying that he is extremely frightening, dangerous, and totally alien to the Lover's view of how the world should be.

148 See <https://www.johnblanke.com/kate-lowe.html>.

149 Sydney Anglo cites several existing and more now missing 'pictorial records of ceremonial, used to augment and clarify verbal records which still abound in the great corpus of heraldic commonplace books'; *Great Tournament Roll* 78, and see 79–80.

is that we notice John Blanke in the Tournament Roll because he is not a clone of his fellow trumpeters. They are drawn on exactly the same template; they might even have been traced. Yet we know that they cannot have looked exactly the same, not only because human beings do not, but also because several of them came from Mediterranean backgrounds: 'Domynyk' Giustiniani, from Italy, 'John de Cesill' from Sicily,[150] Jacquet de Lanoa or Lanos probably from Spain or Portugal. Frank Bocard might well have been French. Their leader, 'Mr. Peter, marshal of the Trumpets', was called Peter de Casa nova, which suggests that he was Italian or Spanish.[151] Yet they all appear as pink-cheeked, auburn-haired clones. Even given that they are a representative selection of the original fifteen, this is unlikely. A visitor from outer space, asked to comment, might well conclude that the Roll was drawn by someone from a distant country to whom all Europeans looked the same.

We were not meant to recognise them by their faces. Concentrating on John Blanke and the trumpeters, commentators fail to mention that everybody else in the Roll also looks the same (FIG. 15). There are slight variations, but nothing so marked as to constitute portraiture. Some of them (such as the King) are just a little larger than the others.[152] There may be a slight attempt to differentiate the King: his face is longer, his nose seems to have been more carefully drawn, and he has been given blue eyes, though the artist has not gone so far as to paint his hair auburn. A viewer might recognise him as a younger version of the c.1520 portrait in the National Portrait Gallery,[153] but I doubt it, if they were to be presented solely with the face. He is meant to be recognised by his role and position in the procession, by the richness of his attire and his collar, by the devices on his horse cloth, and, crucially, by the name written over the top of his head.

---

150   Nadia T. van Pelt writes about him at length in her recent book *Intercultural Explorations and the Court of Henry VIII* (Oxford UP, 2024).

151   See <https://www.dhi.ac.uk/chamber-books/folio/LL_BL_AddMS_21481_f0109r.xml>.

152   The same is true of the figures on the Parliament Roll (see below). There the heralds are drawn half the size of the dignitaries they are escorting; so are the four tonsured clergy carrying the King's canopy. Relative size indicates relative importance.

153   Unknown Anglo-Netherlandish artist, c.1520: King Henry VIII (NPG 4690) <https://www.npg.org.uk/collections/search/person/mp02145/king-henry-viii>.

FIG. 15: *Le Roy desarmey*: Henry surrounded by attendants. London: College of Arms MS Westminster Tournament Roll, 1511, membrane 35 detail. Reproduced by permission of the Kings, Heralds, and Pursuivants of Arms.

The same is true of the other contemporary 'portrait' in the 'Parliamentary Procession Roll' of 1512, a year later (FIG. 16).[154] At first, if you take the King in isolation, it looks more convincing. The artist is better at drawing faces; or rather one particular face, because when you pull back from the figure under the canopy, it turns out that he is good at repeating one quite well-drawn face again and again. The row of abbots and of bishops proceeding before the King all look exactly the same; so do the peers who follow him (FIG. 16). In this row of earls, the only one who looks slightly different is Henry Stafford, 1st Earl of Wiltshire, at the far right, and that is because he has white hair. He was no older than most of his peers, and younger than some of them: one is tempted to conclude that the painter had forgotten to colour his hair because he was on the end of the line on that particular membrane. How then are we supposed

---

154 Trinity College, Cambridge, shelfmark O.3.59; *The Procession of Parliament 1512*, a 5.5-metre-long vellum parchment roll. Facsimile online at <https://mss-cat.trin.cam.ac.uk/Manuscript/O.3.59>. The description comments, 'The drawing is not of the first class, but is fair. The faces can hardly be regarded as portraits. All are beardless'.

FIG. 16: The Earls in *The Procession of Parliament 1512*:
Trinity College, Cambridge, shelfmark O.3.59, recto part 10, detail
<https://mss-cat.trin.cam.ac.uk/Manuscript/O.3.59>.
© The Master and Fellows of Trinity College, Cambridge.

to recognise them? The answer is obvious: by the coats of arms above their heads, and the names written on scrolls above those. Looked at from this point of view, what really draws the eye is that Thomas Stanley, Earl of Derby, is the only one who is not a Garter Knight.

Michael Ohajuru uses the word *caricature* to describe this simplified mode of drawing, an unfortunate choice, because it suggests satirical intent.[155] There is nothing satirical about the presentation of John Blanke in the Roll, any more than there is of the other participants in the event. A better word would be *stereotypical* or *formulaic*. We would not recognise any of Henry's attendants as we might in a group photograph, even if we knew what their faces looked like in the first place. Holbein, who did not turn up in England till 1526, has skewed our perception of what to expect.

The rules of representation are different in heraldic painting. A herald could not count on recognising anyone by his face because it might

---

155 <https://www.johnblanke.com/about.html>. For comic cartoon-like Moors, see the crests of the Gelre Armorial; <https://uurl.kbr.be/1733715>.

well be concealed by his helmet: coat armour evolved for precisely this reason. He was trained to look for the outward, manufactured signs of identity; largely the heraldry. It is noticeable that even in the next formal pictorial record of a procession that survives, that in the Black Book of the Garter (1534),[156] where the artist, possibly Lucas Horenbout, has definitely attempted individual portraits, he identifies the Knights in procession by giving them inauthentic all-enveloping heraldic mantles, even though in the group portrait around the King they are wearing the traditional blue Garter robes.

In the Westminster Tournament Roll, even this does not obtain, because it is a record of an occasion when the chief characters are appearing not as themselves, but as fictional figures: *Joyeulx Penser*, *Bon Vouloir*, *Vaillant Desyr*, and *Noble Cueur Loyal*, and are labelled as such on the Roll. We may know that they were Sir Edward Neville, Sir Wiliam Courtenay, Sir Thomas Knyvet, and the King (and the crown surmounting his pavilion should give that away), but that is not the important thing. When the King is labelled as himself it is when he has removed his disguising helmet to reveal his identity: *Le Roy desarmey*. The coats of arms are not specific to the jousters, but part of the complimentary fantasy presented to the Queen. All the other figures are labelled by their role: *Le Maistre de larmurerye du Roy* (Sir Edward Guildford), *Le grant Escuyer* (Master of the Horse, probably Matthew Baker deputising for Sir Thomas Knyvet), *Le Maistre des pages* (Master of the Henchmen, name unknown).[157] Who they are is not particularly important. For practical purposes, all the heralds need to know is, should this ever be repeated, which officials should be where.

Who is not wearing a hat?

However, there is one thing about the depiction of the procession in the Roll that does not seem to have been remarked upon, and which concerns John Blanke. In their anxiety to point out that he alone of all his fellows

---

156 Windsor: St George's Chapel, Garter Chapter Archives. There are two good if slightly blurry images from it at <https://www.johnblanke.com/blog1/the-black-book-elite-images-before-portraiture>. The judgement that this is 'before portraiture' has not really looked at the faces.

157 Anglo (see note 5) identifies most of the figures except for the Master of the Henchmen. He is not named in this period in *Letters and Papers*; whenever a warrant is issued for his clothing, it is just for the henchmen and their Master.

is wearing something on his head, commentators do not focus on the fact that conversely none of the rest of the trumpeters are wearing any form of headgear, and that this might be significant.

There is no solid evidence that they were issued with hats as part of their livery, yet trumpeters in other drawings and paintings in a rather less formal context are shown wearing hats.[158] It cannot be because the painter could not draw hats (or maybe got bored with drawing them). If you go through the whole Tournament Roll, it suddenly becomes noticeable that the trumpeters are the only people in the procession to be hatless or helmetless, except for *Les Officiers darmes* – the pursuivants and heralds. Only the last herald, whom one assumes to be Garter, is wearing one. Heralds and trumpeters are bareheaded; no one else in the Roll is.

What is going on here? If you look at the Parliamentary Roll of 1512, which also depicts a procession, the same thing seems to be happening, save that there are no trumpeters. The pursuivants[159] and heralds escorting the bishops are also hatless. So is Garter. This is slightly complicated here by the existence of another small group, who are hatless for a well-known reason. Lord Henry Stafford bearing the Sword of State and the Duke of Buckingham bearing the Cap of Maintenance are also bareheaded, as their counterparts would be at the Opening of Parliament today.[160] They are in close physical proximity to the Sovereign, and they are bearing the major emblems of state. They, and Garter, are also bareheaded in the painting of the Opening of Parliament in 1523 in the Wriothesley Garter Book;[161] and in the painting of the Field of the Cloth of

---

158   For example, in the 'Retablo de Santa Auta' (see note 12), the musicians are wearing matching livery, with hats. However, often hat-wearing seems to be a matter of choice, as in Holbein's c.1524 drawing of musicians in a gallery: <https://www.britishmuseum.org/collection/object/P_1852-0519-2>. The two trumpeters in the Field of the Cloth of Gold tapestry are wearing completely different hats; <https://en.wikipedia.org/wiki/Field_of_the_Cloth_of_Gold#/media/File:TapestryHenriFrancois.jpg>.

159   Distinguished, as in the Tournament Roll, by wearing their tabards transversely so the short sides are to the front.

160   So are several other minor figures escorting the Bishop of London and the Archbishop of Canterbury. This seems to indicate their relatively low social status. They are attendants, not an essential part of the procession.

161   See <https://www.rct.uk/collection/1047414/the-wriothesley-garter-book>.

JOHN BLANKE'S HAT AND ITS CONTEXTS

Gold, the Marquis Dorset, bearing the Sword of State in the procession,[162] is also bareheaded, as is Garter Wriothesley.[163]

The other major processional event that is recorded in images, the Procession of Knights of the Garter, seems to show the same kind of protocol. Again, trumpeters are not shown, but there is a clear distinction between the Garter Knights, who wear their caps, and the heralds and pursuivants, who are bareheaded. This includes Garter, despite his pivotal role in the Order. This is most clearly shown in the 1576 engraving by Marcus Gheeraerts the Elder,[164] though it also appears in later images.[165] It is difficult to tell in the Black Book, where the image of the procession is largely limited to the Knights and the Sovereign, but it looks as if Garter, walking next to the clergyman in the bottom right section, is bareheaded, as is the figure bearing the Sword of State immediately before Henry VIII.[166] The clergy are naturally bareheaded, but that is for a different reason.

We seem here to have some form of processional etiquette, too obvious at the time to be noted.[167] The most likely possibility is that since

---

162 Hall *Union* 'Henry VIII' fol. Lxxvj recto. There is an obvious problem of protocol, as when Henry sees that the French Sword of State is being born naked, he commands Dorset to draw his out of the scabbard and also bear it unsheathed.

163 See the usefully enlargeable image at <https://upload.wikimedia.org/wikipedia/commons/0/04/The_Field_of_the_Cloth_of_Gold.jpg>. It is hard to tell if the macebearers are wearing hats, because of the cracking of the paint.

164 See <https://www.britishmuseum.org/collection/object/P_1892-0628-194-6>. Unfortunately, on the website this sheet is mislabelled. Garter (Sir Gilbert Dethick) appears on sheet 8: see <https://www.britishmuseum.org/collection/object/P_1892-0628-194-2>; also, National Portrait Gallery NPG D31854 (uncoloured) at <https://www.npg.org.uk/collections/search/portrait/mw126785/Procession-of-the-Knights-of-the-Garter-sheet-2>. One herald, identified in the notes as 'Hugh Cotgrave, Richmond', appears to be wearing some form of cap. Was he ill?

165 For example, the engravings by Wenceslas Hollar for Elias Ashmole's *The Institution, Laws & Ceremonies of the most Noble Order of the Garter* (London: Nathanael Brooke, 1672). This can be seen online at <https://archive.org/details/gri_33125012878183/page/n9/mode/2up>. The image of the Elizabethan procession is between pages 514–15; it is an adaptation of Gheeraert's sequence. The procession of Charles II is between 576–7.

166 The clearest online image is at <https://tudorfaces.blogspot.com/2017/04/anne-boleyn-as-lady-of-garter.html>.

167 Ashmole's account of the various processions (551–87) goes into great detail about the order of precedence, but does not at any point mention whether

the heralds, and the trumpeters who are their adjuncts, are technically servants of the king and the magnates to whom they are attached, there are occasions on which this was formally acknowledged, and that these were among them. Nowadays, when men no longer wear hats in public as a matter of course, the concept of 'hat-honour' – taking off the hat in the presence of someone of superior status[168] – has fallen into disuse. If this is a form of it that belongs especially to processions, it rather suggests that in the Tournament Roll, where hatlessness is confined to the heralds and trumpeters, whatever John Blanke is wearing, it did not count as a hat.

    certain persons are or are not bareheaded. The closest he comes to it are when he mentions that on the eve of the Grand Feast when the Sovereign arrives, the Knights make their 'Reverences unto him; which being performed, he re-saluteth the Knights-Companions by putting off his Cap. This done, the Sovereign putteth his Cap on again, whereupon every of the Knights-Companions put on theirs, and immediately rank themselves, according to their due place, on both sides of the State'; Ashmole *Garter* 512.

    One problem with other images of processions is that there seem to be variations about how far proximity to the Sovereign extends, in terms of taking off one's hat. In the c.1560 drawing of Queen Elizabeth I in procession, probably proceeding to Parliament, most of the participants are bareheaded, and are labelled as such, but without explanation: 'The squieres and footemen nexte aboute her highnes litter barehed'; 'Garter chef kinge of armes barehed; 'The sworde borne by the erle of [blank] barehed'; 'The duke of norffolk earle mareshall of england barehed'; College of Arms MS M 6 (Manuscript Book of Ceremonies, fols 41v–42; illustrated as PLATE XII of *The Heralds' Exhibition Catalogue 1934* (London: Tabard Press, 1970, enlarged reissue of catalogue of 1936) catalogue entry 65 #86.

168 See Randle Cotgrave *A Dictionarie of the French and English Tongues* (London: Adam Islip, 1611): '**Barretade**: f. Cap-courtesie, hat-reuerence; the vailing of the bonnet; the putting off of the hat, or cap, in a salutation, etc'; also, French *barretade* in Edmond Huguet *Dictionnaire de la langue française du seizième siècle* 7 vols (1925–1967) *1* 493. In Spanish, *bonetada*, 'La cortesía que se hace quitándose el bonete ó sombrero'; Matías Calandrelli *Diccionario filológico-comparado de la lengua castellana* (1880). Maria Hayward refers to it briefly in '"The Sign of Some Degree"?: The Financial, Social and Sartorial Significance of Male Headwear at the Courts of Henry VIII and Edward VI' *Costume 36* (2002) 1–17 at 11–12; Penelope J. Corfield maps the seventeenth and eighteenth-century refusal to grant it; 'Dress for Difference and Dissent: Hats and the Decline of Hat Honour' *Costume 23* (1989) 64–79. Hat-honour is a male preserve. It lingers in the habit of men taking off hats on entering church. Most male hats that are worn today, disregarding uniform, are either for protection against the weather, or sports-based, like the baseball cap.

A Possible Identification

But what is it? I think by now we can declare with a fair amount of confidence that what John Blanke is shown wearing, in a painting also by an heraldic artist, is not meant to be a turban (they would have drawn it differently); nor is it to be read as any form of the characteristic Muslim headgear of either a Turk or a Moor (Henry and his court seem to have had a good idea of what this was). I have just declared that it was unlikely to have been seen as a hat, though we must define precisely what this might have meant at the time.

Nadia van Pelt has already challenged the 'turban' identification in her article in *Notes and Queries*.[169] She cites 'a reference to eight trumpet players from Spain who had been sent by the Spanish king Ferdinand to entertain Archduke Philip and his wife, Juana of Castile – who was Ferdinand's daughter – on their journey to Spain'. They came, somewhat surprisingly, to England, expecting to find Philip and Juana breaking their journey in order to visit her sister Katherine of Aragon, newly married to Prince Arthur.[170] The trumpet players are described (later) as:

> *huyt trompettes du Roy despaigne tous habilliez dung manteaux de rouge drap a la manière despaigne , et vne barette sur leur teste de velours vert.*

> eight trumpet players of the king of Spain all dressed in coats[171] made of red cloth in the manner of Spain, and on their heads a beret of green velour.

She points out that the writer interpreted this combination 'as typical "livery" for a Spanish trumpet player', and suggests that therefore 'Blanke's green hat' might have been 'a typical head-dress as it was worn

---

169 Nadia T. van Pelt 'John Blanke's Hat' (see note 18).
170 Ferdinand, Joanna's father, had insisted that the couple should come to Spain by sea, and presumably when the musicians set off he still expected this. However, Philip decided that they should go by land through France in order to meet Louis XII and his wife Anne of Brittany, with whom he had arranged a marriage alliance between their one-year-old children, Charles (later the Emperor Charles V) and Claude. The land route was probably a wise move, since his sister Margaret of Austria had been shipwrecked on the south coast of England in 1497, and he and Joanna were shipwrecked there in 1506.
171 According to Cotgrave, a *manteau* is 'A cloke', not a coat; Randle Cotgrave *A Dictionarie of the French and English Tongues* (London: Adam Islip, 1611).

by trumpet players at the court of Ferdinand of Aragon', and probably a 'beret'. If so, it would appear in the Tournament Roll either because it was 'an invention by the artist creating the manuscript, so as to symbolically refer to a Spanish connection', or as historical reportage of something that Blanke actually wore. In the latter case, rather than it being his free choice, the court might have 'imposed this head-dress on the trumpet player; if Blanke was not Spanish, the court may still have wanted to pass him off as such'. Either way, this headgear would be meaningful, though because of an implied Spanish connection, not because it denoted a Muslim heritage.

Perhaps fortuitously, the shawm-players in the Portuguese *Retabulo de Santa Auta* painting of c.1525 are wearing precisely the same colour combination, save that they have green sleeves to their red tunics.[172] And they are not wearing turbans, but what Henry VIII's court would have called *bonnets*.

Costume: the problems of translation

Or so we believe. We must be careful when visualising a piece of clothing from its name, especially from language to language and century to century. Nadia van Pelt translates *barette* as 'beret', but it is not a *beret* in our sense; the word in this form did not enter English (with much the same meaning as it has nowadays), until the early nineteenth century.[173] When a version of it (as *baretta*) turns up in 1598, it refers to the Roman Catholic priest's *biretta*.[174] The French word in the quotation, *barette*, seems to have referred to the soft four-pointed cap worn in the sixteenth

---

172 'Shawm band with sackbut player' (see note 12). Detail on cover of *Medieval English Theatre 44*, full image at <https://en.m.wikipedia.org/wiki/File:Bottega_di_lisbona,_retablo_di_sant%27auta,_1522-25,_matrimonio_di_s._orsola_e_il_principe_conan_3_musici.jpg>.

173 *OED* sv *beret*: 'A round flat woollen cap worn by the Basque peasantry' (1850), or (a slightly earlier usage, 1827), a fashion version of this.

174 *OED* sv *biretta*; the first example is spelled *baretta*. Possibly it was not adopted as *bar[r]ette* because the Middle English noun *baret* (from French *barat*) meant 'fraud', or 'strife'; see *OED* sv *barrat* n. The *OED*'s earliest citation under *barrette* is 1901, and refers to 'A bar for supporting a woman's back hair; also, a hair-ornament'.

century by clergy, academics, and lawyers;[175] the same garment was worn by the same professional classes in England – think of portraits of Wolsey (where it is 'a Cardinal's cap'), Fisher, Cranmer, Cromwell, and More. In Latin, the English called it a *birretum*;[176] in English, however, they called it a *cap*.[177] There is no direct one-to-one correspondence between words in different languages, because each language classifies things differently.

Among costume historians today, the consensus seems to be that *bonnet* in English refers to a hat, usually with a small turned-up brim (known as a *turf*),[178] which could be slashed or tabbed and decorated with feathers, brooches, buttons, ribbons, or embroidery. It was made of silk velvet, felt, or knitted. Richard Gibson almost always describes the headgear he provides as 'bonnets'.[179] A *cap* was (probably) closer-fitting and mostly (though not always) brimless, possibly for harder or (except as above) less formal wear.[180] Maria Hayward defines it as 'a small close-

---

175 *Dictionnaire du Moyen Français (1330–1500)* sv barrette 2: 'Petit bonnet plat, à trois ou quatre faces carrées, qui peut se replier'; see <http://www.atilf.fr/dmf>. For a wider definition see also *Trésor de la langue Française informatisé* sv barrette 2 B 1: 'Bonnet de feutre ou de laine foulée, genre de béret qui fut porté au 15e et 16e s. et qui souvent prenait le crâne jusqu'aux oreilles'; see <http://atilf.atilf.fr/tlf.htm>.

176 *DMLBS* sv *birretum*.

177 Its direct descendant is the Canterbury cap, in the sixteenth and seventeenth centuries called the *square-cap*, which was frequently used as an example by the disputants in the Vestarian Controversy. (This was an ongoing and bitter dispute in the Protestant Church of England about suitable liturgical wear for the clergy, and whether some items could be considered acceptable because edifying.) Its academic descendant is the Oxford women's academic cap, which has a buttoned flap at the back which can be lowered as in the portraits of Thomas More (it can now be replaced by the 'mortarboard').

178 *OED* sv †*turf*, n.2. The verb means 'to turn over', as in *topsy-turvy*. See Hayward 'A Sign of Some Degree' 6.

179 We cannot work out the difference from the amount of material used, because they were both supplied ready-made by the milliner. Caps usually seem to be cheaper than bonnets, but not always. It must partly have depended on the amount of decoration.

180 On the subject of men's headgear in general, see Hayward 'The Sign of Some Degree'. She mentions 'questions over terminology' and that a 'fairly limited vocabulary was used to describe headwear in sixteenth-century documents and it is necessary to observe it' but does not really attempt definitions. This probably reflects the loose usage at the time. She discusses 'Headwear' in *Dress at the Court of King Henry VIII* 112–13, but assumes a knowledge of the meaning of

fitting head covering, often of soft material'.[181] On the other hand, just to show the flexibility of vocabulary and frustrations that lie in wait for anyone trying to find a tidy solution, a 1523 grant by Henry VIII refers to *birettis sive pilleis vulgariter vocati French bonettis or cappes*;[182] and later on (1611) Cotgrave translates *barrette* as 'a cap or bonnet'.[183] Any attempt to pin it down further runs up against the inbuilt problem that the object to which it refers keeps on changing with the fashion.

It is possible, therefore, even likely, that Joanna's Spanish trumpeters were wearing *bonnets* like the Portuguese shawm-players in the altarpiece. Frustratingly, most of the trumpeting in contemporary Spanish art seems to be being done by angels. There are a couple of earth-bound examples, both by outside observers: in Vermeyen's 1539 *juego de cañas* painting, the four Portuguese trumpeters (there are Portuguese coats of arms on their trumpet banners) are wearing a variety of headgear, all red: two sport bag-shaped caps with turned-up brims (Richard Gibson's 'hanging coifs'?), one has a pointed cap, and one a round cap with a white torse twisted round it.[184] Christoph Weiditz' Imperial drummer is wearing a round blue cap with a rolled brim.[185] The field for musicians' headgear seems to be wide open.

One thing is certain, though: John Blanke's hat is not a *towel* or turban, either Moorish or heraldic. And I do not think that it is a *bonnet* as reportedly worn by Joanna's Spanish trumpeters. It is visibly not any

---

the terms *bonnet* and *cap*, which she defines very briefly and generally – 'a small head covering'; 'a small close-fitting head covering, often made of soft material' – at 433–4. Another pair of definitions, in the *Great Wardrobe Accounts* 288, 290 [see note 10] enlarge *bonnet* to 'worn by men and women. A small, round, soft headcovering worn as part of fashionable dress and by professional men' and applied to the gable hood for women. *Cap* remains the same, which does not take into account its use in special cases such as the cap of maintenance, and the cardinal's cap.

181 Hayward *The Great Wardrobe Accounts* 290.
182 Thomas Rymer *Foedera* edited George Holmes (The Hague: Joannes Neaulme, 1741) 6:2 4; quoted in *DMLBS* sv *birretum*. An adjacent quotation, dated 1469, from the Scottish Exchequer records is *pro ... birretis, pilleis et aliis minutis expensis ad usum domini regis*.
183 Cotgrave *Dictionarie* sv *barrette* f.
184 See <https://rkd.nl/en/explore/images/49155>, bottom right of painting.
185 See <https://dlib.gnm.de/item/Hs22474/168>.

of the kinds of hat worn by the Portuguese trumpeters in Vermeyen's painting or the Santa Auta retable. So, what is it? If my argument is valid, then it is something that no one would expect him to take off in the procession, possibly because it would be too difficult to do so, possibly because it did not count as a hat for purposes of hat-honour. Here I must confess that when I first saw it, I thought, 'I have seen that before', and it was not in an African, or even a Spanish, context.

Lancaster University

Publisher's Note

This subject will be pursued further in Part 2, in the next volume of *METh*.

DISJOINTED UNISON
Bodily Porousness and Subversion in the Croxton *Play of the Sacrament*

Sadegh Attari

The Croxton *Play of the Sacrament* has been one of the most widely studied texts in relation to depictions of the body, including Christ's body, the body of the 'other' (in this case, the Jewish body), and the medical body.[1] In the majority of such studies, bodies seem to be conceived within and through a dichotomy that privileges bodily 'wholeness' over bodily damage or disintegration. It is fairly easy to find justification for this privileging: one sense of the Middle English word *hole* (*whole* in modern spelling) signified the healthy, undamaged state of the body, and an undamaged body tends to have a more pleasant sensory experience than a damaged one.[2] However, 'wholeness' of the body is not privileged over disintegration in all late medieval contexts: in some examples, the un-whole body is an important signifier. This prompts a reconsideration of how to refer to the quality of being un-whole without invoking the dichotomy and denigrating the un-whole state of bodies to a state of being damaged. My term of choice is *porousness*, defined as the capacity of the body to have its superficial integrity violated without descending into dysfunction or damage; this then enables it to enter relationships and transactions with other bodies through that very state of porousness. Accordingly, to avoid resorting to 'disintegration', I will also refer to the process of achieving such a state as 'becoming-porous'. By suspending the dichotomy between whole bodies and damaged bodies, we can enrich our understanding of the pivotal scene during the Passion sequence of the Croxton *Play*, in which the Host (or the body of Christ) and the hand of the character of Jonathas are joined. The adjusted perspective and the reading that it offers augment existing scholarship on the role of bodies and subversion in the play, as well as affecting how we view un-whole bodies (including the body of Christ), highlighting porousness not as the negation or absence of wholeness, but as a self-sufficient property of bodies.

---

1   The play is cited throughout, by line number, from *Medieval Drama: An Anthology* edited Greg Walker (Oxford: Blackwell, 2000) 213–33.
2   *MED* sv *hōl(e)* adj. 2.

I argue that from such a perspective, the simultaneity of the performance of becoming-porous in the bodies of both Christ and Jonathas (the oppressed and the oppressor) unites Christian and Jewish bodies through the very state of porousness, blurring the purported natural differences between them. Consequently, it offers an opportunity for the subversion of the hierarchy of status between them. It is quite typical of Host desecration narratives – of which the Croxton *Play* is an example – to feature the two instances of becoming-porous: that of Christ and that of the Jewish villain. Each seems intended for its own purpose: one to elicit pity and compassion, as well as to show Christ's power and resilience in the face of adversity, and the other to enact cathartic justice on the Jewish aggressors. Jody Enders notes that Passion plays and Host desecration plays provided a 'golden opportunity to purge audience emotion and give them pleasure by staging the unjust punishment of Christ and the presumably just punishment of the Jews for having punished him'.[3] In the Croxton *Play*, however, the simultaneous occurrence of the two processes confuses the cathartic function: it allows the becoming-porous of the Jewish body to mirror Christ's, and this is then boosted by the Jews' growing understanding of Christ and eventually their conversion. The subversive potential of porousness is augmented by the performance of the two simultaneous processes, since it is in the immediacy of performance that the conflation of the two senses of becoming-porous is most effective.

To demonstrate how this process works, I will draw on the theoretical concept of *becoming*, which refers to what Erika Fischer-Lichte characterises as the capacity to generate 'something that does not yet exist elsewhere but comes into being only by way of the performative act/ the performance that occurs'.[4] The concept will help me account for the play's subversive capacity not as a product of authorial decision, but as a potential and emergent consequence of the simultaneous performances

---

[3] Jody Enders *The Medieval Theater of Cruelty: Rhetoric, Memory, Violence* (Ithaca: Cornell UP, 1999) 183.

[4] Erika Fischer-Lichte *Theatre, Sacrifice, Ritual: Exploring Forms of Political Theatre* (London: Routledge, 2005) 27. This essay adopts Katie Normington's definition of performance as 'an act which has been self-consciously prepared for deliberate spectatorship'. This definition includes rituals (such as the Mass), different forms of drama, music, games, various forms of processions, and even instances of public punishment; Katie Normington *Medieval English Drama: Performance and Spectatorship* (Cambridge: Polity Press, 2009) 2.

of becoming-porous. In what follows, I shall elaborate on my choice of the term *porousness* and expound on the theoretical concept of *becoming* and its applicability to medieval drama. I will then offer a reading of the interaction between Christian and Jewish bodies in the play and its capacity to subvert the hierarchy of status among bodies.

Struggling for Words

Late medieval culture's understanding of the body as a permeating, unstable, and networked entity has been explored by a number of scholars.[5] They emphasise the limited applicability of understanding the medieval body solely as a unified, isolated whole when examining late medieval cultural phenomena. What they suggest emerges instead, is a view of the body as composed of various elements, in constant flux, not necessarily bound by its superficial integrity, and capable of establishing connections with other entities within and without it. They use various terms to characterise this body: 'compartmentalised', 'fragmented', and 'in parts' or 'bits'.[6] Much like 'disintegration' in the dichotomy discussed above, these terms are negative: they insinuate a lack or absence of a privileged quality of wholeness, even if they are used by the authors to argue the contrary. I would like to suggest *porous* as an alternative term to describe the capacity of the body to function as a whole, as well as a fluctuating amalgamation of entities within and without its superficial boundaries, capable of establishing connections with new entities at any given moment.

---

5   There are plenty of studies on the subject; significant interventions include Sarah Beckwith *Christ's Body: Identity, Culture and Society in Late Medieval Writings* (London: Routledge, 1993); Caroline Walker Bynum *Christian Materiality: An Essay on Religion in Late Medieval Europe* (New York: Zone Books, 2011); Katherine Park *Secrets of Women: Gender, Generation, and the Origins of Human Dissection* (New York: Zone Books, 2006); and Miri Rubin *Corpus Christi: The Eucharist in Late Medieval Culture* (Cambridge UP, 1991).

6   David S. Areford *The Viewer and the Printed Image in Late Medieval Europe* (Farnham: Ashgate, 2010) 77; Caroline Walker Bynum *Fragmentation and Redemption: Essays on Gender and the Human Body in Medieval Religion* (New York: Zone Books, 1991); David Hillman and Carla Mazzio 'Introduction: Individual Parts' in *The Body in Parts: Fantasies of Corporeality in Early Modern Europe* edited David Hillman and Carla Mazzio (New York: Routledge, 1997) xi–xxix; Beckwith *Christ's Body* 113.

The phrasing of this understanding is, as we shall see, indebted to posthumanist and New Materialist theories of embodiment; but this conception of the body is itself inspired by medieval medical theories, which place the human being in continuous transaction with a universe-wide network of factors, ranging from the stars to diet.[7] Within this framework, the human body never remains uncontaminated by outside influence. It also never remains a passive recipient of outside influence for, as the Middle English translation of the thirteenth-century Bartholomaeus Anglicus' encyclopaedia notes, the body is 'ful of poores' that have the function of 'puttynge out of superfluitees of fumosite. For by hete þe pores open, and þe superfluite þat is bytwene þe fel and þe fleisch it is iput out by vapoures and swetes'.[8] When pores are blocked, the healthy level of transaction between the body and extracorporeal entities is disrupted, which results in humoral imbalance, and, consequently, illness. Various means of treatment were recommended for such circumstances: from purgatives and anti-inflammatory drugs to topical salves and ointments, and more invasive methods of treatment such as phlebotomy and even surgery. Many of these solutions involved restoring the body to its porous state. Therefore, to make the body 'whole' again often entailed both violating its superficial integrity and making it porous.[9]

---

7   The posthumanist and New Materialist framework that I use is informed by Rosi Braidotti *The Posthuman* (Cambridge: Polity, 2013), Gilles Deleuze and Félix Guattari *What is Philosophy?* translated Hugh Tomlinson and Graham Burchell (New York: Columbia UP, 1994), and the works of Jane Bennett, Manuel DeLanda, and Bruno Latour. For medieval theorisations of networked embodiment, see *Western Medical Thought from Antiquity to the Middle Ages* edited Mirko D. Grmek (Cambridge, MA: Harvard UP, 1998); Julie Orlemanski *Symptomatic Subjects: Bodies, Medicine, and Causation in the Literature of Late Medieval England* (Philadelphia: University of Pennsylvania Press, 2019); Elizabeth Sears *The Ages of Man: Medieval Interpretations of the Cycle of Life* (Princeton UP, 1986); Nancy G. Siraisi *Medieval and Early Renaissance Medicine: An Introduction to Knowledge and Practice* (Chicago UP, 1990).

8   Bartholomaeus Anglicus *On the Properties of Things* translated John Trevisa edited M.C. Seymour, 3 vols (Oxford: Clarendon Press, 1975) *1* 286.

9   Detailed explanation of such processes can be found in Nancy G. Siraisi's and Mirko D. Grmek's works cited in note 7 as well as in Jacques Jouanna *Greek Medicine from Hippocrates to Galen: Selected Papers* edited Philip van der Eijk translated Neil Allies (Leiden: Brill, 2012); Vivian Nutton *Ancient Medicine*

In the medical sense, then, porousness bypasses the problematic dichotomy of *whole* versus *damaged*. It is difficult, however, to view corporeal damage, like that done to Christ's body during the Passion, as a positive or neutral state of porousness from the medical perspective. On the other hand, late medieval devotional culture provides an angle from which porousness, even in the sense of bodily damage, achieves significantly positive powers. Iconography, for example, rather than solely encouraging veneration of Christ's perfect and healthy body, also reveres Christ's crucified, tormented, and wounded body, which becomes the focus of intense piety in meditational literature and portrayals of the scenes of the Passion. The prime example of this is the iconographic trope of the Man of Sorrows.[10] Instances of the trope typically depict Christ with all his wounds, including his nail wounds. However, whereas in many late medieval representations of the Crucifixion, Christ is on the cross with his eyes closed (signifying his death), in the Man of Sorrows portrayals, his eyes are open (therefore he is alive, even though he bears the nail wounds as well as the side wound that signify that he has already died on the cross), and while he bears the wounds caused by his crucifixion, he is not on the cross. There are also instances in which elements from the tropes of crucifixion, the *arma Christi*, the *Pieta*, and even Christ the Judge blend into the Man of Sorrows. In the words of Bernhard Ridderbos, what we have is 'a portrait of the dead Christ who was miraculously standing or sitting', an adaptable anomaly constructed to inspire meditational piety through the representation of porousness. Ridderbos notes that the icon is principally a fusion of 'elements from the representation of

(London: Routledge, 2nd edition 2013); Peter E. Pormann and Emilie Savage-Smith *Medieval Islamic Medicine* (Edinburgh UP, 2007).

10 The origins of the image of the Man of Sorrows go back to a fourteenth-century miraculous appearance of the icon during Mass at the Basilica of the Holy Cross in Jerusalem (or Santa Croce) in Rome. The inception of the image is emblematic, to some extent, of the larger shift of focus from the Crucifixion as the moment of Christ's triumph to one worthy of the viewer's compassion and pity. See Eamon Duffy *The Stripping of the Altars: Traditional Religion in England 1400–1580* (New Haven: Yale UP, 2nd edition 2005) 241–2; Bernhard Ridderbos 'The Man of Sorrows: Pictorial Images and Metaphorical Statements' in *The Broken Body: Passion Devotion in Late-Medieval Culture* edited A.A. MacDonald, H.N.B. Ridderbos and R.M. Schlusemann (Groningen: Egbert Forsten, 1998) 145–81, at 149. A pan-European overview of the trope of the Man of Sorrows can be found in Gertrud Schiller *Iconography of Christian Art* translated Janet Seligman, 2 vols (Greenwich: New York Graphic Society, 1972) *2* 184–230.

the crucified Christ and the representation of the Pantocrator' (usually translated as *all-powerful*), a predominantly eastern icon showing a stern Christ looking directly at the viewer, his right hand making the gesture of teaching or blessing (and often his left holding the New Testament).[11] This suffering yet triumphant Christ is, then, 'a visualisation of theological antitheses', an idealisation of disintegration that infuses the state of porousness with new emotional meaning and fervour.[12]

This adoration was translated into writing in devotional literature, a famous example of which is a meditational treatise on the Passion attributed to the fourteenth-century mystic Richard Rolle. In a series of extended similes, he compares the wounded body of Christ to a number of things, highlighting similarities and differences that always emphasise the superiority of Christ's wounded body to the other image. Christ's body is 'lyk to hevyn, for as heuyn is fill of sterris, so was þy body ful of woundes'. Rolle then exclaims: 'Bot, lord, þy woundes bene bettyr þan sterris, for sterres shynen bot by nyght, and þy woundes bene ful of vertu day and nyght' (lines 195–8).[13] He then prays that 'þese woundes be [his] meditacioun nyght and day, for in [Christ's] woundes is hool medicyne for euche desaise of soule' (lines 202–3). Here, not only are wounds considered virtuous and medicinal, they are also constant, which demonstrates the superiority of Christ's porous body to a night sky punctuated by stars. The next comparisons are even more immediately related to the idea of porousness. Rolle notes, 'lord, swet Ihesu, þy body is lyk to þe nette, for as a nette is fill of holys, so is þy body ful of woundes'

---

11   Ridderbos 'The Man of Sorrows' 158. Michael Camille notes that 'When any character in a painting looks directly at us, conscious not only of being observed but also observing us, this crucially breaks the illusion of reality that has been constructed. Instead of being a historical narrative happening in the past, the internal gaze incorporates the viewer within the scene'. 'Mimetic Identification and Passion Devotion in the Later Middle Ages: A Double-Sided Panel by Meister Francke' in *The Broken Body* edited MacDonald 183–210, at 190. On the Pantocrator, see Hans Belting *The Image and Its Public in the Middle Ages: Form and Function of Early Paintings of the Passion* translated Mark Bartusis and Raymond Meyer (New York: Aristide D. Caratzas, 1990) 91–4.

12   Ridderbos 'The Man of Sorrows' 162. Also see Mitzi Kirkland-Ives 'The Suffering Christ and Visual Mnemonics in Netherlandish Devotions' in *Death, Torture and the Broken Body in European Art, 1300–1650* edited John R. Decker and Mitzi Kirkland-Ives (Abingdon: Routledge, 2016) 35–54.

13   Richard Rolle *Richard Rolle: Prose and Verse Edited from MS. Longleat 29 and Related Manuscripts* edited Sarah Ogilvie-Thompson EETS OS 293 (1988) 74.

(lines 210–11). Further on, he writes, 'þy body is like to a dufhouse, for a dufhouse is ful of holys: so is þy body ful of woundes', and petitions Christ to shelter him from temptation in his nest-like wounds (lines 221–6). Rolle proceeds to compare the wounded body of Christ to a honey-filled honeycomb, a book written with red ink, and a meadow 'ful of swete flours and holsome herbes', all of which emphasise how porousness (even in the form of physical damage) can have positive, protective qualities.[14]

What is evident here is that the quality of porousness, when considered in a broader cultural context inclusive of not only medical theories, but also devotional and theological notions, offers an understanding of the body with sufficient complexity to allow nuanced readings of un-whole bodies. One could also consider the doctrine of concomitance itself, which states that each crumb of the broken Eucharistic wafer contains the unbroken, undiminished blood and body of Christ.[15] Here, we are ostensibly closer to a compartmentalised or fragmented understanding of the body. However, once we consider the process of becoming-porous of Christ's body in the Croxton *Play*, we realise that concomitance is as much about porousness as it is about compartmentalisation. The play depicts the conspiracy of a group of Jews in late medieval Aragon to 'examine' the Host, subjecting it, in the process, to a second Passion that includes gory scenes of the Host being attacked and wounded.[16] Similar to the Passion in scripture, this results in Christ being resurrected and vanquishing doubt. The play concludes with a Corpus Christi procession and the conversion of the Jews, the latter of which is untypical of the genre of Host desecration tales. The bloody becoming-porous of the Host as well as its transformation into the figure of the Christ Child and back into a wafer highlight the significance of porousness in the conception of concomitance throughout the play.

---

14   Rolle *Prose and Verse* 74–5.

15   Miri Rubin 'The Eucharist and the Construction of Medieval Identities' in *Culture and History 1350–1600: Essays on English Communities, Identities and Writing* edited David Aers (London: Harvester/Wheatsheaf, 1992) 43–63, at 50.

16   Typically known as Host desecration narratives, the earliest instance of such stories occurs in Gezo of Tortona's treatise on the Eucharist, written around 981, in which a Jew steals a consecrated host in order to disgrace it. See Phyllis G. Jestice 'A Great Jewish Conspiracy? Worsening Jewish–Christian Relations and the Destruction of the Holy Sepulcher' in *Christian Attitudes toward the Jews in the Middle Ages: A Casebook* edited Michael Frassetto (New York: Routledge, 2007) 25–42, at 38.

The only extant copy of the play is bound in Trinity College, Dublin MS F.4.20. It was originally inscribed independently as a standalone text in the mid-sixteenth century; but the Banns to the play, and a scribal note at its conclusion, claim that the events it dramatises took place in 1461.[17] The association with a village of Croxton (of which there are more than one in the counties of Norfolk and Suffolk) comes from a reference to the town in the Banns. Due to the mention of another village, Babwell Mill near Bury St Edmunds, it has been suggested that the Croxton the text refers to is one near Thetford.[18] At the centre of the miracle play is the notion of transubstantiation, and it is the corporeality and immediacy of transubstantiation that permits the becoming-porous of the Host to be considered as a key element in the study of the play. In the next section, I will explore the significance of the modern theoretical concept of *becoming* for our understanding of this process as well as its subversive potential through performance.

Representation and Becoming in the Performance of the Passion
Becoming in modern theory

In Gilles Deleuze's theorisation, *becoming* is presented as the polar opposite of *representation*. It has been defined as:

> the continual production (or 'return') of difference immanent within the constitution of events, whether physical or otherwise ... becoming is critical, for if the primacy of identity is what defines a world of re-presentation (presenting the same world once again), then becoming (by which Deleuze means 'becoming different') defines a world of presentation anew.[19]

What this means is a shift from the static and fixed presentation of what has already happened – which relies on reference to pre-existing events, objects, or subjects – to the emergence of something that does not reflect

---

17 For a different assessment of the context of the manuscript's production, see Tamara Atkin 'Playbooks and Printed Drama: A Reassessment of the Date and Layout of the Manuscript of the Croxton "Play of the Sacrament"' *The Review of English Studies NS 60:244* (2009) 194–205.
18 Walker '*Play of the Sacrament*' 213–33, at 214.
19 Cliff Stagoll 'Becoming' in *The Deleuze Dictionary: Revised Edition* edited Adrian Parr (Edinburgh UP, 2010) 25–7, at 26.

a pre-existing entity. As Laura Cull puts it, *becoming* marks a shift from representation of 'discrete objects and subjects', to the presentation of something being actualised in real-time in 'processes, relations and happenings'.[20] Deleuze's definitions are less concise and plain, but one could look to the following for his further explication of the term:

> In becoming there is no past nor future – not even present, there is no history. In becoming it is, rather, a matter of involuting; it's neither regression nor progression. To become is to become more and more restrained, more and more simple, more and more deserted and for that very reason populated. This is what's difficult to explain: to what extent one should involute. It is obviously the opposite of evolution, but it is also the opposite of regression, returning to a childhood or to a primitive world.[21]

It is important to emphasise, as Liesbeth Groot Nibbelink notes, that this 'emphasis on process, experimentation, or continuous differentiation [*does not lead*] us beyond representation'.[22] The reason for this is that bypassing representation completely is virtually impossible. Even if we were able to present something that is un-representable (or, in other words, is 'full presence'), in order to comprehend the total non-representation of the event, we would still need representation, signification, representational systems such as language, and repetition. This point is explained succinctly by Jacques Derrida: he notes that for something to make sense, it must have 'iterability', which means:

> it must carry with it a capacity to be repeated in principle again and again in all sorts of contexts ('no context permits saturation'), at the same time as being in some way singular every time ('no meaning can be determined out of context'). Iterability thus entails both 'repetition' (sameness) and 'alterity' (difference).[23]

---

20 Laura Cull 'Introduction' in *Deleuze and Performance* edited Laura Cull (Edinburgh UP, 2009) 1–21, at 3.

21 Gilles Deleuze and Claire Parnet *Dialogues* translated Hugh Tomlinson and Barbara Habberjam (New York: Columbia UP, 1987) 29.

22 Liesbeth Groot Nibbelink *Nomadic Theatre: Mobilizing Theory and Practice on the European Stage* (London: Methuen, 2019) 51.

23 Jacques Derrida 'Living On' translated James Hulbert in *Deconstruction and Criticism* edited Harold Bloom and others (New York: Seabury Press, 1979) 75–176, at 81.

As he further points out in an essay on Antonin Artaud, 'Presence, in order to be presence and self-presence, has always already begun to represent itself'.[24] Therefore, Deleuze's (and, by extension, my) use of *becoming* does not signify a total absence of representation, but rather, a move away from representation. Similarly, and as noted by Derrida above, each iteration of a performance cannot be a perfect representation of the original, because for repetition to occur as repetition, there must be difference. Therefore, it would be more helpful to conceive of the *representation-becoming* dichotomy as a continuum, as opposed to a binary opposition, for there is a simultaneity in the existence of *representation* and *becoming* in all forms of production.[25] This is especially apposite to our understanding of theatrical performance, perhaps in particular to the performance of transubstantiation in Croxton.

Nonetheless, *becoming* tilts performance away from representation. For Deleuze, the stability of representation ensures that meaning and interpretation are regulated, and the hierarchies of power are preserved. Thus, for example, ostensibly innocuous elements such as the preservation of male authority figures, a historically accurate costume design that serves to distinguish noble from common characters, or the sustenance of the source material's original language in every production and iteration of a play all maintain sexist, historical, and linguistic hierarchies of power, which are perpetuated and extended through the stability of continual representation. These elements of power 'are those

---

24 Jacques Derrida, from 'The theatre of cruelty and the closure of representation' in *Antonin Artaud: A Critical Reader* edited Edward Scheer (London: Routledge, 2004) 39–46, at 44.

25 See Jacques Derrida 'Signature Event Context' in *Limited Inc.* translated Samuel Weber and Jeffrey Mehlman (Evanston, IL: Northwestern UP, 1988) 1–23. Mohammad Kowsar refers to this mixed state of representation and non-representation as a kind of 'bilingualism where the trace of the original dialogue and speech exists, albeit with gaps, hiatuses, and partial repetitions'; 'Deleuze on Theatre: A Case Study of Carmelo Bene's "Richard III"' *Theatre Journal 38* (1986) 19–33, at 22. Deleuze extends this simultaneity even to language, in every utterance of which repetition and difference (*representation* and *becoming*) are simultaneously present. He claims that 'Every word is physical, and immediately affects the body'. See Gilles Deleuze *The Logic of Sense* translated Mark Lester and Charles Stivale edited Constantin V. Boundas (London: The Athlone Press, 1990) 87. For a discussion of the debate in the late Middle Ages, see below.

which assure at once the coherence of the subject dealt with and the coherence of the representation on stage'.[26]

The non-representational aspect of performative events enables, on the other hand, the destabilisation of such fixed elements of power, which operate through representation. He further elucidates that this destabilisation can be achieved via:

> [the] elimination of constants or invariants not only in the language and the gestures, but also in the theatrical representation and in that which is represented on stage; thus the elimination of everything which 'makes' power, the power of what the theater represents (the king, the princes, the masters, the system), but also the power of the theater itself (the text, the dialogue, the actor, the director, the structure).[27]

In practical terms, then, to facilitate a move from *representation* to *becoming*, as Deleuze suggests, might include initiatives like preferring improvised noise to dialogue, radically altering the expected succession of events in the play (i.e. narrative), and suddenly changing the setting, the *mise en scène*, or the costume design. As we shall see, all these measures occur, to some degree, in the Croxton *Play*. The existence of these features in the *Play* should not be deemed a haphazard coincidence. Rather, as I will demonstrate, such features highlight the significance of and controversy around the potential of *becoming* in performance. Late medieval debate around the reception of visual art, the written word, and theatre also engages with the *representation-becoming* continuum. Therefore, our consideration of *becoming* as a modern theoretical concept can be utilised as a tool to help us understand better the anxieties around the performance of the Passion in the late medieval context. Such anxieties are, in turn, significant for our appreciation of the Croxton *Play*.

Becoming in late medieval thought

Devotional works on the life and the Passion of Christ and in the tradition of affective piety, such as Nicholas Love's *Mirror of the Life of Jesu*, in which the reader is encouraged to 'behold' Christ's suffering, offer a mode

---

26 Gilles Deleuze 'One Manifesto Less' in *The Deleuze Reader* edited Constantin V. Boundas (New York: Columbia UP, 1993) 204–22, at 207.
27 Deleuze 'One Manifesto Less' 217.

of understanding performance that seems to try to move away from strict bounds of representation.[28] Sarah McNamer defines the practice of affective piety as imagining oneself 'present at scenes of Christ's suffering and [performing] compassion for that suffering victim in a private drama of the heart'.[29] Compassion, here, would entail an attempt to empathise with the suffering via its renewal through 'beholding' it via imagination, sensation, and experience. An early Franciscan tract, Pseudo-Bede's late thirteenth-century *De meditatione passionis Christi*, puts this view more bluntly: 'it is necessary that when you concentrate on these things in your contemplation, you do so as if you were actually present at the very time when He suffered'.[30] Medieval Passion plays, often drawing on works such as Love's *Mirror*, frequently seem to invite the same kind of empathetic response. Fischer-Lichte notes that 'the Church [overall] acknowledged attendance at a religious play as a "good work," and' (in Europe) 'actors and spectators were often granted indulgences'.[31]

On the other hand, it is in Lollard polemics against representations of the Passion (in sacramental or dramatic form) that we find one of the most explicit reflections on the *representation-becoming* continuum. It occurs in a discussion of the difference between iconography and drama. The early fifteenth-century two-part *Tretise of Miraclis Pleyinge* – generally thought to have been written between 1380 and 1425 – is a treatise which,

---

28   Nicholas Love *The Mirror of the Blessed Life of Jesus Christ* edited Michael G. Sargent (Exeter UP, 2005) at various places. See also, Richard Beadle '"Devoute Ymaginacioun" and the Dramatic Sense in Love's *Mirror* and the N-Town Plays' in *Nicholas Love at Waseda: Proceedings of the International Conference, 20–22 July 1995* edited Richard Beadle, Shoichi Oguro, and Michael G. Sargent (Cambridge: D.S. Brewer, 1997) 1–17.

29   Sarah McNamer *Affective Meditation and the Invention of Medieval Compassion* (Philadelphia: University of Pennsylvania Press, 2010) 1.

30   Translation quoted from David Freedberg *The Power of Images: Studies in the History and Theory of Response* (Chicago UP, 1989) 171. Original Latin: *Necessarium etiam esse, ut aliquando ista cogites in contemplatione tua, ac si praesens tum temporis fuisses, quando passus fuit.* PL 94 cols 561–8, at col. 561.

31   Erika Fischer-Lichte 'The Medieval Religious Plays – Ritual or Theatre?' in *Visualizing Medieval Performance: Perspectives, Histories, Contexts* edited Elina Gertsman (London: Routledge, 2008) 249–61 at 254. The early fifteenth-century treatise on the commandments, *Dives and Pauper*, also has a generally approving attitude towards 'pleyys and dauncis þat arn don principaly for devocioun and honest merthe'; *Dives and Pauper* edited Priscilla Heath Barnum, 2 vols EETS OS 323 (2004) 1 Part 1 293.

despite being targeted at 'miraclis pleyinge', a term that seems to denote a wide range of dramatic performances, mainly discusses Passion Plays.[32] Appearing to be from the East Central Midlands in its dialect, the tract is commonly considered to be associated with the Wycliffite or Lollard movement.[33] Each part was written by a separate author. In the first part, the author responds to six reasons that advocates of such performances provide in support of the 'miraclis pleyinge': they are an aid to worship; they convert their viewer to true faith; they (specifically those of the Passion) spur and inspire compassion and piety; they captivate those who would not otherwise heed the church's teaching; they are the lesser of two evils compared to 'pleyinge of other japis' (l. 178),[34] and, perhaps most importantly:

> sithen it is leveful to han the miraclis of God peintid, why is not as wel leveful to han the miraclis of God pleyed, sithen men mowen bettere reden the wille of God and his mervelous werkis in the pleyinge of hem than in the peintinge? And betere they ben holden in mennes minde and oftere rehersid by the pleyinge of hem than by the peintinge, for this is a deed bok, the tother a quick.[35]

Here we find two clues about the *representation-becoming* duality: first, that there is something extra in performance, a kind of liveliness, as the author puts it, which distinguishes it from iconographic representation. A 'quick' book has the potential to reaffirm itself and its powers (to some extent) without a need to refer to pre-existing entities, and this could indeed be unpredictable and/or unintentionally subversive. As the second part of the treatise posits: 'unkindely seyen men now on dayes,

---

32 *A Tretise of Miraclis Pleyinge* edited Clifford Davidson (Kalamazoo: Medieval Institute Publications, 2011) 1. The text exists in London: British Library MS Additional 24202, fols 14r–21r. For an alternative, albeit not overwhelmingly convincing, understanding of the term, which posits that the term refers to parodies of the liturgy or sacred events, see Lawrence M. Clopper '*Miracula* and the *Tretise of Miraclis Pleyinge*' *Speculum* 65:4 (1990) 878–905.

33 Davidson *Tretise* 59.

34 Davidson *Tretise* 98.

35 Davidson *Tretise* 98 (179–85). Many scholars have understood mystery plays as having a predominantly didactic function. For an introduction, see Deane E.D. Downey 'Images of Christ in Corpus Christi Medieval Mystery Play Cycles' in *Images of Christ: Ancient and Modern* edited Michael A. Hayes, Stanley E. Porter, and David Tombs (Sheffield: Sheffield Academic Press, 1997) 206–26.

"Crist doth now no miraclis for us, pley we therfore his olde," adding many lesingis therto so colowrably that the puple gife as myche credense to hem as to the trwthe' (623–6).[36] The problem, here, then, is not just infidelity to the source material and going beyond faithful representation, but also the re-enactment – presenting anew – of Christ's acts.

On this presenting anew of Christ's acts, the first author contrasts 'signes of verrey love' with 'dedis of verrey love', and then argues that 'sithen thise miraclis pleyinge ben onely singnis, love withoute dedis, they ben ... contrarious to the worschipe of God' (197–202).[37] Here, it is made clear that for the *Tretise* authors all representations, and not just performance, are indeed problematic, because representations are mere signifiers (or signs, in the author's words), and they refer to something other than the material reality of the event. Every portrayal of Christ without Christ himself and his actions, then, is invalid. Just as for medieval realists, a representational understanding of things would demote them to an inferior order of existence, so for the reformists, anything other than pure *becoming* (or total presence without the trace of another sign) is deceitful and false. In fact, what makes performance even more threatening is that extra element of 'liveliness' or *becoming* in addition to representation, which renders performance more than 'signs without deeds', but rather deeds without deeds. This is why, for reformists, even the ritual of the Mass is considered against the truth, as it is simultaneously representational and non-representational. The idea that the bread and the wine contain the essence of the body and blood of Christ, as asserted in the first canon of the Fourth Lateran Council of 1215, means that the body and blood *become* present, by transubstantiation, in the bread and wine every time they are administered at Mass. Therefore, every time the Mass is held, the Passion occurs anew. Karl Young points out that 'The central act [*in the Mass*] is designed not to represent or portray or merely commemorate the Crucifixion, but actually to repeat it. What takes place at the altar is not an aesthetic picture of a happening

---

36 Davidson *Tretise* 111. Theodore K. Lerud avers that the *Tretise* considers performative acts and images as part of the same category, which, as my analysis shows, may not be entirely convincing. Theodore K. Lerud 'Quick Images: Memory and the English Corpus Christi Drama' in *Moving Subjects: Processional Performance in the Middle Ages and the Renaissance* edited Kathleen Ashley and Wim Hüsken (Amsterdam: Rodopi, 2001) 213–38, at 216.
37 Davidson *Tretise* 99.

in the past, but a genuine renewal of it'.[38] It is through the Reformists' criticism that we begin to see the subversive potential that performance and *becoming* harbour in relation to theological tenets, which, in Deleuze's theorisation, comprise one set of the 'elements of power'.

The criticism of representation in art and performance is not extended to language and the scripture, however, which implies that for the authors of the treatise, language – at least in relation to the scripture – seems capable of reliably conveying truth without descending into representation, thus serving as their chief and only authority. This is, of course, contrary to the position of contemporary Nominalists – for whom language was capable of producing illusory abstractions such as the universals, as well as to that of orthodox authorities such as Archbishop Arundel who sought to regulate the use of language in preaching via his *Constitutions*.[39] More importantly, however, there seems to be a contradiction between the *Tretise* authors' – and indeed other reformist thinkers' – confidence in language as a system capable of conveying 'the absolute truth and authority of the bible as the Word' and the implied acknowledgement of the opaqueness and unreliability of language in Wycliffite translators' reliance on commentaries (the dominance of which over exegesis they opposed) in their efforts to produce a vernacular version of the Bible.[40] This suggests that the supposed radical literalism

---

38   Karl Young *The Drama of the Medieval Church* 2 vols (Oxford: Clarendon Press, 1933) *1* 84–5. Miri Rubin also points out that from the High Middle Ages, the Eucharist emerged 'as a re-enactment, not merely memorial, of the central act of sacrifice which had been foretold in the Last Supper, and suffered in the Passion'; Rubin 'The Eucharist' 46–7.

39   On Nominalism and the problem of universals, see Alastair Minnis '"Authorial Intention" and "Literal Sense" in the Exegetical Theories of Richard Fitzralph and John Wyclif: An Essay in the Medieval History of Biblical Hermeneutics' *Proceedings of the Royal Irish Academy: Archaeology, Culture, History, Literature* 75 (1975) 1–31; Roberto Pinzani *The Problem of Universals from Boethius to John of Salisbury* (Leiden: Brill, 2018). Penny Granger views the *Play of the Sacrament* and the Towneley Shepherds' plays as evidence that Arundel's constitutions may not have been as influential as sometimes presented: *The N-Town Play: Drama and Liturgy in Medieval East Anglia* (Cambridge: D.S. Brewer, 2009) 58.

40   Ruth Nisse 'Reversing Discipline: The *Tretise of Miraclis Pleyinge*, Lollard Exegesis, and the Failure of Representation' *The Yearbook of Langland Studies* 11 (1997) 163–94, at 166; Anne Hudson *The Premature Reformation: Wycliffite Texts and Lollard History* (Oxford: Clarendon Press, 1988) 257; Ralph Hanna, Tony Hunt, R.G. Keightley, Alastair Minnis, and Nigel F. Palmer 'Latin Commentary Tradition

that is associated with the Wycliffite movement(s) appears to have been fuelled by more than just theoretical opposition: there was a political dimension to their struggle, one which opposed the clergy's regulation of interpretation and, indeed, representation. Regardless of the *Tretise* authors' positions on language, it is evident that when accompanied by visual representation and performance, even the status of language did not remain unsullied.

In terms of visual representation, the first *Tretise* author, in their response to that last proposed benefit of 'miraclis pleyinge', writes that 'peinture, yif it be verry withoute menging of lesingis and not to curious, to myche fedinge mennis wittis, and not occasion of maumetrie to the puple, they ben but as nakyd lettris to a clerk to riden the treuthe' (372–8).[41] The three conditions here can be reformulated as: the absence of any form of *becoming* (i.e. going beyond the text, with infidelity ('lesingis') as its weakest example and emergent, subversive, and self-referential ('curious') elements as stronger examples); incapacity to be affective (not appealing to people's senses or 'wittis'); and not inviting veneration of the image itself (idolatry or 'maumetrie'). Only by removing layer after layer of any imaginable additional element that has the potential to go beyond the 'nakyd' truth (i.e. scripture) does the author finally acknowledge that a painting could conceivably be considered a faithful representation.[42] This view, however, was obviously not shared by the majority of the reformists, who did not consider even such pictorial depictions as valid.[43]

---

and Vernacular Literature' in *The Cambridge History of Literary Criticism, Vol. 2: The Middle Ages* edited Alastair Minnis and Ian Johnson (Cambridge UP, 2009) 363–421, at 396.

41 Davidson *Tretise* 104.

42 For a study of the *Play* proposing that it is, similar to the *Tretise*, a critique of performances of the Passion, see Christina M. Fitzgerald 'Performance Anxiety and the Passion in the Croxton *Play of the Sacrament*' *Journal of Medieval and Early Modern Studies* 46:2 (2016) 315–37.

43 Margaret Aston *Lollards and Reformers: Images and Literacy in Late Medieval Religion* (London: The Hambledon Press, 1984) 139. An example of such disapproving views can be found in a tract on images in the same early fifteenth-century manuscript that contains the *Tretise*, London: British Library MS Additional 24202, fols 26–28v. It notes that while there were images, by God's command, in the Temple of Solomon, by Christ's new law, such images are prohibited; 'Images and Pilgrimages' in *Selections from English Wycliffite Writings* edited Anne Hudson (Cambridge UP, 1978) 83–8, at 84.

The second clue about the *representation-becoming* duality in the passage quoted from the *Tretise* above is the implication that viewers are moved more greatly when watching the tangible performances as opposed to still, iconographic representations. This second clue re-emphasises that for medieval viewers just as for modern theorists such as Fischer-Lichte and Deleuze, the affective power of *becoming* in performance was significant. Furthermore, as Carolyn Muessig argues, this is especially true for performances of the Passion, in which 'there is no gap between what happened at one moment in salvation history and what happens in real time, [so] the religious events are brought to the present and can occur at any moment'.[44] It is thus evident that what is extra in performance in comparison with iconography – and, consequently, threatening for the reformists' penchant for literalism and/or independence from the Church's monopoly over exegesis – is this move away from representation towards *becoming*, which creates a more tangible, immediate experience with a potentially subversive affective power.

How might this examination of the *Tretise* affect our understanding of the play? First, it highlights that *becoming* (or 'liveliness' in the discourse of the *Tretise*) was an equally legitimate concern for late medieval thinkers. The affinities between the late medieval conception of performance and modern theorisations of *becoming* in performance, then, enable the adoption of the concept of *becoming* as a critical tool for the examination of the play. Second, the late medieval understanding of performance's subversive capacity is itself quite germane to Deleuze's theorisations of *becoming*, discussed earlier. In both cases, a performative event has the potential to dissociate itself from either historical reality or narrative accompanied by exegetic addenda that aimed to provide the 'correct', sanctioned contextualisation and explanation for the event. This potential, in turn, is what made performance problematic for reformists. The addenda must necessarily rely on representational systems such as language to disseminate and be understood. In our particular case, such exegetic addenda would aim to differentiate between the piety-inducing becoming-porous of Christ and the cathartic becoming-porous of Jewish characters by putting the performance in its appropriate context. Once this context is bypassed, such *becomings*, untied to any

---

44 Carolyn Muessig 'Performance of the Passion: The Enactment of Devotion in the Later Middle Ages' in *Visualizing Medieval Performance: Perspectives, Histories, Contexts* edited Elina Gertsman (Aldershot: Ashgate, 2008) 129–42, at 137.

theological explanation, enable emergent, unintended interpretations of performance through their affective power, and make possible the conception that Christ and the Jew are actually united through becoming-porous. In the next sections, I will bring the two previous areas of discussion together, first by considering how the more nuanced idea of porousness opens up the possibility for alternative readings of the Croxton *Play*, and then by examining the subversive potential of specific performative instances of becoming-porous from this perspective.

Wholeness versus Porousness: A False Dichotomy?

There have been extensive and conflicting discussions of the Croxton *Play* as an example of anti-Lollardy or antisemitism, and at the same time of its openness towards heterodoxy and alterity.[45] While many have persuasively written against the Lollard connection, Ann Eljenholm Nichols notes that the author must at least have been familiar with anti-Lollard discourse as well as the vocabulary used by Lollards themselves, for the text 'uses Lollard vocabulary to characterize the non-believing Jews'.[46] Thus, the text is aware of the issue of exclusion at work within it. Similarly, the reason for scholarly attention in relation to the play's antisemitism is that, apart from the body of Christ, the text foregrounds the Jewish body and its porousness, as well as its role in the torture of Christ. Critics generally fall into two broad camps: those who see the play as emblematic of the exclusionary forces of antisemitism at work within late medieval society, and those who see a challenge to such forces in the play's depiction of the interaction between Jews and the Host.[47] It could be said that each camp emphasises one function of

---

45 For the frequently challenged connection with Lollardy, see Cecilia Cutts 'The Croxton Play: An Anti-Lollard Piece' *Modern Language Quarterly* 5:1 (1944) 45–60; Gail McMurray Gibson *The Theater of Devotion: East Anglian Drama and Society in the Late Middle Ages* (Chicago UP, 1989) 34–42.

46 Ann Eljenholm Nichols 'Lollard Language in the Croxton *Play of the Sacrament*' *Notes and Queries* 36 (1989) 23–5, at 23, 25. For the vocabulary used by Lollards, see Anne Hudson *Lollards and Their Books* (London: Bloomsbury, 1985); especially 165–80.

47 The former camp includes Robert L.A. Clark and Claire Sponsler 'Othered Bodies: Racial Cross-Dressing in the *Mistere De La Sainte Hostie* and the Croxton *Play of the Sacrament*' *Journal of Medieval and Early Modern Studies* 29:1 (1999) 61–87; Lisa Lampert 'The Once and Future Jew: The Croxton "Play of the Sacrament," Little Robert of Bury and Historical Memory' *Jewish History* 15:3 (2001) 235–55;

becoming-porous introduced at the beginning of this chapter: the first sees antisemitism as manifesting itself in the cathartic function, and the second camp sees Eucharistic and affective piety bringing bodies closer.

With regard to catharsis, the play situates itself within a context of violence against Jews, which goes beyond the charge of Host desecration and forms the basis of the narrative. David Nirenberg emphasises that violence against Jews, literally and symbolically, was a ritualised aspect of Holy Week festivities in mainland Europe, sometimes following performances of the Passion of Christ.[48] As Nirenberg suggests, one of the aims of the Holy Week cycle was to 'make brutally clear the sharp boundaries, historical and physical, that separated Christian from Jew'.[49] In practice, these boundaries were also enforced via biopolitical means that sought to regulate Jews' activities and movements through separating them from Christians throughout Holy Week.[50] Furthermore, rumours of Host desecrations were often followed by riots against Jews.[51] However, the play's engagement with bodies, as Nichols points out, is also informed

---

Steven Kruger 'The Spectral Jew' *New Medieval Literatures 2* (1998) 9–35; Stephen Spector 'Time, Space, and Identity in the Play of the Sacrament' in *The Stage as Mirror: Civic Theater in Late Medieval Europe* edited Alan Knight (Cambridge: D.S. Brewer, 1997) 197–8. The latter camp could be said to include Sarah Beckwith 'Ritual, Church and Theatre: Medieval Dramas of the Sacramental Body' in *Culture and History 1350–1600* 65–89; Richard L. Homan 'Devotional Themes in the Violence and Humor of the *Play of the Sacrament*' *Comparative Drama 20* (1986) 327–40; Elisabeth Dutton 'The Croxton Play of the Sacrament' in *The Oxford Handbook of Tudor Drama* edited Thomas Betteridge and Greg Walker (Oxford UP, 2012) 56–71; Greg Walker 'And Here's Your Host … : Jews and Others in the Croxton *Play of the Sacrament*' *Jewish Culture and History 11:1–2* (2009) 40–56.

48   David Nirenberg *Communities of Violence: Persecution of Minorities in the Middle Ages* (Princeton UP, 1996) 214–15.

49   Nirenberg *Communities* 217–19.

50   Shlomo Simonsohn *The Apostolic See and the Jews: History* (Toronto: Pontifical Institute of Mediaeval Studies, 1991) 131–2. This was, one must bear in mind, at the same time as lepers were allowed into the community to participate in rituals or collect alms, especially before the Black Death; Anna M. Peterson 'Connotation and Denotation: The Construction of the Leper in Narbonne and Siena before the Plague' in *Leprosy and Identity in the Middle Ages: From England to the Mediterranean* edited Elma Brenner and Francois-Olivier Touati (Manchester UP, 2021) 323–43, at 333.

51   Jestice 'A Great Jewish Conspiracy?' 25–42.

by its engagement with the elements of Eucharistic and affective piety popular in the fifteenth century.[52] She reminds us that the:

> symbols of the Passion are ubiquitous in East Anglian parish churches; they are carved on baptismal fonts and porch facades, decorate roodscreens, and are held by myriads of angels on hammerbeam roofs from which the reserved Eucharist was suspended.[53]

This image is fused with the Eucharist in the iconography of the Mass of St Gregory, in which the Man of Sorrows appeared or came to life on the altar during a Mass held by Pope Gregory praying to convince doubters of transubstantiation.[54] We see a form of this fusion at the climax of the Croxton *Play*, where the Host transforms into the figure of the Christ Child. The narrative backbone of the *Play* is similarly concerned with the Eucharist and shaped by Host miracles or Host desecration stories that, as Miri Rubin notes, developed from an account from 1290 Paris and became popular in the late Middle Ages.[55]

Thus, both positively and negatively, the play seems to be already centred on bodies, and the first step in that direction is taken by Jonathas, the Jewish merchant, who intends to put the Host 'in a prefe' (*to a test*); Jason, the first of his attendants, proposes:

> Yff þat thys be he that on Calvery was mad red,
> Onto my mynd, I shall kenne yow a conceyt good:
> Surely wyth owr daggars we shall ses on thys bredde,
> And so wyth clowtys we shall know yf he have eny blood.
>
> 369–72

The Jews' subsequent suggestions are equally disturbing and sacrilegious: one says that 'wyth our strokys we shall fray hym as he

---

52 Anne Eljenholm Nichols 'The Croxton *Play of the Sacrament*: A Re-Reading' *Comparative Drama* 22:2 (1988-9) 117–37. See also, Michael Jones 'Theatrical History in the Croxton *Play of the Sacrament*' *ELH* 66:2 (1999) 223–60.

53 Nichols 'The Croxton *Play*' 122.

54 Nichols 'The Croxton *Play*' 122; see also note 10. For similarities between the image of the Man of Sorrows and the image of the Christ Child appearing at the end of the play, see below.

55 Rubin 'The Eucharist' 54; Nichols 'The Croxton *Play*' 123. See also, W.C. Jordan *The French Monarchy and the Jews: From Philip Augustus to the Last Capetians* (Philadelphia: University of Pennsylvania Press, 1989) 191–4.

was on þe Rood', another tells his companion to 'smyte ye in the myddys of þe cake | And so shall we smyte þeron woundys five!' (375, 377–8). When inflicting those wounds, thus initiating the becoming-porous of the Host, the characters emphasise the force with which they bore into the Host, describing their every strike and its intended goal, while the Host remains silent and ostensibly passive. But this turns into confusion as soon as Jonathas pierces the middle of the Host – the equivalent of Christ's side. The Host starts bleeding profusely, and before they can immerse it in the cauldron full of boiling oil that they have prepared, it sticks to the hand of Jonathas, who starts running around in desperation. The Jews tie the Host to a post, drive three nails into it, and then try to remove it from their master's hand; but somehow they end up ripping the hand off his arm: 'Here shall thay pluke þe arme, and þe hand shall hang styll with þe Sacrament' (436 sd).

This moment is significant in relation to the validity of the binary opposition between wholeness and porousness. Robert Clark and Claire Sponsler highlight that '[l]ike women, Jews were frequently defined as "body," and, again like women, their bodies were often seen as dangerously porous and open, threatening contamination of those (Christian males) who came into contact with them'; they argue that the same dynamic is at work in the threat of contamination posed by Jewish bodies to the Host in this scene.[56] For them, it is the Jewish body that has the potential to 'pollute' the Host. However, their reading is quite unbalanced in its characterisation of the attachment of the Host to Jonathas's hand. They emphasise that when Jonathas's 'hand becomes so strongly attached to the Host that it is actually ripped from his body, pollution is vividly explored as the body of the Jew conjoins with the body of Christ'.[57] It is true that the conjoining highlights an anxiety in terms of the proximity of the threatening, polluting, and excluded body to a perfectly pure one, mirroring the anxieties about the proximity of Jews in mainland Europe (and Lollards in England) to the unpolluted within the urban environment. Jews were associated with a variety of diseases and conditions, some of which involved bleeding (such as menstruation, haemorrhages and haemorrhoids), and the unease around contact with

---

56   Clark and Sponsler 'Othered Bodies' 72.
57   Clark and Sponsler 'Othered Bodies' 72.

a Jewish body must have been recreated among the play's audience.[58] However, characterising what occurs here as the hand becoming 'so strongly attached ... that it is actually ripped from [the] body' misses the point. The hand is not detached from Jonathas's body in order to signify that the polluted and the pure cannot naturally co-exist at any cost; it is ripped off his body, but remains attached to the Host, in the middle of an attempt at treatment – which itself aimed to separate the Host from the hand. The hand itself is still Jonathas's hand, the hand of a Jew attached to the Host, and nowhere in the scene or in the play is the hand disowned and treated as an entity that no longer belongs to Jonathas. At the same time, we cannot ignore that for an 'othered body' to become melded with the body of Christ, a boundary must be crossed – a network has to be established. If the sole concern had been pollution, the Host would have had to reject the hand, not take it and keep it.

Clark and Sponsler go on to argue that 'the dismemberment of Jonathas is the counterfigure of the wafer's enduring wholeness', and that this dismemberment is materialised in order to 'uphold the wholeness of Christian community'.[59] The proposition here is based on the mistaken binary opposition discussed above, which privileges wholeness over porousness, and it is through this privileged sign that they read the entire text. For them, the Host must remain intact the whole time, otherwise the play will become too subversive to remain contextually, representationally, and discursively stable: wholeness is only for the same (Christ and Christians), and porousness and damage only belong to

58 Joshua Trachtenberg *The Devil and the Jews: The Medieval Conception of the Jew and Its Relation to Modern Anti-Semitism* (Skokie: Varda Books, 2001) 50, 149, 228 note 27. Anthony Bale disagrees with characterising the medieval understanding of the Jewish body as something degenerate and contaminating. Rather, in his analysis of Chaucer's 'The Prioress's Tale', he emphasises that 'The Jewry is not a contagious or leaking corrupt body, but rather an entity which is entered by non-Jews'. Here, Bale reverses the direction of the Jewish body's flow of power, underlining that the absorptive porousness of the Jewish body, its adaptive instability, is one of the reasons why it is treated with hostility; Anthony Bale *The Jew in the Medieval Book: English Antisemitisms, 1350–1500* (Cambridge UP, 2006) 132, 83.

59 Clark and Sponsler 'Othered Bodies' 73. David Lawton opposes this view by casting doubt on the whole ideas of 'wholeness' and 'community' in relation to dramatic performances. 'Sacrilege and Theatricality: the Croxton *Play of the Sacrament*' *Journal of Medieval and Early Modern Studies* 33:2 (2003) 281–309, at 295.

the other (Jews). It is due to this hierarchic binary opposition that Clark and Sponsler underline a 'risk of [the audience's] self-implication in the disavowed qualities projected onto racial others' as their conclusion.[60] The self-implication, by which is meant the realisation by Christians that they, too, doubt transubstantiation, is not necessarily a deconstructive glitch in the play's discursive system that has somehow made its way into the play. Rather, it is the result of a parallel conception of the two bodies as porous and permeable, allowing for the Jewish body to be conjoined with that of Christ. As briefly noted at the beginning of this chapter, porousness was indeed idealised and invoked in order to secure the Passion's redemptive and protective powers. Here, too, it cannot be any more obvious that the bleeding, bored-through Host is not intact, and if we were to tear the dichotomy down and dethrone wholeness, we would discover that when Jonathas's hand is ripped off, porousness is the only thing in common between him and the Host; it is what unites Christ with the Jews.

The result of this disjointed unison is, first, the investment of the Host with a further degree of materiality and corporeality, as the Jewish body was considered a more visceral 'body', as Clark and Sponsler put it. Consequently, the idea that the Host is the body of Christ becomes more immediately tangible. Second, Christ, Christianity, and God enter into the Jewish body through the union, which will then render the Jewish body capable of becoming Christian and entering the communal Body of Christ. It is here in this episode that the Passion moves beyond the representation of already existing discourses, and the narrative that typically emphasises the exclusion of the Jewish body, towards *becoming*, where the boundaries between same and other are crossed beyond the narrative through a positive, simultaneous violation of bodily integrity. As opposed to porousness negating the status of bodies and reinforcing exclusion, this *becoming* unites the ostensibly excluded Jewish bodies and the Body of Christ. *Becoming*, of course, is not a single, static action occurring during the performance of the scene. Rather, it is, as discussed in the previous section on the *Tretise*, interactive and cumulative. *Becoming*, then, is the aggregate of the simultaneous processes of becoming-porous, its affective impact, and the potential resultant interpretation that proposes that a porous Jewish body can be as favourable an entity as the porous body of Christ.

60   Clark and Sponsler 'Othered Bodies' 80.

Becoming-Porous and Subversion

The interaction between porous bodies has thus provided the potential to pose a challenge against the dominant medieval position of antisemitism. This form of becoming is further strengthened by the absence of any verbal explication of the theological significance and implications of what goes on in the sequence, leaving communication predominantly to affective and non-representational means. This is exemplified by the silent Host or the Body of Christ and how it overcomes adversity and communicates with the audience, as well as the Jewish characters, through the process of becoming-porous. The Host remains ostensibly passive and silent throughout most of the sequence of the renewal of the Passion. I propose that the absence of language in the performance of the becoming-porous of Christ's body activates a new mode of communication that depends on affective communication through corporeal damage (in other words, speaking via wounds). In turn, this new mode further destabilises the centrality of the representational system of language, through which sanctioned interpretations of events are disseminated.

The motif of speaking wounds enjoyed considerable popularity in late medieval iconography. For instance, an illustration in an early fifteenth-century Book of Hours, a collaboration between Flanders or France and England, allows the reader to view the heart through Christ's side wound, which is mandorla-shaped. Around the side wound, there is a labial caption, which reads *Hec plage Christi sint ad veniam michi cuncti; Quinque vulnera dei sint medicina mei* ('May Christ's wounds be my forgiveness for all, and the Lord's five wounds be my medicine').[61] Apart from the shape's gynaecological connotations, David S. Areford reads the shape as approximating a mouth, which would suggest that the wound is speaking.[62] In the opening folios of London, British Library, MS Egerton 1821 (c.1480–c.1525), we see the wounds evolving into an entire

---

61 Oxford: Bodleian Library MS. Lat. Liturg. fol. 2, fol. 4v; at <https://digital.bodleian.ox.ac.uk/objects/55dbf4b2-d614-4f46-80de-c7de81ab47b6/surfaces/d02a0df6-2109-43f1-8944-e64d06812904/>.

62 David S. Areford 'The Passion Measured: A Late-Medieval Diagram of the Body of Christ' in *The Broken Body* 211–38, at 238 note 87. The mouth motif is even more pronounced in a modern impression of a German late fifteenth-century woodcut in the Staatliche Graphische Sammlung, Munich 1929: 268 (Schr. 1788); see Areford *The Viewer* 236–7.

book. The manuscript is catalogued as a Psalter and Rosary of the Virgin but includes other devotional texts, as well. Folios 1r–2r are painted black, punctuated by bright drops of blood; in folios 6v–9v, the pages are painted entirely red, featuring bleeding wounds of darker shades. On several of these are pasted devotional woodcuts of the *arma* as well as the wounds, at the centre of which is displayed the bleeding heart. The whole content of the book thus becomes part of a conversation with Christ. It is noteworthy that even with the efforts of Egerton 1821, all the above-mentioned examples still rely on the representational system of language to initiate contact between the reader and Christ. On folio 9v, for instance, there exists a conversation between a severely wounded Christ and a Carthusian monk, in which Christ guides the monk to salvation by the following words: *Fili fuge vince tace quiesce* ('Son, flee, vanquish, be silent, be still'). Below the illustration a caption proclaims, 'The greatest comfort in all temptacyon is the remembraunce of crystes passion'. Despite the multisensory experience offered by the manuscript, the only way to truly interact with Christ is, the manuscript's maker seems to suggest, to *read* him; thus, Christ's ability to speak depends on the devotee.[63]

By contrast, in the play the performative wounds are active: they rely neither on language nor on the devotees to be able to speak, and even if a spectator averts their eyes, the act of speaking continues through means other than visual connection – for example, kinetic, auditory, olfactory, or even tactile. This woundly form of communication is not achieved via language. Until the denouement of the play, no word is spoken by the Host/Christ; it/he remains silent throughout the Passion, meekly undergoing the ordeal as per the narrative. In addition to the Gospels,

---

63 London: British Library MS Egerton 1821, fols 1r–2r, 6v–9v; at <http://www.bl.uk/manuscripts/Viewer.aspx?ref=egerton_ms_1821_f001r>. For the multisensory engagement in Egerton 1821, see Michelle M. Sauer 'Audiotactility and the Medieval Soundscape of Parchment' in *Sounding Out* at <https://soundstudiesblog.com/tag/ms-egerton-1821/>. On the gynaecological representations of the side-wound, see Martha Easton 'The Wound of Christ, the Mouth of Hell: Appropriations and Inversions of Female Anatomy in the Later Middle Ages' in *Tributes to Jonathan J.G. Alexander: The Making and Meaning of Illuminated Medieval and Renaissance Manuscripts, Art and Architecture* edited Susan L'Engle and Gerald B. Guest (Turnhout: Harvey Miller, 2006) 395–414; Flora May Lewis 'The Wound in Christ's Side and the Instruments of the Passion: Gendered Experience and Response' in *Women and the Book: Assessing the Visual Evidence* edited Lesley Smith and Jane H.M. Taylor (London: The British Library, 1997) 204–29.

Christ's silence is a significant aspect of the narrative of the Passion elsewhere in the Bible and devotional literature: it is suggested in Isaiah 53:7, which reads 'He was oppressed, and he was afflicted, yet he did not open his mouth; like a lamb that is led to the slaughter, and like a sheep that before its shearers is silent, so he did not open his mouth'. The performance of the Passion, however, enables the establishment of the active, material, and affective mode of woundly communication that relies on *becoming* (specifically, the process of becoming-porous of Christ) and overcomes Christ's ostensible passivity.[64] As Cull points out, affective impact is itself a kind of *becoming* and cannot be engineered.[65] The Jewish tormentors, by contrast, during their stabbing of the Host use language only to emphasise either the affective force of the violence and cruelty being performed or their own confusion when their scheme is disrupted.[66] The innocence and truth of Christ and the depravity of his/ the Host's offenders, then, are not communicated explicitly via language. Rather, they are demonstrated by their non-representational becoming-porous in real time. As mentioned earlier, the becoming-porous of Christ reveals his innocence and inspires the audience with pious reflection, as well as portraying the Jews as the culprits in Christ's Passion. The becoming-porous of the Jews, in contrast, might be supposed to have

---

[64] Christ's silence has been examined in a number of studies: Alexandra F. Johnston '"His Langage Is Lorne": The Silent Centre of the York Cycle' *Early Theatre 3* (2000) 185–95; Clare Wright 'Acoustic Tyranny: Metre, Alliteration and Voice in "Christ before Herod"' *Medieval English Theatre 34* (2012) 3–29; Daisy Black 'Commanding Un-Empty Space: Silence, Stillness and Scopic Authority in the York "Christ before Herod"' in *Gender in Medieval Places, Spaces and Thresholds* edited Victoria Blud, Einat Klafter, and Diane Heath (University of London Press, 2019) 237–50, at 247. The closest anyone has come to an understanding of Christ's silence as an action rather than inaction is Rosemary Woolf, who argues that 'Far from Christ's silence being solely a manifestation of his unquestioned submission to human suffering, it becomes rather a sublime expression of his divinity'. *The English Mystery Plays* (London: Routledge and Kegan Paul, 1972) 257.

[65] Cull 'Introduction' 8. Deleuze and Felix Guattari emphasise this in *A Thousand Plateaus: Capitalism and Schizophrenia* translated Brian Massumi (Minneapolis: University of Minnesota Press, 1987) 256.

[66] The Jews' comments on their actions serve a practical purpose in performance of ensuring that anyone who cannot see what is happening can nonetheless understand it. The Jews' words are here very different in function from their rehearsal of liturgical phrases, especially from the Apostles' Creed, immediately before their assault on the Host (397–440).

a cathartic function, through which justice is restored, as well as emphasising their felony even more. In the absence of any sanctioned exposition that would clarify what each action should signify, the impact of the performed becoming-porous during this specific sequence is rendered predominantly affective. By bypassing language, then, the simultaneous becoming-porous of Christ's and Jonathas's bodies confuses the purpose of each separate becoming-porous and opens up the possibility of a disjointed unison between them. In this unison, the becoming-porous of Jonathas might be read along the same lines as that of Christ. In turn, this emergent interpretation destabilises the pre-existing narrative of Host desecration within which the play may also be read.

Becoming here seems to instigate an irreversible chain reaction of further *becoming*, for at this point, the famous quack doctor interlude takes place, which removes the performance from its supposed source material by another degree.[67] The episode does not move the plot forward in any way, but it transports the setting of the play from Heraclea in Aragon to Norfolk when Colle, the doctor's assistant, says 'Inquyre to þe colkote, for ther ys hys loggyng, | A lytyll besyde Babwell Myll, yf yhe wyll have und[er]stondyng' (540–1).[68] As soon as we are transferred from a narration of something that happened in Aragon to something that is happening now, we have crossed the threshold separating representation from *becoming* once again. The initial authority of the narrative derives from the recording of its occurrence in Aragon, which is mentioned in the Banns: the transposition to here and now destabilises the representational structure of the play.[69] Furthermore, if we consider the confrontation between the Host and the doubters, the moment of the doctor's entrance marks the first stage of the Jews' defeat. Once we have suspended the privileging of wholeness over un-wholeness, Christ's silence and torture no longer seem to be passivity; instead, they can be

---

67 Ruth Nisse suggests that the episode harbours some of the animosity directed towards the migrant Flemish, Dutch, Walloon, and Brabantine communities active in East Anglia since the mid-fourteenth century; *Defining Acts: Drama and the Politics of Interpretation in Late Medieval England* (University of Notre Dame Press, 2005) 118.

68 Walker 'Croxton, *Play of the Sacrament*' 226.

69 Also see Thomas Betteridge 'Playing with the Past: History in the Croxton *Play of the Sacrament* and *King Johan*' in *Staging History: Essays in Late Medieval and Humanist Drama* edited Peter Happé and Wim Hüsken (Leiden: Brill, 2021) 62–77.

seen as the Host fighting back. As noted in the previous section, the plight of the Jews begins once the Host starts bleeding. Thus, the Host can be said to be repelling attacks by being violated and wounded – by affectively communicating to the audience Christ's innocence through becoming-porous, thus coming to life and moving beyond passive representation. In other words, the blood functions both as a sign of physical damage, through which Christ speaks, and a weapon with which the Host disrupts the aggressors' scheme.[70] We can even view the farcical pandemonium of the Jews in this light and see it as the point when their defeat is laid bare. The fooling around serves to deflate the built-up tension in the situation and establish Christ's dominance in the power play; the comedy is, in effect, the humiliation of the losers and a show of dominance by the Host.

At the same time, however, due to the absence of representational communication and through the attachment of the Host to Jonathas's hand, the Host and Jonathas are paradoxically united, undermining the Christian-Jew dichotomy in the struggle between the Host and the Jews. This alternative interpretation is assisted by the Jews' conversion and inclusion in the Christian community at the end of the play, and therefore, it can be viewed as the moment the woundly mode of communication begins to affect Jews alongside Christians.[71] By becoming-porous, the Host overpowers and convinces the Jews, and the Jews begin to understand Christ's righteousness and register the woundly speech. After the doctor episode, the doubters, already on the back foot, pull the nails out of the Host, wrap it in a cloth, and toss it into a cauldron. Then, however, 'shall þe cawdron byle, apperyng to be as bloode', consequently overflowing (592 sd). Bewildered, they resort to trying other means to get rid of the Host, and Jonathas suggests that they should 'make an ovyn

---

[70] Estella Ciobanu similarly argues that Christ's becoming-porous is part of an 'argument' or contesting of claims to power by Christ and his torturers. *Representations of the Body in Middle English Biblical Drama* (The New Middle Ages; Cham: Palgrave Macmillan, 2018) 125–88.

[71] At the same time, it could be argued that when the Jews set off on a voyage at the end of the play (884–91), they are once again excluded from the community even after conversion. Based on such a reading, the subversive implications of the conjoining of the bodies of Jonathas and Christ could more easily be seen as a deconstructive glitch in the narrative the play seeks to present, what Pierre Macherey calls the work's 'unconscious' – 'the inscription of an *otherness* in the work', which exposes the 'decentred-ness' of the text; Pierre Macherey *A Theory of Literary Production* translated Geoffrey Wall (London: Routledge, 1978) 94, 79.

as redd hot | As ever yt can be made with fere', throw the Host in it, and shut the lid (mirroring the entombment of Christ) (603–4). The scene concludes with the explosion of the oven and blood gushing out of the cracks. A victorious Christ, or rather, 'an image [which we later learn is one of the Christ Child] appere[s] owt with woundys bledyng' (632 sd), calling on the Jews:

> *O mirabiles Judei, attendite et videte*
> *Si est dolor [sicut] dolor meus!*
>
> Oh ye merveylows Jewys,
> Why ar ye to yoyr kyng onkynd,
> And [I] so bitterly bowt yow to My blysse?
> Why fare ye thus fule wyth yowre frende?
> Why peyne yow Me and straytly Me pynde,
> And I yowr love so derely have bowght?
> ...
> Why blaspheme yow Me? Why do ye thus?
> Why put yow Me to a newe tormentry,
> And I dyed for yow on the Crosse?[72]   637–44, 651–3

Richard Homan finds a similar depiction of a wounded victorious Christ Child in a fifteenth-century exemplum in Lincoln Cathedral Library, MS 50, fols 126v–127r, and while he refutes the connection between the image of the child and the Man of Sorrows, the similarities are not easy to overlook, as Nichols's reading and my analysis illustrate.[73] Similar to

---

72 The Latin may be translated as: 'O you strange Jews, behold and see if any sorrow is like unto My sorrow'. See Lamentations 1:12.

73 Richard L. Homan 'Two *Exempla*: Analogues to the *Play of the Sacrament* and *Dux Moraud*' Comparative Drama 18:3 (1984) 241–51. Furthermore, the role of blood libel stories must not be underemphasised. For instance, the analysis of visual representations of the story of Simon of Trent (alleged death in 1475), one of the most famous iterations of blood libel canards, by David S. Areford demonstrates the parallelism between its iconography and that of Christ: the child is depicted among the instruments of his torture (similar to the *arma Christi*), in a wounded state (like the Man of Sorrows), dead (as in the *Pieta*), and in a triumphant state (mirroring Christ's resurrection), highlighting that the portrayal of Christ as a triumphant child would certainly not have been deemed outlandish by the audience; Areford *The Viewer* 165–227. On the story of Simon and its impact, see Klaus Brandstätter '*Antijüdische Ritualmordvorwürfe in Trient und Tirol: neuere Forschungen zu Simon Von Trient und Andreas von Rinn*' Historisches Jahrbuch 125 (2005) 495–536.

the Man of Sorrows, the Christ Child here invites the viewers to behold the wounds. This time, however, the Jews are the direct addressees of the spectacle: they are encouraged to engage in woundly communication with Christ, which is, on this final occasion, framed within verbal speech to elicit from them the desired response: contrition. It is only after completely vanquishing the Jews, once they have been virtually beaten into submission and are unable to harm Christ anymore, that Christ begins to speak verbally. During this whole sequence, the wounds and the blood speak to the audience and Jews simultaneously about how Christ was wronged and his power in overcoming his enemies and death.

Much like the oxymoronic protective power of wounds in iconography, here the blood performs three functions: on the one hand, it dramatically illustrates and emphasises Christ's innocence. In contrast to iconographic representations of the Passion, in which Christ is presented 'as passively exposed to the gaze of the devotee', it is the blood that actively disrupts the Jews' scheme and makes a mess of their arrangements.[74] On the other hand, it unites Christians and Jews by fusing the Body of Christ and the Jewish body, blurring the hierarchy of status between Christian and Jewish bodies as well as signifying the Jews' registration of Christ's woundly power of communication. Consequently, differently from what we find in other Host desecration narratives, the Jews repent, and they are told by Jesus that they should go to a priest to become his 'servauntys' (682; Luke 17:14).[75] Jesus also restores Jonathas's amputated hand, which has by this point been 'soden' and boiled to the point of tissue disintegration, and tells him:

> Thow woldyst preve thy power Me to oppresse.
> But now I consydre thy necesse;
> Thow wasshest thyn hart wyth grete contrycyon.
> Go to the cawdron, þi care shal be the lesse,
> And towche thyn hand, to thy salvacyon.   693–7

Nisse avers that the play's mode of converting the Jews – through miracle rather than exegetical reasoning – 'offers a critique of the predominant

---

74 Alexandra Barratt also links this passivity to femininity in iconographic representations of Christ. Alexandra Barratt '*Stabant Matres Dolorosae*: Women as Readers and Writers of Passion Prayers, Meditations and Visions' in *The Broken Body* 55–71, at 55.

75 Ruth Nisse locates this scene within an apocalyptic context, in which the conversion of Jews is a necessity for the Christian teleology; *Defining Acts* 102.

English urban dramatic model, the typological play cycle in which the spiritual or allegorical senses attempt to neatly resolve history and the carnal, literal Jews ultimately disappear'.[76] This signifies the affective mode through which the play makes its impression on the audience and undermines the discursive/representational system governing the play. After this, the Jews go to the bishop and explain what they have done. This time, however, the woundly speech gives way to language, the representational system within which legitimate interpretation of events is regulated. The plot, however, does not return to type, for no cathartic revenge is enacted. The bishop petitions Christ that 'From thys rufull sight þou wylt reverte', which then leads to a procession to the church (similar to Corpus Christi and certain feast processions) headed by the now reverted Host (737).

The second narration of the second Passion also takes place through language. The emphasis is still on the wounds, and the Jews describe what they have done, which includes admitting 'Wyth daggars styckyd Hym wyth grevos wonde | New naylyd Hym to a post, and with pynsonys pluckyd Hym down' (854–5). Jason avows that 'in a cawdron we dyd Hym boyle' and 'In a clothe full just we Hym wounde | And so dyd we seth Hym in oyle', while another notes 'In an hott ovyn we speryd Hym fast' (857–9, 861). The narration emphasises, once again, the overwhelming power of Christ in the face of such brutal attacks. This time, too, in spite of a return to the representational system of language, it does not seem that this return has any effect on the hierarchy of status between Christian and Jewish bodies, which could be interpreted as the irreversible consequence of their simultaneous processes of becoming-porous.

The final procession to the church could have potentially included the audience – if the play was ever actually performed.[77] Dutton notes that the church here would probably have been 'another scaffold or another theatrical re-designation of a single stage' and not a real church as suggested by several critics.[78] Furthermore, Dutton suggests that the line 'The Bysshope commythy [in] processyon with a gret meny of

---

76 Nisse *Defining Acts* 103.

77 David Lawton dismisses this idea as a fantasy, arguing that the stage is simply cleared at the end; 'Sacrilege and Theatricality' 296.

78 Dutton 'The Croxton Play of the Sacrament' 68. Lawton also casts doubt on the idea of the play being performed near an actual church; 'Sacrilege and Theatricality' 294.

Jewys' (763–4) implies the identification of the audience, 'by the miracle of theatre, as a Jewish crowd'.[79] This would be another instance of destabilisation of the distinction between Christian and Jewish bodies. Here, the union between the Host and the Jewish body is extended to the entire audience, blurring the lines of exclusion of bodies at work in the play's context. In addition, the Bishop's words, typically addressed to a Christian crowd, are applied, this time, to ethno-religious others, thereby removing the discursive exclusionary power surrounding the play. Greg Walker highlights that:

> the Croxton play seems perversely to insist on alienating its audience, unsettling familiar conventions, and blurring the very distinctions between the domestic and the foreign, the familiar and the alien, virtue and vice, that such drama conventionally takes for granted.[80]

And it is indeed this effect that comes with a successful move from *representation* (conventions) towards *becoming*. This is achieved, most prominently of all, I suggest, by the porousness that links various bodies in the performance space as well as in the audience.

Conclusion

Victor Turner describes public performances as part of a culture's 'subjunctive' mood, which opens up a realm of desire and possibilities.[81] To fully appreciate this realm and the emergent interpretations generated within it, we must stop privileging wholeness, marked by the supposed intact superficial integrity of the body, over un-wholeness, which is defined as anything other than this perfect state. As I have illustrated, the body was never understood as immaculately whole and isolated in late medieval culture: medical theories acknowledged the

---

79 Dutton 'The Croxton Play of the Sacrament' 68. Also see David Bevington 'Staging and Liturgy in *The Croxton Play of the Sacrament*' in *Staging Scripture: Biblical Drama, 1350–1600* edited Peter Happé and Wim Hüsken (Leiden: Brill, 2016) 235–52.
80 Walker 'And Here's Your Host' 45.
81 Victor Turner 'Liminality and the Performative Genres' in *Rite, Drama, Festival, Spectacle: Rehearsals toward a Theory of Cultural Performance* edited John MacAloon (Philadelphia: Institute for the Study of Human Issues, 1984) 19–41, at 21.

skin's pores as well as other orifices as ports through which matter is absorbed into and excreted from the body. Furthermore, violating the integrity of the body was often an essential part of treating illness, as the state of health required an optimal level of exchange between *within* and *without* the body. Similarly, devotional culture offered an idealised state of un-wholeness in the wounded bodies of holy figures, highlighting the unsuitability of privileging wholeness. The state of porousness, as I have proposed, can function as a more useful alternative: it incorporates the ambivalent function of bodily un-wholeness as a simultaneously unfavourable and favourable state that can even include, but is not limited to, bodily damage. It is by means of this concept that Christ's bodily disintegration can be understood not just as a sign of passivity, oppression, and defeat, but also as a show of power, a means of retaliation, and a mode of communication. In the Croxton *Play*, the silence of the Host/Christ is only silence within the representational system of language, which is the representational system associated with the liturgical culture authorising legitimate interpretation of events, miracles, offences, etc. Porousness enables communication through non-representational means (performance, *becoming*, and the woundly speech), which then opens up opportunities for emergent, unsanctioned, and potentially subversive interpretations of acts and events within and without the play. In this woundly mode of speech, Christ and the Host speak through their wounds, circumnavigating, and, at the same time, convincing or overpowering their adversaries – the Jews.

Within this realm of possibilities, not only does the performance of becoming-porous in the Croxton *Play* destabilise the authority of language and the location of Christ's Passion, it also, crucially, obliterates the distinction between Jewish and Christian bodies. Moreover, the play moves beyond the representation of scriptural material and towards a non-representational form of communication by renewing the Passion and transubstantiation in real time and on the spot. It also subverts late medieval liturgical convention by holding the Mass in the performance space, and modifies the tonality of priestly address by including the Jews in the same group as Christians. Lastly, the dissolution of boundaries in Croxton, materialising through the fusion of the Host with a Jew's hand and the inclusion of Jews in the concluding procession, would have further destabilised the exclusionary forces regarding Jews within the play itself as well as in late medieval culture. Such emergent and potentially subversive outcomes depend on the recognition that late medieval culture understood the body as an open, interactive entity for which wholeness is not an essential property, and recognised performance as an interactive experience within which it is possible to move beyond mere representation.

University of Birmingham

Acknowledgements

An earlier version of this chapter was presented at Medieval English Theatre 2023: I thank the conference organisers and attendees, especially the chair of my session, Sarah Carpenter, whose kind and warm reception of the paper encouraged me immensely. I also thank my anonymous reviewer and my doctoral supervisors, Olivia Robinson, Victoria Flood, and David Griffith, for their incisive comments. I gratefully acknowledge the Wolfson Foundation's support of my doctoral thesis, on which this chapter is based.

THE DISABLED BODY *AS* PERFORMANCE
'Disabled' Performers in the Records of Early English Drama

Mark Chambers

The study of historic disability has enjoyed increasing interest among scholars working across the arts and humanities. The role of disability on the early modern stage has drawn particular critical attention, as scholars look to shed further light on some of those 'thousand natural shocks' to which Hamlet says all flesh is heir.[1] Richard III's deformity, Gloucester's blindness, Lear's madness, the ubiquitous bodily mutilation in revenge tragedies such as *Titus Andronicus*, for example – many of these iconic staged 'impairments' have featured in recent studies of historic disability.[2] This chapter takes a different tack. Drawing on the substantial evidence offered by the *Records of Early English Drama* (*REED*) project, which identifies record references to pre-modern performances across Britain, it ultimately looks at some of the evidence for *actual* performance by those with physical disabilities, in order to begin to place these examples alongside the well-known fictional representations. Attempting to draw together some of the different kinds of evidence for disability and premodern performance raises a couple of key questions: beyond the much studied literary and artistic examples, what might the evidence offered by *REED* have to say about the physically disabled body as it played a part in premodern performance?

---

1   *Hamlet*, 3:1, 63. See Allison Hobgood and David Woods 'Introduction, "Disabled Shakespeares"' *Disability Studies Quarterly 29:4* (2009) <https://dsq-sds.org/article/view/991/1183>, and their edited collection *Recovering Disability in Early Modern England* (Columbus: Ohio State UP, 2013); *Disability, Health, and Happiness in the Shakespearean Body* edited Sujata Iyengar (London: Routledge, 2015); Genevieve Love *Early Modern Theatre and the Figure of Disability* (London: Bloomsbury, 2019); Katherine Schaap Williams *Unfixable Forms: Disability, Performance, and the Early Modern Theatre* (Ithaca: Cornell UP, 2021).

2   For *Richard III*, for example, see Allison P. Hobgood 'Teeth Before Eyes: Impairment and Invisibility in Shakespeare's *Richard III*' and Geoffrey A. Johns 'A "Grievous Burden": *Richard III* and the Legacy of Monstrous Birth' both in *Disability, Health, and Happiness* edited Iyengar, chapters 2 and 3. Other examples may be found in the works listed in the previous note.

And can records for performers with apparent physical disabilities tell us anything about how they might have been conceptualised, characterised and/or accommodated in premodern British society? This chapter hopes to initiate potential responses to such questions.

Derived from a wider study of the performance of disability in the early British and Irish record,[3] this chapter highlights the surviving record evidence in order to reframe how such performers contributed to wider premodern performance culture. The latter part of the chapter presents the evidence that relates specifically to musculoskeletal difference in the *Records of Early English Drama*. It suggests that the published and forthcoming *REED* collections can tell us a good deal about those performers whose physical impairment and/or difference affected their conceptualisation as performers. I do not include the references to so-called dwarfs or giants, as focus here is trained solely on performers identified as differently shaped rather than differently sized.[4] Examples include the handful of records for performers identified with some manner of amelia, amputation or other related physical abnormality of limbs, that potentially served a performative function – either as is shown by its mention alongside the performer's talent or skill, or, as in one case, is featured in performance.

Before turning to these records, however, the opening sections consider a couple of examples from the medieval drama where amelia is feigned through a stage effect – that is, where actors feign dismemberment as part of their role. Indeed, the use of staged dismemberment has proven one of the most popular ways of addressing historic physical disability as an aspect of performance.[5] The medieval drama contains numerous examples of characters rendered 'disabled', often temporarily, by the loss of a limb or other body part. The first section addresses a prime example of bodily dismemberment in the medieval drama, the

---

3 See my book-length study *Performing Disability in Premodern Britain*, to be published by Arc Humanities Press in early 2024; some of the evidence discussed here features in Chapter 4.

4 See Chapter 4 of *Performing Disability* (forthcoming).

5 See Margaret E. Owens *Stages of Dismemberment: The Fragmented Body in Late Medieval and Early Modern Drama* (Newark: University of Delaware Press, 2005); Cameron Hunt McNabb 'Croxton Play of the Sacrament (ca. 1461–1546)' in *Medieval Disability Sourcebook: Western Europe* edited Cameron Hunt McNabb (Santa Barbara: Punctum Books, 2020) 458–9; <https://doi.org/10.2307/j.ctv11hptcd>.

loss-of-hand scene in the Croxton *Play of the Sacrament*, alongside other related late medieval play scenes. This common piece of medieval stage business then facilitates a brief introduction to some of the key concepts in disability theory that are often applied to the medieval drama. In the second half of the chapter I will turn to some of the *REED* evidence for musculoskeletal difference in premodern performance.

While the overall approach is thus a bifurcated one, the intent is to suggest ways in which further study of disability in premodern performance might benefit from drawing together actual record and the famous fictional confections. The literary and artistic representations may tell us much about how disability was conceptualised and enacted, but they arguably tell us less about disability as a real lived experience. The *REED* evidence is fascinating and arguably underutilised. Yet it can also be frustratingly brief and ambiguous. Both kinds of evidence, from plays and from records, have much to offer. Neither on its own, I suggest, is capable of offering a complete picture.

Staging Conversion: A Show of Hands

An English play that often features in discussions of medieval disability in performance is the infamous Croxton *Play of the Sacrament* (c.1461–1546).[6] A deeply antisemitic work, the Croxton play is the premier English dramatic example of the 'Host desecration' tale that was popular in Europe from at least from the thirteenth century. Its subject matter draws on and is related to the recurring late medieval antisemitic canard known as the 'blood-libel', the play being frequently considered in those terms.[7] The Croxton play is also a fascinating, if challenging, drama for analysing some of the practicalities of late medieval stagecraft, requiring numerous special effects, including pyrotechnics, flowing stage blood

---

6   *The Croxton Play of the Sacrament* edited John T. Sebastian (TEAMS Middle English Texts; Kalamazoo: Medieval Institute Publications, Western Michigan University, 2012); further references to the text will be from this edition and indicated by line number(s).

7   See Elisabeth Dutton '*Macbeth* and the Croxton *Play of the Sacrament*: Blood and Belief in Early English Stagecraft' in *Blood Matters: Studies in European Literature and Thought, 1400–1700* edited Bonnie Lander Johnson and Eleanor Decamp (Philadelphia: University of Pennsylvania Press, 2018) 183–97; Owens *Stages of Dismemberment* 76–7; *The Croxton Play* (Introduction) 3–12.

and bodily dismemberment.[8] Dismemberment in the play – the loss and restoration of a character's hand – has drawn particular attention from scholars of historical disability.[9] Ultimately, the Croxton play's Host desecration narrative thus compounds its framing of the medieval Jew as 'Other', or social outsider, with another common form of 'othering': punitive and visible physical disablement.

Early in the play, a group of Syrian Jews obtain a specimen of consecrated bread for Christian Mass from a merchant; they intend to use the Host to disprove and defame the doctrine of transubstantiation. The conspirators first torture the Host by stabbing it, and then attempt to throw it into a cauldron of hot oil. The *de facto* leader, Jonathas – to his horror – becomes stuck to the Host, as his hand miraculously adheres to it. When his fellow conspirators nail the Host to a post in an attempt to free it, Jonathas's arm pulls away, leaving his severed hand still attached: '[Malchus:] Alas, alas, what devil is this? | Now hath he but oon hand, iwyse!' (516–17). Hand, Host and post are all then tossed together into the cauldron, which boils over with blood (672, sd). Jonathas is thus rendered 'disabled', we might say, by his loss of a limb. Physical and spiritual deficiency are thus elided in the play's stage business, as the impaired body becomes equated with impaired belief.

Typical of the miracle play genre, this piece of violent action provides opportunity for a conversion. Jonathas's amputation allows for his miraculous healing later in the play, which in turn initiates the mass conversion of the Jews at its turning point. So far, so hagiographic: in plays staging saints' lives, an act of violence typically initiates a miraculous conversion. The characters identified as evil are converted, either through their interaction with the play's tortured or murdered subject – as with the other Jews in this play following their 'torture' of the Host, or with various witnesses to Christ's Death and Resurrection in Passion Plays – or through their miraculous restitution by the intervening saint or relic – as with Jonathas here, the curing of the Roman centurion's blindness at the Crucifixion (from John 19:34), or St Paul's blinding and

---

8   *Croxton Play* (Introduction) 3–12; Philip Butterworth *Theatre of Fire: Special Effects in Early English and Scottish Theatre* (London: Society for Theatre Research, 1998) 48–9 and 51–3; Daryll Grantley 'Producing Miracles' *Aspects of Early English Drama* edited Paula Neuss (Cambridge: D.S. Brewer, 1983) 78–91.

9   McNabb 'Croxton *Play of the Sacrament*' 458–9; see also Owens *Stages of Dismemberment* 42–3, 72–8.

subsequent healing conversion on the road to Damascus (Acts 3:3–18). This kind of miraculous conversion is a common feature of medieval hagiography, and it proved very popular in the medieval drama.[10]

In the Croxton play, the conspirators go on to throw the Host into an oven, which then bursts open in a display of pyrotechnics and flowing blood. This is followed by the appearance of an image of the Christ Child. The figure of Christ then blames Jonathas himself for his disabling impairment: 'Jonathas, on thyn hand thow art but lame, | And ys thorow thyn own cruelnesse | For thyn hurt thu mayest thiself blame' (770–2). Bodily disablement is thus equated specifically with depravity and iniquity – that is, with the Jew's spiritual 'disability' as non-believer.[11] However, this is not to say that dismemberment is always associated with depravity in the medieval drama – certainly it is not. After all, Christ's wounded and bloodied body was itself an essential metaphor for late medieval Christian devotion (discussed more fully in Sadegh Attari's chapter on the Croxton play, this volume). Members of the Christian community were framed as members of that fractured body. Indeed, the Feast of Corpus Christi and worship of the Host celebrated Christ's fragmented body as *the* means to Christian salvation. Yet in many constructions of Christian miracle, such as in the Croxton play, the impaired human body is equated with spiritual ill-health. In such constructions, the 'healing' of a dismemberment or disfiguration is effected only in correlation with the successful conversion of the disbeliever. This is precisely what happens to Jonathas.

In the wider drama it is clear that the use of dismemberment as a means of divine punishment or corrective is not unique to the Croxton play. Nor is it unique to English drama: a near-identical dramatisation

---

10   Many saints' lives featuring the 'healing' of disability were adapted from Jacobus de Voragine's popular *Legenda Aurea* (orig. c.1260), including the story of the blind centurion Longinus and St Paul's conversion on the road to Damascus; see Jacobus de Voragine *The Golden Legend: Readings on the Saints* translated William Granger Ryan, 2nd edn, edited Eamon Duffy (Princeton UP, 2012) 84, 119–21. The Longinus (or Longeus) story was dramatised in the York *Mortificacio Christi*, the Towneley *Crucifixion*, the N-Town *Burial*, and the Chester *Passion* plays. St Paul's blinding and conversion feature in the fifteenth-century play of *The Conversion of St Paul* from the Digby Manuscript.

11   See McNabb's excellent (brief) discussion in 'Croxton' 458–9; on the scene's religious symbolism, see Anne Eljenholm Nichols 'The Croxton *Play of the Sacrament*: A Re-Reading' *Comparative Drama* 22 (1988–1989) 117–37.

of the 'Host desecration' tale occurs in Continental drama, as in versions of the French *Mistere de la Sainte Hostie*.[12] In a cycle of miracle plays prepared for the city of Bourges in 1536, a stage direction indicates similar dismemberment effected by similar stage business (*fainctes*): in a part of the cycle showing the Death of the Virgin, a Jewish prince named Belzeray *meetant les mains a la lectiere où lon porte la Vierge Marie et ses mains demeurent atachées a Lad. lectiere* ('puts his hands on the litter on which the Virgin Mary is being carried, and his hands remain attached to the said litter').[13] The action continues (in the modern English translation):

> and much fire in the form of lightning [*fouldre*] is thrown at them, and the Jews must fall to the ground, blinded. Belzeray's hands must be detached and joined back onto his arms. Then he is given the palm which he carries to the others, by which those who wanted to believe were enlightened [*illuminez*].[14]

Again, miraculous loss of a limb occasions miraculous healing and conversion. Momentary sensory impairment is also thrown into the mix, as the blinded disbelievers are also *illuminez*.

This episode is paralleled in and likely derived from the medieval prose apocrypha dealing with the miracles of the Virgin, such as Jacobus de Voragine's popular collection the *Legenda Aurea*, or *The Golden Legend*.[15] *The Golden Legend*'s version appears elsewhere in the English drama, although without the specified loss-of-hand: in the N-Town *Assumption of Mary* (Play 41), a Jewish prince (*princeps*) has his hands attached to the Virgin Mary's funeral bier: *saltat insanus ad feretrum Marie et pendet per manus* ('the madman leaps to Maria's bier and hangs

---

12 Apparently staged in Paris in the late fifteenth century and Metz in 1513: see Owens *Stages of Dismemberment* 71–3; *Croxton Play* (Introduction) 6, 21.

13 *Mystère des actes des Apôtres* edited Auguste Théodore baron de Girardot (Paris: V. Didron, 1856) 15.

14 Translation in *The Staging of Religious Drama in Europe in the Later Middle Ages: Texts and Documents in English Translation* edited Peter Meredith and John E. Tailby (EDAM Monograph Series 4; Kalamazoo: Medieval Institute Publications, Western Michigan University, 1984) 101–2; also quoted and discussed by Owens *Stages of Dismemberment* 31.

15 In this version the incident involves a 'chief priest' whose hands become stuck and 'withered' in pain; see *The Golden Legend* 467 (see note 10).

there by his hands').[16] In the now lost York Linenweavers' (formerly Mercers') play, the uniquely named character Fergus gets similarly stuck to Mary's bier, as recorded in the surviving 1416 *Ordo paginarum*:

> *Quatuor Apostoli* [...] *Marie et Fergus pendens super feretrum* [...] *is Iudeis cum vno Angelo*
>
> Four apostles [carrying the bier] of Mary, and Fergus hanging upon the bier [the two oth]er Jews and one angel.[17]

The extra-biblical character Fergus and his momentary dismemberment seems to have proven a highlight of York's Corpus Christi cycle. Indeed, the scene finds itself depicted in a mid-fourteenth-century stained-glass window in York Minster.[18]

Over time, the play of Fergus and his handlessness seems to have encouraged quite a raucous response from the audience – so much so that, by the 1430s (just over a decade after its mention in the *Ordo*) things appear to have got 'out of hand'. Now the responsibility of the Goldsmiths, the play 'in which Fergus was beaten' apparently prompted vigorous audience participation. The Goldsmiths petitioned the city's mayor and council in order to rid themselves of responsibility for the play, arguing that the cost of producing two plays (for which they were now responsible) was too great. Moreover, they argued that they should not stage the play:

> *pro eo quod materia pagine illius in sacra non continetur scriptura & magis risum & clamorem causabat quam deuocionem Et quandoque lites contenciones & pugne inde proueniebant in populo ipsamque paginam suam raro vel nunquam potuerunt producere & ludere clara die sicut faciunt pagine precedentes*

---

16 *The Assumption of Mary* in *N-Town Plays* edited Douglas Sugano and Victor I. Scherb (TEAMS Middle English Texts; Kalamazoo: Medieval Institute Publications, Western Michigan University, 2007) 422.

17 *REED: York* edited Alexandra Johnston and Margaret Rogerson, 2 vols (University of Toronto Press, 1979) *1* 23, *2* 709 and 732.

18 The window is in the south clerestory of the Lady Chapel. See Clifford Davidson and David E. O'Connor 'York Art: A Subject List of Extant and Lost Art' *EDAM 4* (2003) 68 <https://scholarworks.wmich.edu/early_drama/4>.

THE DISABLED BODY AS PERFORMANCE

FIG. 1: 'Death of the Virgin, funeral procession' (c.1340), detail.
Lady Chapel south clerestory window SIV, panel 4b, York Minster. Photo by
The York Glaziers Trust, reproduced by kind permission of the Chapter of York.

because the subject of this pageant is not contained in the sacred scripture and used to produce more noise and laughter than devotion. And whenever quarrels, disagreements, and fights used to arise among the people from this, they have rarely or never been able to produce their pageant and to play in daylight as the preceding pageants do.[19]

A dramatic tradition producing noise and laughter, alongside quarrels, disagreements and fights must surely have proven controversial, if popular. And at this stage in York Corpus Christi's history, the Goldsmiths successfully petitioned the civic authority to take it off their hands.

19 REED: York 1 47–8, 2 732.

Clearly, scenes enacting a sinner's temporary bodily paralysis or dismemberment have form in the miracle and saints' plays. Indeed, the sinner's miraculously restored body part proved a popular trope across late medieval European hagiographic art and literature more generally. In the case of hands, arms, or legs, sinful characters like Jonathas, Belzeray, and (probably) Fergus are taught the error of their ways by amputation and subsequent restoration (as Margaret Owens points out, the loss of heads – via decapitation – is reserved for holy martyrs and the elite).[20] Such 'corporeal hagiographics' of dismemberment also feature in other miracles attributed to the Virgin Mary, although not all make their way into the English drama.[21] The following section will outline briefly how recent disability theory responds to some of these dramatic confections.

Early drama and disability theory

I have outlined some of the context of the Croxton's dismemberment and healing scene here – Jonathas's disablement and miraculous restoration – to highlight a couple of common approaches to the medieval drama that draw on disability theory. The first involves narrative: Jonathas's disablement and subsequent restoration provides a perfect example of what has been called *narrative prosthesis*. The term was coined by David Mitchell and Sharon Snyder and suggests how, in traditional Western literature, a disability, an illness, or monstrosity gets introduced into a storyline to give it its shape. For the narrative to proceed, the anomaly must then be erased, elided, or else reformed ('cured' to use a medical/spiritual term) for it to reach a satisfactory conclusion.[22] Physical,

---

20 Owens *Stages of Dismemberment* 29.

21 The phrase is Richard Rambuss's: 'Devotion and Defilement: The Blessed Virgin Mary and the Corporeal Hagiographics of Chaucer's *Prioress's Tale*' in *Textual Bodies: Changing Boundaries of Literary Representation* edited Lori Hope Lefkovitz (Albany NY: University of New York Press, 1997); see also Owens *Stages of Dismemberment* 42–3; other related miracles of the Virgin can be found in Caxton's fifteenth-century English version of *The Golden Legend* edited Frederick Startridge Ellis, 12 vols (London: J.M. Dent, 1900) 'The Life of St. Leo' 4 294; and 'Miracles of the Virgin: The man who cut off his foot' in Oxford: Bodleian Library MS Vernon 150 fol. 125v b–c.

22 David T. Mitchell 'Narrative Prosthesis' in *Disability Studies: Enabling the Humanities* edited Sharon L. Snyder and others (New York: MLA, 2002) 15–30; for their more in-depth study, see Mitchell and Snyder *Narrative Prosthesis: Disability and the Dependencies of Discourse* (Ann Arbor: University of Michigan Press, 2000).

mental, or sensual abnormality must thus be expunged for a story to reach an acceptable end – to achieve narrative harmony. In the Croxton play, Jonathas's arm is made whole again, prompting his conversion to Christianity. He is healed corporeally, and, we might say, is brought to heal in terms of late medieval orthodoxy. To use the terminology of disability studies: his temporarily *non-normate* body is rendered *normate* by the narrative's conclusion.[23] In the terms of narrative prosthesis and medieval storytelling, the differentiated Other – the disabled Jew – was often simply done away with or silenced. This is what happens in Continental versions of the tale like the *Sainte Hostie*, where the Jewish figure who takes and abuses the Host ultimately meets his death.[24] But in Croxton, the Other's punitive disability provides means for his eventual conversion and assimilation. As Owens explains:

> The miraculous coupling of fragmentation and regeneration marks out a dialectic in which difference is both constructed and dissolved. If Croxton seems more enlightened than the *Sainte Hostie*, it is because the strategy for containing the Other in the English play is one of assimilation rather than annihilation. The Jew's body is knit together once again, but at a cost that most Jewish communities of the Middle Ages could not accept.[25]

Medieval hagiography, much more obviously than other genres, provides grist-to-the-mill for that notion of narrative prosthesis. Saints' and miracle plays stage various narratives of broken bodies being made whole again: the 'blind' being restored their sight (both physically and metaphorically), or the ostensibly abnormal rendered normal by an intervening saint or relic.[26] This is, of course, the very stuff of hagiographic drama. And it is a way of introducing, then erasing, ostensive 'disability'.

A forthcoming study that appears to take this approach (although I have not yet had opportunity to read it) is Cameron Hunt MacNabb's *Dramatic Prosthesis: Disability and Drama*, under contract with the University of Michigan Press.

23 For these terms, see Mitchell 'Narrative Prosthesis'.

24 Robert L.A. Clark and Claire Sponsler 'Othered Bodies: Racial Cross-Dressing in the *Mistère de la Sainte Hostie* and the Croxton *Play of the Sacrament*' *Journal of Medieval and Early Modern Drama Studies* 29 (1999) 61–87, at 75–7.

25 Owens *Stages of Dismemberment* 77.

26 Biblical examples of converting blindness that were often staged include Christ's curing of the blind man from John 9:3 (staged in the Chester *Glovers' Play* [play

Beyond the notion of narrative prosthesis, another popular related if basic theoretical model of disability relevant to the medieval drama is Edward Wheatley's 'religious model' (also referred to as the 'spiritual' or 'moral' model).[27] This way of thinking is ubiquitous in the so-called 'pre-medicalised' societies of premodern Europe: one's physical ailment or deviation is equated with one's spiritual ill-health. Premodern art and literature – and especially the homiletic and religious literature – provides numerous examples of metaphorised disability along the lines of the religious model. It is key to the long allegorical poem *Piers Plowman*, for example, where disability is used as a metaphor for spiritual error. During the fourteenth-century poem's recurring anxieties about the so-called 'undeserving poor' (as opposed to the 'deserving' or worthy recipients of charity), 'false' hermits are contrasted with true ones. In doing so, the poem etymologically equates *lameness* with the heresy of Lollardy:

> As by the Engelische of oure eldres, of olde mennes techynge,
> He that lolleth is lame or his leg out of ioynte
> Or ymaymed in som member, for to mischief hit souneth,
> Rihte so sothly such manere ermytes
> Lollen ayen the byleue and the lawe of holy churche.[28]

> As in the English of our elders, from old men's teaching,
> He who lolls is lame or his leg is out of joint
> Or he's maimed in some member, a hint of an accident.
> Just so indeed such manner of hermits
> Loll against the faith and the law of Holy Church.[29]

The poem thus attempts to redefine that relatively new Middle English term *lollen*, meaning 'to move unnaturally, [to] be lame' (thence *lollares* =

13]), Saint Paul's miraculous conversion on the road to Damascus, and the 'curing' of the centurion Longinus's at the foot of Christ's Cross (see note 10).

27 Edward Wheatley 'Blindness: Evolving Religious and Secular Constructions and Responses' in *A Cultural History of Disability in the Middle Ages* edited Jonathan Hsy, Tory V. Pearman, and Joshua R. Eyler (*A Cultural History of Disability*; London and New York: Bloomsbury, 2020) 68–9.

28 William Langland, *Piers Plowman: A New Annotated Edition of the C-Text* edited Derek Pearsall (University of Exeter Press, 2008) 170, Passus IX 215–19.

29 *William Langland's 'Piers Plowman': The C Version. A Verse Translation* edited and translated George Economou (Philadelphia: University of Pennsylvania Press, 1997) 85–6, Passus IX 214–18.

'lollards'), in a way that metaphorises physical-spiritual impairment, along similar lines to Christ's scolding of Jonathas in the Croxton play.[30]

There are of course other well-worn theoretical models applied to historic disability. The long-established 'social' model, for example, characterises disability as essentially a social construct, focusing attention on a particular society's and/or period's construction of the disabled Other. The social model stands in contrast to the older 'medical' model, which sees disability as something to be fixed or treated, or something requiring accommodation or prosthesis.[31] And there are myriad other evolved models: Tom Shakespeare's 'critical realist' model, for example (although the term is not his own), is an attempt to capture the nexus of impairment, disability, and identity. He points out, for example, that at certain points in our lives, we are all to a degree 'disabled'.[32] More than approaches like narrative prosthesis – which obviously foregrounds fictive storytelling – or the 'religious' or 'moral' model of disability so easily applied to literary, theological and philosophical texts from the medieval period, the 'critical realist' model arguably reminds us of the quotidian nature of disability.

Many of these models have been informed by art and literature. Often, approaches to historic disability rely solely on instances of 'cripping up' or feigning disability such as those written into the plays. To begin to form a rounded approach to disability as a performed phenomenon, however, it may be helpful to consider different kinds of evidence alongside the period's scripted plays – including those offered by *REED*. If the dramatic texts have helped inform current notions of disability as an aspect of premodern performance,[33] what might the evidence for real 'disabled' or ostensibly impaired performers from the period add to our understanding?

---

30 For the senses of the Middle English terms see *MED* sv *lollen*.
31 See Joshua Eyler *Disability in the Middle Ages: Reverberations and Reconsiderations* (Burlington: Ashgate, 2010) 4–5; McNabb *Medieval Disability Sourcebook* 15.
32 Tom Shakespeare *Disability Rights and Wrongs* (London: Routledge, 2006) 68.
33 See, for example, MacNabb *Medieval Disability Sourcebook* 14–19 and 419–70.

Orthopaedic 'impairment' in *REED*

There are now a number of excellent formal histories of disability as a condition and/or construct in premodern Europe.[34] But their interest is geographically wide-ranging and not focused specifically on disability in performance. Readers of *Medieval English Theatre* will of course be interested in what the play texts have to say about the performance of medieval disability, as well as the experience of acting, producing, and staging such parts. But they will also be aware of that other valuable source of evidence for medieval performance: the historic record. The records of performance, such as those provided by the *Records of Early English Drama* project, have the potential to offer valuable evidence for actual disabled performance in the medieval period, beyond the imaginative confections of the play texts. This chapter will now consider some of the evidence for performers with musculoskeletal difference in *REED*, positing that such evidence provides real potential for developing further some of the theoretical models used to approach historic disability, as well as disability as part of early performance.

Performers with specifically orthopaedic or musculoskeletal difference are, in fact, rare in *REED* as a whole. However, the few that do survive are worth considering in some detail. One of the most remarkable performers with apparent musculoskeletal difference to appear in the *REED* collections so far is also one of the latest (and is certainly post-medieval). In a fascinating record from David Galloway's volume for early modern Norwich, we find a record from 1633 in the Mayor's Court Book concerning one Adriane Provoe and his wife.[35] In July of that year, the Provoes were allowed to 'make their shewes' in the city. And it is Mrs Provoe that draws attention here, as 'she beinge a woman without hands is licenced to shew diverse works &c done with her feete'. Skilled pedal performance of tasks normally done by hand seems to be the nature of the handless woman's act. The couple (or at least Mrs Provoe) must have

---

[34] Such as Irina Metzler's three works: *Disability in Medieval Europe: Thinking about Physical Impairment During the High Middle Ages, c. 1100–1400* (London: Routledge, 2006); *A Social History of Disability in the Middle Ages: Cultural Considerations of Physical Impairment* (London and New York: Routledge, 2013); and *Fools and Idiots? Intellectual Disability in the Middle Ages* (Manchester UP, 2016). Also, *A Cultural History of Disability in the Middle Ages* edited Hsy and others (see note 27).

[35] *REED: Norwich 1540–1642* (University of Toronto Press, 1984) 211.

been popular, as the record tells us they were in possession of a (royal) licence from the Master of the Revels. In short, they seem to have been on tour.

The fact the Provoes moved around the country with their act is supported by another record, this one from Dorchester in Dorset a year later (1634). Here, the town records mention 'a French woman that had no hands, but could write, sow, wash, & do many other things with her feet'. It adds that the woman 'had a commission vnder the seale of the Master of the Reuelles' but that her performance was 'not allowed here'.[36] This is undoubtedly the same Mrs Provoe. She was apparently at least thought to be a French woman whose handless act included her performing domestic tasks with her feet. What we might now classify as 'intersectional' othering in her performance is readily apparent: not only is her ostensible disability – her handlessness – part of the act, but she is also marked out by her nationality and language (French), as well as by gender (she performs 'women's' tasks). Madam Provoe's record is a late one for *REED*. Sadly, it is also atypical.

The earliest record of a performer of note in the current *REED* evidence comes from medieval Hereford. Its appearance in *REED* is a lucky one, as technically it fails to meet the project's criteria for inclusion, and the *Herefordshire* editor David Klausner relegates it to an Appendix.[37] As stated on *REED*'s website, the criteria include 'all known references to dramatic, secular musical, and mimetic ceremonial performances' up to the year 1642 (when the Puritan-led government closed the London theatres).[38] This is clearly a very wide remit and the huge scope of the project necessitates more precise editorial guidance for inclusion and exclusion. Records of those identified as performers, but not as performing, are excluded. Regarding music, for example, the *REED Handbook for Editors* specifies only the inclusion of 'musical performance by secular musicians' and 'musical instruments for secular performances' – not, we note, the mention of secular musicians when

---

36 *REED: Dorset and Cornwall* edited Rosalind Conklin Hays and C.E. McGee (University of Toronto Press, 1999) 206.

37 See criteria listed in *REED: Handbook for Editors* compiled by A.F. Johnston and Sally-Beth MacLean (1980) revised by Sally-Beth Maclean (1990) 11–13; <https://reed.utoronto.ca/wp-content/uploads/2013/12/Handbook.pdf>.

38 *REED Online* 'About the Records' 2016–23; <https://ereed.library.utoronto.ca/about/>.

they are not involved in performing.[39] The rationale behind such limits is self-evident. The aim of the project is to capture evidence of performance, not simply performers *per se*.

In the case of the *Herefordshire* appendix, however, an exception was made for a musician on pilgrimage. In a Vatican Library manuscript containing testimony from the canonisation hearings of St Thomas de Cantilupe, who was bishop of Hereford from 1275 until his death in 1282, we find the case of the so-called 'Miracle of Philip the Harper'.[40] Philip's 'miracle' is said to have taken place in the cathedral on Good Friday 1287. A pilgrim to the cathedral, to the shrine of Thomas de Cantilupe, Philip is described as having been *alius contractus pedibus* (or 'crippled in the feet' in Klausner's translation). Philip's perceived disability was *miraculose curatus* ('miraculously cured') as he was made *erectus* in the presence of St Thomas's tomb. The miracle was related by another physically disabled pilgrim named Juliana Knock, who was similarly healed by the same intervention. Now, formally, this is not a *REED* record, as there is no suggestion of performance of any kind. There is simply reference to a named performer: a *citharist*. And, in Philip's case, there is no evidence that his apparent bodily impairment played any formal part in his role as a musician. Nonetheless, the record from Hereford does provide a vivid glimpse into that high and late medieval culture of ostensive disability 'cured' or erased through miraculous intervention or saintly healing. It may not be factually true, but the details of Philip's 'restoration' are no less valid a representation of the period's performance of physio-spiritual therapy than Jonathas's mended hand (and faith) in the Croxton *Play of the Sacrament*. Of course, both Jonathas's wickedness and his Jewishness are simultaneously 'cured' alongside his handless arm. His is a fictitious example of that intersectionality that often characterised constructions of the 'healing' of disability in the religious model. No mention is made of Philip's spiritual state, and we cannot presume that he was, or was thought to be, any more or less wicked than your average musician; nor was he Jewish. But the record of his miraculous transformation by an intervening saint tells us a great deal about how the conceptualisation of disability may have played a part in the lives of everyday people. It

---

39 *REED: Handbook for Editors* 12; <https://reed.utoronto.ca/wp-content/uploads/2013/12/Handbook.pdf>.
40 *REED: Herefordshire & Worcester* edited David Klausner Appendix 1: 'A Minstrel's Miracle' 199–201, translated 271.

also suggests that his disability had not hindered his successful career as a working performer. The record thus speaks to both the social and religious models of disability as much as the medieval play texts.

Those coming to pray with impairments – what might be framed as 'disabilities' – are, of course, well recorded around the shrines of medieval saints and their relics. The practice of offering a votive at the shrine of an intervening saint, often in the form of a wax body part, crutches, carvings of eyes, etc., is quite well attested in later medieval European art (indeed, there is a famous English example in the St William Window in York Minster, featuring a pilgrim offering a wax effigy of a leg at the saint's shrine with other body parts represented above).[41] Such literalising rituals are also well attested in the records. For Hereford's canonisation of Thomas de Cantilupe, for example, there are two inventories surviving from the papal inquisition of 1307.[42] These record the various votive objects left in the vicinity of the saint's tomb (*in circuitu dicti tumuli*). Tellingly, the first one lists a number of votives, including:

> 170 silver and forty-one wax ships.
> 129 silver images of whole and diverse body parts.
> 436 wax images of people.
> 1,200 wax images of body parts.
> Seventy-seven figures of horses, animals and birds.
> An uncountable multitude of wax images of eyes, breasts, teeth, and ears.
> Ninety-five silk and linin [*sic*] garments.
> 108 walking sticks.[43]

Votive offerings were clearly big business, and it is tempting to speculate that Philip the Harper may also have left some *ex-voto* offering behind to mark his miraculous healing.

---

41 'The Saint William Window, 21b' in York Glaziers' Trust and York Minster's 'Stained Glass Navigator'; online at <https://stainedglass-navigator.yorkglazierstrust.org/window/st-william-window/panel/21b>.

42 Ian L. Bass 'Bishop Cantilupe is Dead! Long Live St Thomas of Hereford! The Effects of St Thomas of Hereford's Miraculous Cult' *History* (2014); online at <https://onlinelibrary.wiley.com/doi/full/10.1111/1468-229X.13032>.

43 Vatican Library (VL) MS 4015 fol 74r-v; translated Ben Nilson in 'The Medieval Experience at the Shrine' in *Pilgrimage Explored* edited J. Stopford (York: York Medieval Press, 1999) 105; see also Ronald C. Finucane *Miracles and Pilgrims: Popular Beliefs in Medieval England* (Totowa: Rowman and Littlefield, 1977) 98.

The Scottish royal court

The record of Philip the Harper survives only in a *REED* appendix, and there are disappointingly few surviving *REED* records besides those for Mrs Provoe where musculoskeletal difference seems to have formed some part of the conceptualisation of a performer's performance. However, one particular tranche of records in which a number of contenders do appear is found in the accounts of the Scottish royal court.[44] These are arguably early modern rather than medieval, but they do offer valuable, if sporadic, insight into the relative socialisation of disabled performers at the premodern Scottish court.

King James IV of Scotland left record of numerous payments to musicians and other performers throughout his reign (1488–1513). Some of these stand out in the accounts because of an intriguing detail or idiosyncrasy. For example, for 3 August 1496 there is record of a payment of nine shillings to 'ye harpar*e* with ye a hand' (the harper with the one hand), while the king was at Linlithgow.[45] The apparently one-handed harper's dexterity and skill must have played a part in his performance, otherwise it would hardly merit mention in the account. In an account the following year (10 April 1497), the remarkable harper appears to be named: again, while the King was in Linlithgow, there is record of another nine shillings paid to 'Johne harpar witht ye ane hand at ye king*is* command'.[46] Sadly, this is the last we hear of John the one-handed harper. However, in May 1497 several musicians benefited from the king's generosity, including another nine shillings paid to 'ye brokin bakkit fithelar in Sanctandro*is*'.[47] Here, courtiers at St Andrews were apparently entertained by this 'broken-backed fiddler', with no doubt his

---

44 I am grateful to Sarah Carpenter, editor of the forthcoming *Scottish Royal Court* collection for *Records of Early Drama: Scotland* (*RED:S*), for providing me with the following records and transcriptions. There are no *RED:S* records yet published for *REED*, apart from a few late sixteenth-century samples on the *REED Pre-Publication* site; <https://reedprepub.org/>. But there are extensive though slightly selective editions of the full Scottish *Treasurer's Accounts* in twelve volumes (published 1877–1971), covering 1473–1574.

45 National Records of Scotland MS E22/4 (1496) fol. 12r; *Accounts of the Lord High Treasurer of Scotland Vol 1 1473–1498*, edited by Thomas Dickson (Edinburgh: HM General Register House, 1877) 288.

46 E22/4 (1496) fol. 56v; *Treasurer's Accounts 1* 329.

47 E22/4 (1497) fol. 61r; *Treasurer's Accounts 1* 333.

orthopaedic irregularity playing some part in the conceptualisation of his performance. It is presumably possible that these payments to John the one-handed harper of Linlithgow, as well as to the broken-backed fiddler at St Andrews, could suggest that they were charity cases. There is no further information about the nature of their performance, if, indeed, they performed for the court at all. But the way they are recorded and the sums they received are in line with those for other local musicians where the king stayed, or who visited the court in Edinburgh. Charity payments to the poor and sick, including those with impairments, in the same places around this time are significantly lower. For example, on 13 March 1497 in St Johnstone we find the following two adjacent records:

> Item þe xiij day of march giffin to dauid hay *and* a lutare in Sanct Johnstoune xviij s
> Item þat samyn day in Sanct Johnstoune to a woman by [*out of*] hir mynd at ye King*is* command iij s

The lute player (presumably sharing with David Hay) receives nine shillings, the woman with a mental impairment three shillings. If the payments are not simply charitable, to what degree might we consider these orthopaedically challenged players' potential performances for the peripatetic Scottish court as evidence for their 'agency' as jobbing musicians? It is difficult to say for certain, but the records leave tantalising details.

There is ample evidence beyond *REED* that King James IV was fond of entertainments and entertaining. Remembering his time in the king's service as a young man, for example, the playwright and courtier Sir David Lyndsay (c.1486–c.1555) recalls fondly the king's love of sporting 'pastimes', the '[t]riumphand tournayis, justing and knightly game / With all pastyme according to ane king'.[48] It is clear that the *REED* evidence for James's support of ostensibly 'disabled' or impaired performers formed part of the wider nexus of entertainment, pastime, and charity associated with his reign.

---

48 Sir David Lyndsay *The Testament of the Papyngo* in *Selected Poems* edited Janet Hadley Williams (Glasgow: Association for Scottish Literary Studies, 2000) 58–97, lines 502–3. See also Sarah Carpenter 'Towards a Reformed Theatre: David Lyndsay and *Ane Satyre of the Thrie Estaitis*' in *Yearbook of English Studies* 43, Early English Drama (2013) 203–22, at 211.

A vivid and intriguing account, though not strictly a contemporary record, gives a description of another pair of 'disabled' potential performers as having entertained the Scottish court, as well as 'the common people', in James IV's reign. As with Philip the Harper, this evidence is not strictly appropriate as a *REED* record but it nonetheless offers some striking insights into recorded attitudes to performers with impairments. Two Scottish historians, both writing in the 1570s, report on these performers, both claiming to have drawn their information from eyewitnesses in the late 1490s. The chronicler and would-be historian Robert Lindsay of Pitscottie (c.1532–1580), in his lively though not strictly dependable vernacular work *The Historie and Chronicles of Scotland, 1436–1565*, leaves a colourful account of conjoined twins, who were apparently raised either in James's court or under his direction, at the end of the fifteenth century. Pitscottie was writing nearly a century after many of the events he was recording, although he claims eyewitness testimonies as his sources and includes much circumstantial detail. While we must take the full details of this particular passage with a pinch of salt, his description of the court maintenance of the pair of conjoined twins may well contain some kernels of truth. Undoubtedly, the twins, who were apparently joined at the waist and shared their lower limbs, would have had significant physical challenges. The king apparently took it upon himself to have the twins raised and supported. Pitscottie also notes that the king had them instructed:

> to pley and singe wpoun the instrumentis of musick quho war become in schort tyme werie [*very*] ingeneous and cunning in the art of musick quhairby they could pleay and singe tuo pairtis, the on [*one*] the tribill [*treble*] the wther [*other*] the tennour quhilk [*which*] was werie dulse [*very dulcet*] and melodious to heir be the common pepill quho treatit thame wondrous weill. Allso they could speik sindrie and dyuerse langagis, that is to say Latine, Frinche, Italieans Spanis Dutch Dens [*Danish*] and Inglische and Earische [*Gaelic*].[49]

Pitscottie's emphasis on the twins' apparently humane treatment, their education and their seemingly welcome reception suggests a degree of

---

49 Robert Lindsay of Pitscottie *The Historie and Chronicles of Scotland* edited A.J.G. MacKay *Scottish Text Society* 3 vols (Edinburgh: William Blackwood and Sons for the STS, 1899) *1* 233. Again, I am grateful to Sarah Carpenter for these references.

positive accommodation on the part of the Scottish court and people. If the twins did indeed become musically proficient and gifted polyglots, the account also suggests that their striking physical abnormality could be socially accommodated through performance. A similar accommodation exists, one might argue, with Mrs Provoe's dexterous footwork described in the Norwich and Dorchester records. The implications for disability theory are numerous, and clearly records like these offer valuable 'real-world' evidence for the evolving theoretical models.

Now, we may ask ourselves: is Pitscottie's description of the conjoined twins appropriate to include as record evidence in REED? It does claim that the conjoined twins were providing musical entertainment to the Scottish royal court. They also appear to have publicly demonstrated their skills with languages. However, much of Pitscottie's fanciful description of the death of one of the twins, with the other suffering despair, smacks of sensational invention.[50] I suggest this record might certainly belong in an appendix, though with caution urged regarding its accuracy. Even if heavily embroidered, it is revealing of attitudes to 'disabled' performers. Clearly, Pitscottie was impressed with what he understood to have been humane treatment of the unusual pair by the wider public. And the twins must have served some sort of performative function: they must have offered diversion or spectacle, whether or not they were truly 'performers'. Pitscottie's record also suggests that they were considered a special charity case by the king. Like the much earlier record of Philip the 'lame' harper, this record may arguably speak to a compassionate impulse towards the physically disabled in some corners of pre-Reformation society. Such impulse was almost certainly supported by the period's long-established commitment to Christian charity.[51]

Luckily another historical account of the Scottish conjoined twins survives. Writing around the same time as Pitscottie or just after, the historian and internationally famed humanist scholar George Buchanan composed his Latin chronicle *Rerum Scoticarum Historia* in the years leading up to his death in 1582. His report of the twins is arguably less melodramatic than Piscottie's, if not necessarily more reliable. Buchanan, too, claims to have drawn on first-hand evidence, and is at pains to

50 Pitscottie *Historie and Chronicles* 1 234.
51 For general discussion of late medieval charity, see Eamon Duffy *The Stripping of the Altars: Traditional Religion in England c.1400–c.1580* (New Haven: Yale UP, 2nd edition 2005 [1992]) 357–66.

emphasise his credentials, concluding his report: *Hac de re scribimus eo confidentius quod adhuc supersunt homines honesti complures qui haec viderunt* ('I am the more confident in relating this story because there are many honest and creditable persons yet alive who saw this prodigy with their eyes').[52] Buchanan's description of what he terms the 'monster' is in fact broadly similar to Pitscottie's, perhaps suggesting that they shared the same sources.[53] But he has a more scholarly interest in the medical and physical details than Pitscottie, noting how:

> *inferiore quidem corporis parte specie maris, nec quiquam a communi hominum forma discrepans. Umbicilum vero supra trunco corporis ac reliquis omnibus membris geminis.*
>
> [i]n the lowest parts of its body it resembled a male child not much differing from the ordinary shape of an humane body newly born, but above the navel the trunk of the body and all the other members were double.[54]

Regarding their role as performers, Buchanan offers a briefer and less colourful description than Pitscottie's. He does note, though, that the king *diligenter et educandum et erudiendum curavit, ac maxime in musicis, qua in re mirabiliter profecit. Quin et varias linguas edidicit* ('gave special order for its [the monster's] careful education, especially in musick, wherein it arrived to admirable skill. And moreover it learned several tongues'). Despite the differing emphases, then, both Buchanan and Pitscottie record the twins' apparent musicianship and skill with languages. Both also indicate the apparent charitableness of the Scottish court.

In terms of disability theory, in these accounts of the conjoined twins we do not see any real-world attempt to erase, elide, or otherwise 'cure' potential disability. Rather, the Scottish court of James IV appears to have attempted to facilitate and accommodate physical difference by enabling

---

52 George Buchanan *Rerum Scoticarum Historia* (1582) edited and translated Dana F. Sutton (University of California, Irvine: The Philological Museum, 20 February 2003, revised 7 January 2009) Book 13 paragraph 5; <https://philological.cal.bham.ac.uk/scothist/index.html>.

53 While not specifically referencing this episode, both Buchanan and Pitscottie in their histories acknowledge Sir David Lyndsay as one of their first-hand sources for events from the reigns of James IV and V.

54 Buchanan *Rerum Scoticarum Historia* Book 13 paragraph 5.

performance. Indeed, Pitscottie seems to suggest that it was *because* of the twins' performance – their musical ability – that 'the common pepill ... treatit thame wondrous weill'.[55] At the same time, there was undoubtedly a degree of voyeurism associated with any performance by the remarkable pair, one piqued by their unusual physical difference. Scholars of historic disability have written on the pet-like status accorded to certain 'othered' early modern household retainers like court fools and dwarfs.[56] While power dynamics in the case of the conjoined twins was undoubtedly one-way, however, the records left by Pitscottie and Buchanan do suggest they were afforded status as performers – perhaps even with a degree of what we might consider agency.

Unfortunately, REED has not yet tackled the substantial records contained in the English royal household. These may well provide many more instances of orthopaedically challenged or differentiated performers whose lived experiences can help further explore how physical differences such as musculoskeletal abnormality might help further illustrate disability as an element of premodern performance culture. Further evidence for performers similarly characterised as having orthopaedic variance or potential impairment occasionally surfaces in the published and forthcoming regional *REED* volumes. But, because this category of ostensible 'disability' is so variant and is frequently non-congenital, its representation in the records for performance and social custom is necessarily sporadic and limited. For example, the *REED Cheshire* volume includes, in its appendix, a reference to the burial of the Malpas-based piper named John Kersey (8 October 1620). Kersey merits mention here because he was a performer (a piper) and his nickname was apparently 'Clubfoot'.[57] But little else can be said about 'Clubfoot' John. Did he make a virtue of his apparent podalic variance as part of his piping? It is impossible to say. What we *can* say is that orthopaedic issues do occasionally make their way into the *Records*

---

55   Robert Lindsay of Pitscottie *Historie and Chronicles* 1 234.

56   Metzler *Fools and Idiots?* 187–9 (see note 34); Chambers *Performing Disability* (forthcoming, see note 3) especially chapters 2 and 4; for theoretical discussion see also Yi-Fu Tuan *Dominance and Affection: The Making of Pets* (New Haven: Yale UP, 1984).

57   *REED Cheshire: Including Cheshire* edited Elizabeth Baldwin, Lawrence M. Clopper, and David Mills, 2 vols (University of Toronto Press; London: The British Library, 2007) 2 905.

of Early English Drama, and that they can, as in the records discussed above, 'play a part' in a particular performer's act.

A Call for Coalescence

So far, my assessment of current and forthcoming *REED* volumes suggests that musculoskeletal difference is the least represented of any of the traditional or legal categories of so-called 'disability' identified for performers in the premodern British and Irish records. Those with mental, intellectual, or sensory difference – musicians described as being blind, for example – are far more numerous in the extant records. This is undoubtedly because, from around 1500, and increasingly in the early modern period, such performers were likely to be retained in royal and elite households. One-armed harpers and broken-backed fiddlers were not. While the *REED* evidence for musculoskeletal difference is sparse, it remains clear that any study of disability as an aspect of premodern performance that relies solely on the literary models is missing out on evidence of lives as they were actually lived.

Although often piecemeal, what the evidence offered by the records suggests is that physically disabled performers seem to have rarely attracted the kinds of moral or spiritual judgement most often expressed through the dramatic representation of fictional characters with such impairments. The records of those with congenital or accidental orthopaedic disabilities may reveal a degree of charitable support and dependence, but they do not suggest either moral condemnation, or usually attempts at 'cure'. It is also clear that some individuals could develop a degree of professional 'agency', as with Mrs Provoe and her undoubtedly impressive *shewes*. Further, accounts like those from late medieval/early modern Scotland for the conjoined twins indicate desire on the part of the court to try to accommodate and facilitate further agency through performance. The records sometimes testify to the humane treatment of the ostensive disabled – those otherwise othered by their obvious physical difference. There are also records that can contribute to the evolving theoretical models of disability, such as the 'miracle' of Philip the harper in Hereford, a performer physically 'healed' by apparent spiritual intervention.

While the *REED* evidence for physically disabled performers is inevitably sporadic and can be frustratingly piecemeal, it can also contribute valuable evidence for the socialisation of disability in premodern Britain and Ireland. Such evidence speaks to the quotidian nature of disability as a part of any past society, arguably much more than the celebrated literary models. Such records, however scanty, leave evidence of lives actually lived, of performers actually performing, and of disability as informing that performance.

University of Durham

FROM HUY TO PRIMROSE HILL
An Early Twentieth-Century English Re-Playing of a Fifteenth-Century Liégeois Nativity Play

Janet Cowen

Richard Aldington (1892–1962) was a prolific reviewer and translator in his time, though probably better known to later readers as an Imagist poet and author of the First-World-War novel *Death of a Hero*. In autumn 1924 he published *The Mystery of the Nativity*, his translation of a fifteenth-century text in Walloon French.[1] In December 1924 there was a performance of his translation in the Church Room of St Mary the Virgin Primrose Hill, London. Neither this performance nor Aldington's translation itself have made their way into standard accounts of the revival of religious drama in England in the early twentieth century. This chapter will make a brief analysis of Aldington's handling of the text and consider what inferences can be drawn about the performance of it at St Mary's from materials preserved in the parish archive and in the archive of George Allen & Unwin Ltd, and from the brief press notices I have found to date.

Beyond the citation of his source text Aldington does not indicate in the published edition how the play first came to his notice or what in particular prompted him to undertake the translation.[2] But correspondence preserved in the archive of his publishers, George Allen & Unwin Ltd,[3] reveals that the initiative for the publication came from Aldington himself, who enclosed a copy of his translation in a letter dated 24 March 1924, in which he notes that he had permission from Gustave Cohen, the editor of the French text, to publish his translation of it

---

1   *The Mystery of the Nativity* translated Richard Aldington (London: George Allen & Unwin, 1924). It was issued simultaneously by the Medici Society, the two issues differing only in the imprints on the respective title-pages, the colophons on the verso of the title-pages, and the verso of the final page of the text, which in the George Allen & Unwin issue bears the publishers' device and in the Medici Society issue is blank, the publisher's device appearing above the imprint on the title-page.

2   In a note following his brief foreword, Aldington cites as his source the scholarly edition of the original text published four years previously: *Mystères et Moralités du Manuscrit 617 de Chantilly* edited Gustave Cohen (Paris: Champion, 1920).

3   University of Reading: Special Collections AUC 7/1.

without charge. Aldington's friendship with Cohen at a later stage of his life is documented by his most recent biographer.[4] But the letter of 1924 indicates that he was already in correspondence with him at this point, and a batch of letters written in 1921 by Aldington to Cohen, published in 2003, shows that Aldington had sent his translation to Cohen for comment, and identifies Aldington as the author of an anonymous review of Cohen's edition in the *Times Literary Supplement* 31 March 1921.[5] The choice of text reflects Aldington's deep interest in medieval French literature, amply attested in his translation and reviewing work. The particular subject matter of the play evidently attracted him for what he saw as its poetic power rather than for its ostensible doctrinal import.[6]

Aldington's Translation

Synopsis of the play as in Aldington's translation

The action encompasses the Purification of the Virgin Mary, Herod's command that all the children of Judaea in their first two years of age should be slain, and the apocryphal visit by the Virgin Mary's sisters and their mother Saint Anne to adore the baby Jesus. Aldington's text consists of five numbered scenes as follows:

Scene i   [Characters: Mary Jacob; Mary Salome; Saint Anne; Mary]
A brief scene in which the two sisters ask their mother's permission to stay behind and help Mary, but Mary tells them not leave their mother alone.

---

4   Vivien Whelpton *Richard Aldington: Novelist, Biographer and Exile 1930–1962* (Cambridge: The Lutterworth Press, 2019) 231, 362 alludes to his 1924 translation of the text in covering the commencement of his friendship with Gustave Cohen in the 1930s.

5   Stephen Steele 'Richard Aldington et Gustave Cohen, l'un pour l'autre: quatre lettres inédites d'Aldington à Cohen' *French Studies Bulletin 24:86* (2003) 11–16. References to *Times Literary Supplement* are cited from <www.the-tls.co.uk/archive>.

6   For his translation and reviewing work at this period see Vivien Whelpton *Richard Aldington: Poet, Soldier and Lover 1911–1929* (Cambridge: The Lutterworth Press, revised edition 2019) *passim*, and Whelpton *Aldington: Novelist, Biographer and Exile* 328–30; for his attitude to religion see Whelpton *Aldington: Novelist, Biographer and Exile* 77–9.

JANET COWEN

Scene ii [Characters: Mary; Joseph]
Mary tells Joseph that as forty days have passed since the birth of Jesus it is the due time to go to the temple for the offering of the child and her purification. When Joseph says this is not required because she is still a virgin, she replies that the law must nevertheless be observed. Joseph provides two turtledoves and they set out. Joseph says he will go ahead to advise 'the bishop Saint Symeon' of their arrival, but Mary replies that the Holy Ghost will inform him.

Scene iii [Characters: Saint Symeon; Mary]
Symeon greets Mary and adores Jesus.

Scene iv [Characters: Herod; The Fool; Seneschal; Knights (non-speaking)][7]
Herod rages against the three kings, who have broken faith with him by failing to return, and he vows to slay them. The Fool warns him that they have superior forces. Herod threatens the Fool, who replies insolently. Herod commands the Seneschal to destroy the kingdom of Tarse. The Seneschal replies that it is too late to set out that day but he will go first thing in the morning. Herod declares that when he himself has come back from Rome he will go and destroy the kingdoms of Saba and Arabie. Again the Fool accuses him of folly and is berated. Herod summons his knights and commands them to seek out and slay all the children of Judea aged less than three years.

Scene v [Characters: Mary; Saint Anne; Joseph; Mary Jacob; Mary Salome]
Mary and Joseph greet St Anne and the two sisters. Mary tells them of her painless delivery and sends Joseph to fetch Jesus. She holds Jesus 'upright upon her lap' (sd) while St Anne and the sisters speak words of adoration. In reply to a question from St Anne about whether she received any visitors since the birth, Mary relates that angels worshipped the child with

---

7   Herod's words of command imply the presence of the Knights, but Aldington has omitted five lines of dialogue in which they accept his orders (*Mystères et Moralités* 33, lines 152–6). This is Aldington's only substantial alteration to his original.

song which brought shepherds from the fields to adore him in the manger, and then three kings, named Jaspar, Melcior, and Baltazar came 'from a far country' guided by a star, and offered gold, myrrh and frankincense, confessing her son as king of heaven and earth. St Anne replies that the prophecies of Balaam have been accomplished. Mary Jacob and Mary Salome remark on the beauty and gentleness of the child and how he seems to recognise them. St Anne tells them his beauty fulfils the prophecies of David, and that he is God and man, who opens the way to paradise for them. She takes leave of Mary and Joseph.

Aldington's sequence of scenes follows the present order of material in the manuscript, where scenes are not numbered. As it stands, it is difficult to make thematic sense of the first scene, unless perhaps it could be taken as an allusive reference to some earlier visit, but neither Aldington, nor Cohen in his 1920 edition, comments on this apparent awkwardness. Subsequently, in his revised edition of 1953, Cohen argued from palaeographical evidence that the folio containing the original text of Aldington's scenes *i–iii* had been displaced from its original position in the manuscript, and thus the original sequence of action is the equivalent of scenes [*iv, v, i, ii, iii*], the dialogue of *i* being in fact the conclusion to *v*, and in his revised text he restored the misplaced material to its presumed original place in the sequence of action, which thus opens with the rage of Herod and concludes with the Purification.[8] Even with this rearrangement, Cohen considered the text to be fragmentary, a view that Aldington echoes in his Foreword.[9]

---

8   *Nativités et moralités Liégeois du moyen-âge* edited Gustave Cohen (Brussels: Académie Royale de Belgique, 1953) 193–201. For his presentation of the palaeographical evidence see the footnotes marked * to pages 191 and 198, and Pl. I. For a more recent study of the manuscript and analysis of the play see Olivia Robinson 'Chantilly, Musée Condé, Ms. 617: *Mystères* as Convent Drama' in *Les Mystères: Studies in Genre, Text and Theatricality* edited Peter Happé and Wim Hüsken (Amsterdam: Rodopi, 2012) 93–118, which does not, however, draw attention to Cohen's emendation of the scene order in his revised edition, and somewhat misleadingly (112) summarises the opening scene in the manuscript as an announcement by Mary's mother and sisters of their visit to her, whereas the dialogue implies they have already arrived.

9   *Mystères et Moralités* cxxxii; *The Mystery of the Nativity* 9. The play as it stands in Cohen's text is 307 lines long.

It should be noted that this play is preceded in the manuscript by another Nativity play, the two forming the opening items of the manuscript, which contains five plays in all. Cohen's title for the first of these, *Jeu de la Nativité*, is derived from the manuscript heading to the text. The second, which has no manuscript heading, he titles in his 1920 edition *Fragment d'un Mystère de la Nativité*, and in his revised edition of 1953 *Suite de la Nativité*. In his introductory discussions he refers to them as *Nativité I* and *Nativité II* respectively, a nomenclature that I shall adopt in the present discussion. *Nativity 1*, to anglicise Cohen's shorthand title, encompasses the birth of Jesus, the angelic appearance to the shepherds, the shepherds' visit to Bethlehem with gifts, their adoration of the child, the meeting of the three kings and their visit to Herod, their visit to Bethlehem, offering gifts and adoring the child, and the angel's warning to them not to return to Herod.[10] *Nativity 2* is thus continuous in action with *Nativity 1*, and Cohen surmised that it may have been intended to be played, or indeed actually played, continuously with it, though it is different in origin.[11] Although Aldington was aware of *Nativity 1* (see below), he makes no allusion to it in his Foreword, and there is no indication that it influenced his treatment of the text of *Nativity 2*.

---

10 An adaptation of *Nativity 1* into French, incorporating the Herod and Fool scene from *Nativity 2*, was made in the early seventeenth century at the convent of Huy, where the fifteenth-century playbook had been copied. For an account of this adaptation and of an enactment of a present-day English translation of it in 2017 see Aurélie Blanc and Olivia Robinson 'The *Huy Nativity* from the Seventeenth to the Twenty-First Century' *Medieval English Theatre 40* (2018) 66–97.

11 *Mystères et Moralités* cxxii; on variations of dialectal forms between the two texts see pages cii–ciii. For questioning of some of Cohen's linguistic analysis see *Recueil général de moralités d'expression française 1* edited Estelle Doudet, Jonathan Beck, and Alan Hindley (Paris: Garnier, 2012) cited in Matthew Cheung-Salisbury, Elisabeth Dutton, and Olivia Robinson 'Medieval Convent Drama: Translating Scripture and Transforming the Liturgy' in *A Companion to Middle English Translation* edited Jeanette Beer (Leeds: Arc Humanities Press, 2019) 63–74 at 65 note 9. See <http://medievalconventdrama.org> for filmed extracts of a presentation of the original French text of both plays enacted as a continuous performance at the University of Fribourg in December 2017 under the title 'The Huy Nativities'. The filmed extracts include only the rage of Herod from *Nativity 2*; for a photograph of the scene of the visit of St Anne from this performance see the cover image of *Medieval English Theatre 42* (2020).

Aldington's translation method

Aldington for the most part follows the original line by line, without additions or embellishments. He does not attempt to replicate the rhyme scheme of the original. In places his close word-for-word translation flows into modern English without any great sense of distance – for example:

>O ma doulce mere Sainte A<u>n</u>ne,
>mo<u>n</u> cuer fut remplie d'amour gr<u>a</u>nde   (177–8)[12]
>
>O my sweet mother Saint Anne
>My heart was filled with great love,

And:

>mon arme fut tout en doulceur,
>qu<u>a</u>nt je veiit, en char humaine,
>le fils de Dieu soueraine,
>gissant deua<u>n</u>t moy en forme d'enfant,   (182–5)
>
>My soul was all in sweetness
>When I saw in human flesh
>The son of God the sovereign,
>Lying before me in child's form.

But in general, his choice of vocabulary and syntax lends a pervasive patina of archaism to his translation. Perhaps he had in mind Cohen's identification of older forms in the extant French text,[13] or perhaps he simply wanted to create for his twentieth-century audience a sense that they were listening to a medieval play. Sometimes he uses obsolete or archaic words, sometimes he retains the corresponding English form of the original in a sense that has become obsolete in modern English. Examples of the former include: 'scurvy kings': *mechan ... roys* (96); 'incontinent': *tout mentena<u>n</u>t* (116); 'and eke': *et* (120); 'Mickle': *Grande* (124 sd); 'thereof': *en* (133); 'sith': *car* (197); 'right faithful': *bien crea<u>n</u>t* (261). Examples of the latter include: 'Certes': *Cert* (101); 'gentle' (in the

---

12   Aldington's text has no line references. References are given here to *Mystères et Moralités*. Readers consulting Cohen's revised edition *Nativités et moralités* should be aware that the line numbering differs there in accordance with his emended scene order.

13   *Mystères et Moralités* xcv.

sense 'noble'): *gentils* (136, 246); 'granddam': *grandame* (210); 'puissance': *puissance* (250).

A similar effect is produced by pervasive use of certain archaic or obsolete syntactic and morphological features such as the inversion of subject-verb order, for example: 'Pleaseth you': *vous plaiste* (2); 'speak we': *nous deuissons* (174); 'have I brought forth': *'j'aie ... enfanteit'* (188); 'shall we go': *nous yrons* (291). Obsolete or archaic verb forms include 'be', used throughout as third-person plural: 'Here be': *vechy* (54), *vechi* (211); 'be': *sont* (145, 267), and once as first-person singular: 'I be': *je suy* (95), and 'gone' used as third-person plural: *passent* (137). The third-person singular ending appears almost invariably as a *-(e)th*, for example, 'pleaseth': *plaise* (60); 'dwelleth': *habite* (69); 'speaketh': *parrolle* (76); 'beareth': *porte* (78), and is the invariable form in the stage directions, for example: 'ANSWERETH': *RESPONT* (8 sd, 12 sd); 'KISSETH': *BAISE* (159 sd); 'ADORETH': *ADORE* (201 sd, 214 sd, 221 sd); 'GO' (plural): *VOISENT* (73 sd). A prominent archaising feature, though one easily or effortlessly absorbed by an early twentieth-century audience familiar with the King James Bible and the Book of Common Prayer, is Aldington's deployment of the second person singular pronoun form *thou* and its attendant verb forms. In the original, the use of *tu* forms is restricted to the exchanges between Herod and the Fool, where it signifies contempt and derision, respectively. Between the other speakers, *vous* forms are invariable, whatever the relationship of status or intimacy. In Aldington's text a mixture of *thou* and *you* forms is the norm in exchanges between all the characters. His introduction of *thou* forms, thus, simply adds a pervasive touch of archaism, it does not distinguish one social or interpersonal dynamic from another.

In these various ways Aldington sets his text at a certain distance while rendering it recognisable. In just a couple of places he deliberately interjects a bizarre note by retaining exclamations in their original form: *Hahay!* (94); *Or cha!* (115). Significantly, both these are expressions of rage and frustration in the mouth of Herod. A curious typographical feature of his text is that where numbers in the original text appear in Roman numerals Aldington's almost always replicates the form, for example: 'Unto the sum of an hundred XLIIII thousand': *jusque à la some de cent XLIIII mille* (146); 'And here be my II daughters': *et vechi mes II fille* (211). Similarly adopted from the original is the spelling of the names 'Ihesus' and 'Symeon', spelling forms that were, of course, common in medieval English texts. These small details, along with the invariable use of *-(e)th* verb endings in the stage directions, noted above, are indications that Aldington envisaged his translation as a text for silent reading as much as a potential performance text.

In his brief foreword Aldington does not comment on his translation technique or on any specifically linguistic features of the original. His appreciation of the play's religious quality perhaps encompasses his perception of its language: 'There was nothing remote and forbidding in their religion; it was familiar and poetic'.[14] Although the brevity of his introductory comments is a temptation to argue from silence, it is arguable that he writes as if he expected these qualities of the original to shine through in a translation palatable to his potential audience, if they will attend to it:

> Whatever our own convictions or doubts may be, this pure poetry of religion is not a thing to be scoffed at ... And that complete acceptance, that poetic faith, have not yet vanished from the world.[15]

He views the play as the product of the simple faith of a distant age, exhibiting 'a charm which is both wistful and tranquillizing', which is not merely to be smiled at but respected for the simplicity and familiarity of its idiom.[16] Compare the review of Cohen's edition attributed to Aldington, as noted above, which comments on: 'a primitive and naïve charm in at least two of the plays which will delight any lover of medieval literature', and 'delightful mingling of sacred persons with humble common life'.[17]

Materials in the archive of George Allen & Unwin Ltd

A folder dated 1924 contains letters to and from Richard Aldington mainly concerning publication of his long poem *A Fool i' the Forest* and his translation *The Mystery of the Nativity*.[18] Aldington's principal correspondent at the publishers is Edgar Louis Skinner. Skinner's letters are often signed with an indecipherable initial, but his authorship can be confidently inferred from the content and sequence of the letters. Items

---

14   *The Mystery of the Nativity* 5.
15   *The Mystery of the Nativity* 6.
16   *The Mystery of the Nativity* 5–8.
17   *Times Literary Supplement* (31 March 1921) 207.
18   University of Reading: Special Collections AUC 7/1.

of particular interest in tracing the process of the publication of *The Mystery of the Nativity* are as follows.

(i) 24 March 1924 Aldington to Skinner
Encloses his translation for consideration, noting that the original manuscript has been printed only recently and that he has permission from Cohen to publish the translation without paying him. He suggests that the text, which he refers to as a 'little poem-play', would make a suitable Christmas gift book if it were provided with several coloured illustrations contemporary with the text, 'the sort of thing people would pick up in Smith's or Mudie's when desperately hunting gifts for a pious maiden aunt or something of that sort'.

(ii) 26 March 1924 Skinner to Aldington
Accepts the text enthusiastically while noting that such small booklets are difficult to handle from a publishing point of view, and the need to produce it inexpensively (he estimates an optimum purchase price of a shilling or one shilling and sixpence) will reduce the margin for illustrations. He proposes approaching the Medici Society about the possibility of joint publication.

(iii) 27 March 1924 Aldington to Skinner
Replies that he is content to leave the publication arrangements to them and for them to approach other publishers but would be reluctant to give the copyright on anything other than a royalty basis.

(iv) 2 April 1924 Skinner to Aldington
Reports that de Grey of the Medici Society is delighted with the play and prepared to do a joint publication with them. As cheapness is essential it probably won't run to more than one illustration; more than 10 per cent royalty fees would raise the cost of the book. Further discussion of costings follows in correspondence of 3 and 4 April. Aldington agrees to a straight 10 per cent royalty; Skinner advises him that costs are unlikely to run to more than one non-coloured illustration, but paper and printing will be top quality.

(v) 5 April 1924 Aldington to Skinner

Encloses his translation of what he terms 'another play of the same sort made from the same collection'. This is clear evidence of his acquaintance with the *Jeu de la Nativité*, the first item in Chantilly, Musée Condé, Ms. 617, although, as noted above, there is no indication of this in his treatment of the other play. Two further points of interest emerge from this letter. One is that he considered the *Jeu de la Nativité*, 'not as good' as the one now accepted for publication, but of sufficient possible interest to send it for consideration. The other is the implication that he had completed the enclosed translation some time before but it had not been occupying the forefront of his attention: he says he came across it while hunting through his manuscripts, an indication of the numerous projects with which he was occupied at this time.

The terms of Skinner's reply, dated 11 April, are also suggestive. He agrees that the play is 'not so attractive' as the other one, but they might be able to make use of it later on, commenting 'it is longer and, I think, would be actable', with the possible inference that the marketability of the text already accepted was not seen solely or primarily in its potential as an acting text. Meanwhile he returns the manuscript, and it seems that nothing came of the idea of publishing it.

(vi) 21 May 1924 Aldington to Skinner

Returning the proofs Aldington says he likes the typeface very much, and asks for ten instead of six free copies as he will have to send three or four to Professor Cohen. His hope that there will be 'a "Madonna" cover' implies that the question of illustration had not been settled at this stage.

(vii) 21 May 1924 Skinner to Aldington

Conveys de Grey's suggestion of the Mabuse 'Adoration' in the National Gallery for the illustration.[19]

---

19   This will be the altar piece by Jan Gossaert, known as Mabuse from his birthplace, Maubeuge; see <https://www.nationalgallery.org.uk/paintings/jan-gossaert-jean-gossart-the-adoration-of-the-kings>. In the event this suggestion was not adopted. Both the George Allen & Unwin and the Medici Society issues have as a frontispiece affixed to the verso of the half-title page a monochrome reproduction captioned 'THE NATIVITY (*after Botticelli*)'. See <https://www.nationalgallery.org.uk/paintings/sandro-botticelli-mystic-nativity>.

JANET COWEN

(viii) 24 May 1924 Aldington to Skinner

Is inclined to follow de Grey's advice (see letter of 2 April), since he must know what takes the public eye and a National Gallery picture will be more liked than one from a foreign gallery.

(ix) 15 September 1924 Aldington to Skinner

Acknowledges a notification of the forthcoming publication of the Nativity play on the thirtieth of the month, and asks whether there is any news from the United States. Allusions to various ultimately unsuccessful attempts to find a co-publisher in the United States are found throughout the correspondence, in letters of 3 April, 11 April, 30 April, 3 May, 24 May, 26 May, 3 June, 16 September, and 17 September.

(x) 17 September 1924 Aldington to Skinner

Expressing his disappointment at Skinner's report of another failure to interest an American publisher, Aldington writes: 'Perhaps the size has something to do with it, but personally I believe that modern people are so prejudiced against Christianity that they cannot see how beautiful a Christian poem can be'. This is a notable counterpoint to his ostensibly cynical and dismissive comments in the letter of 24 March, and is in line with his appreciative comments in the Foreword to his edition.

(xi) 8 December 1924 Skinner to Aldington

Informs him that his Nativity play is to be performed at the church of St Mary the Virgin, Primrose Hill, on 18–20 December, and that: 'The Vicar is the man who reviewed the Play in "The Guardian", and is enthusiastic about it'.[20]

(xii) 9 December 1924 Aldington to Skinner

Expresses his pleasure that 'the little Nativity play' is to be performed at St Mary's, and the hope that 'the Vicar will point out to the audience that this is the first revival performance since the 15th century!' He

---

20   This is not the *Manchester Guardian*, but a church newspaper of the time for which the Vicar, Arthur Duncan-Jones, was a regular reviewer; see Christopher Kitching *St Mary the Virgin Primrose Hill: A Church and its People, 1872–2022* (Market Harborough: Matador, 2022) 160.

136

asks whether it would be possible to arrange for copies to be sold by making the Vicar an offer whereby a certain proportion of the price went to Church Funds.[21] He relates that his mother has been assiduous in promoting the sales of the play in her neighbourhood and among her associates, the Church being one of her hobbies.[22]

(xiii) 18 December 1924 Aldington to Skinner

Thanking him for cuttings received, alludes to a review in the *Observer* and an announcement of the performance of the Nativity in that day's *Times*.

(xiv) 22 December 1924 Aldington to Skinner

'I wish I could have seen the performance of the Nativity, but I have been slaving to get all things straight for Christmas.' He goes on to talk about sitting up late to meet various publishing deadlines.[23]

Two undated linked items relating to the marketing of the volume are of particular interest in relation to the performance at St Mary's. A typewritten postcard with the publishers' printed letterhead gives details of the forthcoming publication, drawing the reader's attention to it as an 'exquisite little play', and citing from *The Guardian* review: 'This is a jewel ... and would form an excellent basis for parochial nativity plays', and from the *Times Literary Supplement*: 'A valuable addition to the literature of devotion'. The price is given as one shilling and sixpence.

Filed with the postcard is a typewritten list of names and addresses headed: 'Attached postcard sent to the following' (pin holes are visible though no pin remains). The addresses are those of local clergy in various parts of the country, with one exception, which is to a Miss Hayler at

---

21 It is to be inferred from the accounts in the St Mary's parish magazine for November 1925 cited below that copies of the book did go on sale on such a basis.

22 Aldington's mother was at this time living in the south-east of England. She ran the Mermaid Inn in Rye for thirteen years from 1911, and by Christmas 1925 had moved to the Dover area; see Whelpton, *Aldington: Poet, Son and Lover 1911–1929* 34, 279.

23 For an account of Aldington's demanding work schedule at this time see Whelpton *Aldington: Poet, Son and Lover 1911–1929* 271, and, more allusively, Richard Aldington *Life for Life's Sake: A Book of Reminiscences* (London: Cassell, 1941) 266.

Walsingham Grammar School. The implication is that, while aiming for the widest possible sales, the publishers saw a particular marketing opportunity among parish clergy. This targeted sales pitch is clearly projected in the wording of the Revd Arthur Duncan-Jones's *Guardian* review. His choice of phrase 'basis for' in his assessment of the potential of the text for parish drama also gives pause for thought in relation to what can be inferred about the performance at St Mary's, which will be explored below.

Performance at the Church of St Mary the Virgin, Primrose Hill

Records of the performance

The materials in the parish archive consist of the following:

(a) Six photographs, apparently a set taken at the same time:

[I] (See Fig. 1) Mounted on card, labelled 1924 on the back in the top left corner; any notation on the reverse of the photograph itself is concealed by the card; number inferred from the numbering II–VI of the remainder. It depicts the Adoration of the Kings: three Kings and three attendants kneeling on the steps, the latter all apparently played by children; Joseph and Mary seated at manger (which is distinct from the cradle in IV and V).[24]

(II) Numbered and labelled 'Christmas 1924' in pencil on the back top left corner. Left to right: Joseph kneeling, holding what is presumably a covered dove-cage; Mary standing, holding the baby; Simeon kneeling, dressed in clerical vestments with bared head.

(III) Numbered and labelled 'Christmas 1924' in pencil on the back top left corner. Left to right: Joseph standing; Mary and Saint Anne centre, standing and embracing; Mary Jacob and Mary Salome (or vice versa) on steps as if approaching; cradle not visible.

(IV) (See Fig. 2) Numbered and labelled 'Christmas 1924' in pencil on the back top left corner. Left to right seated: Saint Anne; Mary; seated on the ground to each side: Mary Jacob and Mary Salome (or vice versa); standing at the back to the left: Joseph; cradle visible on the left.

---

24   Reproduced in Christopher Kitching *St Mary the Virgin Primrose Hill* 136.

FIG. 1: The Adoration of the Kings.
Original photograph of a scene from the performance of 1924.
Reproduced by kind permission of the Church of St Mary the Virgin, Primrose Hill.

FIG. 2: The Virgin Mary with St Anne, Mary Jacobi, Mary Salome, and Joseph.
Original photograph of a scene from the performance of 1924.
Reproduced by kind permission of the Church of St Mary the Virgin, Primrose Hill.

(V) Numbered and labelled 'Christmas 1924' in pencil on the back top left corner. Left to right, gathered around cradle: standing: Mary Jacob (or Mary Salome); Joseph; Mary; kneeling Mary Salome (or Mary Jacob); standing to the right: Saint Anne.

(VI) Numbered and labelled 'Christmas 1924' in pencil on the back top left corner. Mary alone, seated, holding the baby (the rest of the stage is not visible in the shot).

The set as visible in the photographs consists of a backdrop of curtains behind a platform approached by five steps. Two plain chairs positioned centre back are visible in (III) and (V), and presumably also in use in (IV).

(b) Items in the parish magazine (designated at this period the Parish Paper):

(i) November 1924 page 92:

The Society is as usual providing for a Nativity play before Christmas to which all members of the congregation are invited. A new play will be done this year, the words of which have just been published. It is a translation of a fragment of a play which used to be annually performed by the nuns of a Convent near Liège in the 15th century. The dates of the performances will be December 17th, 18th and 20th (afternoon).[25]

(ii) December 1924 page 103:
A further announcement, written when the preparation was obviously well under way:

The Nativity Play has in previous years been a real spiritual preparation for Christmas, and as such has been valued by many people. We have every hope that the new form of the Play will be no less beautiful than the one previously used. It brings out in a very striking way the simple faith which finds no difficulty in holding our Lord's Divinity and Humanity quite easily side by side, a faith which we should all desire to share and nourish.

25 'The Society' was the name of the parish organisation responsible for various social and cultural activities in this period, see Kitching *St Mary the Virgin Primrose Hill* 137.

The dates are reiterated as above, with the specification of 8.15 for the two evening performances and 5.30 for 20 December, and the gloss that the 5.30 performance is intended specifically for children but not intended to exclude others who might find the time more convenient. Admission is free but a collection will be taken for the Save the Children Fund.

(iii) January 1925 page 5:
A note signed A.S.D.-J. (sc. the Vicar, Revd Arthur Duncan-Jones) recording thanks to all those involved in 'the Nativity play', referring to it as 'at once an act of thanksgiving and a blessing', commenting on 'the joy' that seemed to take hold of both presenters and spectators, and alluding to 'the critic whose appreciative words are found elsewhere' (presumably a reference to the review in the same issue, pages 8–9, cited below).

(iv) January 1925 pages 8–9:
A very appreciative review, signed R.E.R:[26]

> I have seen a good many productions, parochial and other, of mystery plays; but never one that gave me such complete pleasure as that of the Society of S. Mary's Primrose Hill. Its great merit was the entire harmony achieved by actors, singers, musicians, wardrobe-mistress, stage-manager and electricians. Nothing and nobody was allowed to stand out, there were no star performers, and the result was that the performance had a unity very rarely seen either at professional or amateur shows. Nor was this subdual of the parts to the whole effect entirely the work, I should say, of the stage-manager. It was a natural result of the spirit in which most things are done at S. Mary's. It would be impossible as well as unsuitable to single out separate performers for praise. It accorded with tradition that none of the actors, except he who took Herod's part, should be excessively dramatic; and the very simple text of the old play lent itself rather to recitation than to acting. I must be allowed, however, to praise the extraordinary beauty of the materials; the simplicity of the stage setting, and the success of the Angels. It is not too much to say that all theatrical producers from Max Reinhardt to Miss Lilian Baylis could learn something from the brief appearance of the heavenly Host to the

---

26 Christopher Kitching advises me that it has not at present been possible to identify these initials among the parish archives.

shepherds. I have never before seen a tolerable stage Angel. The music I expected to be perfect; but it was even more moving than I had hoped, and it was not perhaps surprising, though regretable [sic], that the audience did not feel equal to joining in the hymns.

The various implications contained in this review about the scope and style of the production will be discussed more fully below.

(v) February 1925 page 8:
A report that 'The Nativity Play', as well as being 'a great spiritual help to very many people', brought in contributions amounting to £36 19s 6½d, which after expenses had been met enabled a payment of £20 to the Save the Children Fund and £7 to the Waifs and Strays.

(vi) November 1925 page 101:
Further, detailed accounts for the Society under the heading 'Nativity Play' break down the income into collections £34 5s 6d and programmes £2 14s, and, interestingly, record income from Sale of Books, £2 13s 6d. It seems a reasonable inference that the books sold were copies of Aldington's translation. Regrettably, no copies of the programme survive.

(c) Press references included in the parish archive:

(i) An unidentified press cutting (in a separate plastic slip case) consisting of a copy of photograph number [I] above with a caption:

NATIVITY PLAY

A scene from *The Mystery of the Nativity* translated from the 15th-century Liegeois which was given for the first time in its English dress at St. Mary's Church Room, Primrose Hill, London, at Christmas time.

Note: An item on the reverse that might help in a further search for the source of the cutting is headed 'Giant Fossils in East Africa: Seeking the Dinosaur'.

(ii) An unidentified press notice pasted into the Parish Chronicle covering the years 1867 to 1937, page 81, under the entries for 1924, beside

FROM HUY TO PRIMROSE HILL

the hand written date '17 Dec:' and beneath the handwritten heading '1st representation of 15th Century Nativity Play':[27]

> 'The Mystery of the Nativity', translated from the Liegeois of the 15th century by Richard Aldington, will be presented for the first time in English dress at St. Mary's Church Room, Oppidans Road, Primrose Hill, to-day and tomorrow at 5.30 pm. Admission is free.

Note: These times are discrepant with those given in the parish magazine item for December 1924, page 103, and in the announcement in *The Church Times*, 12 December 1924, cited below.

(d) Other press references found to date:

(i) Notice in *The Church Times* 12 December 1924, 699:[28]

> ST. MARY'S, PRIMROSE HILL. – THE MYSTERY OF THE NATIVITY (translated from the Liégeois of the Fifteenth Century by Richard Aldington) will be presented in the CHURCH ROOM, OPPIDANS ROAD, N.W.3. DEC. 17 and 18 at 8.15, and DEC. 20 at 5.30. Tube, Chalk Farm; 'bus 31.

Note: This not the same notice as that pasted into the 1924 parish chronicle, or the unidentified loose press cutting noted above. These dates and times correspond exactly to those given in the parish magazine item for December 1924, page 103 (see above).

(ii) Notice in *The Church Times* 24 December 1924, 744:

> ST. MARY'S, PRIMROSE HILL. – 'The Mystery of the Nativity' (translated by Richard Aldington from the Liégeois of the 15th century) will be presented again, after Evensong, on SUNDAY NEXT, in response to many requests, at 6.30. Tube: Chalk Farm; 'bus 31. The Carol Recital is postponed to January 4th.

Note: This not the same notice as that pasted into the 1924 parish chronicle, or the unidentified loose press cutting noted above, neither of

---

27 The Parish Chronicle was compiled initially by Vivian H. King (parish clerk 1916–1934, d. 1935). Christopher Kitching has identified the hand of these notes as his.
28 All references to *The Church Times* are cited from <www.churchtimes.co.uk>.

which refer to a repeat performance. The context of this item is worth noting: it appears under the heading 'Nativity Plays' in a list of five productions in London venues, including the Chester Nativity Play at the Old Vic.

We know the identities of only a few of the people involved in the production. On the back of photograph number IV, in pencil, probably in the hand of the numbering and labelling,[29] roughly positioned behind the characters in the photograph, are the names: 'Vivian King "Joseph"'; 'Susan Shaw' [positioned behind Mary]; 'Mrs Geoffrey Shaw "Ann"'; 'Mary O'Malley? [original query] (now Mrs Dunlop)'; 'Ruth Leach (later Mrs Hardcastle)' [positioned behind Mary Jacob/Mary Salome respectively]. Of these Vivian King was parish clerk at the time, as noted above. Mrs Geoffrey Shaw was Mary Shaw, married to Geoffrey Shaw, the church organist at the time, who along with his brother Martin Shaw, the previous organist, played a major part in the flourishing musical tradition at St Mary's. Susan Shaw was the daughter of Geoffrey and Mary Shaw.[30] Mary O'Malley was a member of the congregation who in 1935 married Colin Dunlop, who had been curate in the parish between 1922 and 1927.[31] The Revd Anthony Hardcastle, Vicar of St Mary's 1934–1952, married in 1940 a wife called Ruth, but her unmarried name was Seth-Smith, not Leach.[32] The reference on the back of the photograph to Ruth Leach appears to be an error either of naming or of identification, a confusion perhaps indicated by the fact that the annotator made two attempts at writing the name, the first of them not entirely legible. An alluring detail in the Vicar's note of appreciation cited above, singling out for mention by name, as he came to help from outside the parish, 'Prince Ocherrin of Haeju' who played the part of 'one of the Kings of Orient', may be a humorous allusion to someone well-known to the congregation.

---

29 I am advised by Christopher Kitching that this is not the hand of Vivian King. It is clear from the phrasing that it significantly post-dates the taking of the photographs.
30 On the musical contribution of Geoffrey and Martin Shaw to dramatic performances at St Mary's, see Kitching *St Mary the Virgin Primrose Hill* 135–7. For the identification of Susan Shaw, I am grateful to Isobel Montgomery Campbell.
31 Kitching *St Mary the Virgin Primrose Hill* 148, 179, 182.
32 Kitching *St Mary the Virgin Primrose Hill* 192, 210.

The Nature of the Performance

What inferences can be drawn from the above materials?

Although photograph number [I] indicates that the production involved some children, and one of the performances was specifically directed at children, the production was not envisaged primarily as a children's play: an earlier report from the Society (November 1924 page 93) had made clear that the Junior Guild were at the same time putting on their own show, a performance of Mabel Dearmer's morality play *Brer Rabbit*, after Christmas, revived for the occasion with the Vicar's approval.[33]

The provision of an extra repeat performance, not originally scheduled, is one of numerous other indications that this performance in December 1924 took place in the context of a lively tradition of dramatic productions at St Mary's during that period.[34] The performance at St Mary's so soon after the publication of the translation suggests in itself that someone in the parish was sufficiently *au fait* with that area of the literary world to have quickly spotted the potential of the new publication, and, given the vicar's review of it in *The Guardian* and his attested enthusiastic support for drama in the parish, it is reasonable to assume that he was the driving force behind the production. None of the available records names the director, or those responsible for the music, which evidently contributed so significantly to the success of the production, and, as noted above, the naming of the actors on the reverse of the photographs is a bit of informal and retrospective in-house record keeping, not a part of the original publicity. A convention of anonymity in church drama was general in this period, as formulated in the precepts of directors such as Nugent Monck and E. Martin Browne.[35]

The notable absence of Aldington's name in the notices and reviews in the parish magazine seems a little curious. One possible implication is that his name would not have been immediately familiar to most of the intended readers. Another is that his published translation of the dialogue had been to an extent appropriated and modified by the addition of further spectacle (note the phrasing 'the words of which have

---

33 Kitching *St Mary the Virgin Primrose Hill* 136.
34 Kitching *St Mary the Virgin Primrose Hill* 126, 135–8.
35 Cited in John R. Elliott Jr *Playing God: Medieval Mysteries on the Modern Stage* (University of Toronto Press, 1989) 60.

just been published' in the November 1924 notice). The generic title 'the Nativity Play' alludes as if to an expected event in the parish calendar. The reference to 'the new form of the Play' (December 1924) absorbs Aldington's text and reiterates it as a variation of a familiar recurring local event within a familiar larger tradition. There is an intriguing analogy here with the auspices of the original French text: a performance undertaken by a set of people who knew each other well, in a particular place, as a specific local instance of a larger tradition of sacred drama.

A number of inferences about the scope and style of the production can be drawn from the review of January 1925. The comment that 'It accorded with tradition that none of the actors, except he who took Herod's part, should be excessively dramatic' implies that Aldington's scene between Herod and the Fool was included, though it does not feature in any of the photographs. The reference to the effectiveness of 'the brief appearance of the heavenly Host to the shepherds' implies an expansion of Aldington's text, even if only in tableau form, and photograph number [I] is a clear indication of a similar expansion of the role of the Kings. In Aldington's text, as in his French original, neither Shepherds nor Kings are represented in person, but only by allusion in the retrospective narrative speech by the Virgin Mary in Scene v. It seems clear that the production at St Mary's had devised some way of amplifying the Virgin's reminiscences into a staging of the two Adoration scenes so familiar in local Nativity pageants by this time.[36] It is notable that a feature singled out for praise by this reviewer should have been one added to the original text. The evident appeal of this device, the visual incorporation of familiar iconographical scenes into the action of the play, points to a dramatic idiom expected, even take for granted, by a Nativity play audience of the 1920s, a stylistic idiom underpinned in part by the revived tradition of pageants of national and local history that became so pervasively popular in the early twentieth century.[37] Such an appeal displays the distance between the 1920s audience and the audience of the original French text, which, drawing perhaps consciously

---

36   Elliott *Playing God* 62 remarks that for the average theatregoer of the 1920s 'the term "mystery play" was virtually synonymous with nativity pageants at Christmas time'.

37   On this topic see the valuable resource, Paul Readman and others *The Redress of the Past*; <http://www.historicalpageants.ac.uk/pageants>.

on a practice of affective meditation, requires the audience to visualise these scenes for themselves.

This raises the question of what kind of familiarity with medieval mystery play texts might be assumed, at this date, before any large-scale professional and commercial revival or academic reconstructions, and what an audience's expectations might have been. A London play-going public with memories stretching back a couple of decades would have had the chance to see sporadic productions of the Wakefield and Chester Shepherds Plays, most recently at the Old Vic under the management of Lilian Baylis, where the production the Chester Shepherds Play in 1923 was revived in 1924. Although the coupling of this in a holiday bill with Dickens's *Christmas Carol* in 1923 suggests that the play was valued for the light-heartedness of its comic business, it is notable that contemporary reviewers valued the play for its perceived qualities of simplicity and dignity and its poignant and moving effects.[38] The allusion to Lilian Baylis in the January 1925 review of the St Mary's production cited above may well be to this production, which was running at the same time as that at St Mary's.

The photographs corroborate the comment in the January 1925 review about the simplicity of the stage setting, showing only a plain backdrop of curtains and minimal furniture for essential seating. How the angelic appearances that so impressed the reviewer were contrived is unfortunately not apparent in the records. The reviewer's general comments imply that costuming, lighting, acting style, and music will all have contributed to the particular effect, but the allusion to Reinhardt is tongue-in-cheek, since Max Reinhardt was celebrated as the populariser of a genre of religious spectacular notably exemplified in London by his production *The Miracle*, staged in 1911 at the Olympia exhibition centre in Earl's Court. This work, based on a legendary story of a run-away and ultimately penitent nun, enacted a sensational scenario involving thousands of actors, singers, and dancers, and was hailed with critical acclaim anachronistically and confusingly conflating it with the Passion Plays of the Middle Ages.[39] The reviewer is presumably implying that stirring visual and audial effects can be achieved on a smaller scale and with considerably less ostentation.

38   Elliott *Playing God* 63.
39   Elliott *Playing God* 48–9.

The music, the high standard of which is noted in the January 1925 review, was clearly a major factor in the effect and success of the production. Once again, no names are mentioned, but it is reasonable to assume that the musical direction would have been undertaken by Geoffrey Shaw, Organist and Choir Master at St Mary's since 1919, who had built on the strong musical tradition there in collaboration with and as successor to his brother Martin Shaw, and who was involved in various parish plays and other entertainments in the 1920s.[40] Martin Shaw himself, although by this time employed as organist elsewhere, continued to play a part in the production of dramatic entertainments at St Mary, along with his wife Joan,[41] and it is possible that he had some hand in in this one too.

The enthusiasm with which Aldington's text was enfolded in to an already existing tradition of parish drama at St Mary's is testimony to a hospitable attitude to the performance of religious plays on church premises, and touches on the wider questions of the ecclesiastical oversight of church drama and the vexed question of censorship of religious subjects in drama in this part of the twentieth century.[42] Since performances in church buildings that did not charge for admission fell outside the Lord Chamberlain's licencing regulations it was within the purview of the diocesan bishop to regulate such performances. There is ample evidence that in the diocese of London as a whole, religious drama in churches was thriving in the 1920s. A scan of the columns of *The Church Times* will produce a wealth of examples in the form of notices and reviews of parish plays, particularly in the Christmas and Easter periods, as well as articles discussing the purpose and effect of religious plays. Notable productions of specially composed plays on scriptural subjects

---

40   Kitching *St Mary the Virgin Primrose Hill* 135–7, 155–6; see also note 30.
41   See Kitching *St Mary the Virgin Primrose Hill* 136, and the reference in the parish magazine for December 1925 cited below.
42   For a summary of the protracted twentieth-century campaign against censorship of religious subjects in the commercial theatre, see Elliott *Playing God* 17–24. For a fuller and important discussion of the topic which draws attention to the frequently confused and often erroneous assumptions which affected the implementation of theatrical censorship in Britain before the ending of the Lord Chamberlain's powers in 1968, see Olga Horner 'The Law That Never Was: A Review of Theatrical Censorship in *Britain*' *Medieval English Theatre* 23 (2001) 34–96, and Olga Horner 'The Law That Never Was – A Codicil' *Medieval English Theatre* 24 (2002) 104–15.

were taking place in a neighbourhood not far away from St Mary's, where B.C. Boulter's *The Mystery of the Epiphany*, *The Mystery of the Passion*, and *Paul and Silas* were performed in the church of St Silas, Kentish Town, in various years between 1918 and 1930.[43] These attracted considerable attention at the time and were published and performed in various other places. *The Mystery of the Passion* has a claim to being the first instance in the twentieth century of a play performance calling for the appearance of the adult Christ on stage.[44]

Aftermath

Two items in the St Mary's parish magazine provide evidence that the production of December 1924 was repeated the following year.

(i) December 1925, page 107:
An announcement that 'The Nativity Play' will be presented on Thursday 17 December at 8.15, Saturday 19 December at 5.30 and also after evensong on the Sundays before and after Christmas, 20 and 28 December. 'The play and the performers will be the same as last year.' On the same page is an announcement of a separate Christmas pageant designed by Martin Shaw featuring separate aspects of Christmas, an indication that, as in the previous year, St Mary's was able to mount Christmas productions of different types in the same Christmas season. It is again notable that there is no mention of Aldington's name in this announcement of the production. The additional performance dates anticipate the popularity that had given rise to a last-minute repeat performance after Christmas the previous year, as evidenced in the notice in *The Church Times* 24 December 1924 cited above.

(ii) January 1926, page 7:
A review commenting on the 'intense reverence, dignity and simplicity' that characterised the production of 'this quaint fifteenth century play'. The reviewer finds it effective and moving despite 'the mingling of medieval ideas with the Scriptural story', and characterises the Virgin Mary's anachronistic naming of her mother as 'Saint Anne' as 'curious

---

43 See *The Church Times* (15 February 1918) 129; *The Church Times* (23 November 1923) 600. The website of the church of St Silas <https://www.saintsilas.org.uk> includes some photographs.
44 Elliott *Playing God* 55.

naïvete'. This review provides a clear indication that of the material added to Aldington's text, at least some was in tableau form, thus making explicit the implication in the review of the previous year's production: 'The tableaux of the Annunciation were most beautiful, as were the scenes of the adoration of the Shepherds and the Magi'. The review is signed 'C. C.'.[45]

This repeat production of December 1925 seems to have been the last time the play was performed at St Mary's. There is no subsequent reference to it in the parish records, and reports for the following two years indicate a modified pattern of dramatic activity at Christmas time. Thus, in the parish magazine for November 1926 there is mention of the Christmas pageant to be given as in the previous year by the children of the catechism (page 106), but no mention of a Nativity play, and there is a similar absence of mention in December 1926, January 1927, and February 1927. An entry in December 1927 (page 128) refers to the difficulty of procuring the Church Room for rehearsals, leading to the decision not to perform 'a Nativity Play' [sic] but instead to perform a play at Passiontide.

Thus, on the evidence of references found so far, the timely and evidently successful dramatic initiative taken by St Mary's in 1924 did not set much of a precedent, although one documented production elsewhere seems to be evidence of an equally successful venture under different auspices. Reviews of a performance in December 1925, by a newly formed children's theatre in Birmingham, of what is termed '"The Mystery of the Nativity" ... [a] quaint archaic version ... written five hundred years ago by the Nuns of Liege' presumably refer to the same play.[46] None of these reviews names Aldington as the translator or refers to any previous performance. Although none describes the action in detail, all praise the artistic merit and success of the production, and the *Birmingham Mail*'s description of it as 'a series of four tableaux vivants – simple little scenes, beautifully grouped and mounted' raises a question of how much of the original dialogue was actually used, and also implies a picturesque and formal style of production, though embellished by a

---

45 Christopher Kitching (private communication) thinks this is likely to be Sir Cyril Cobb, a member of the Parochial Church Council at the time.
46 *The Stage* (17 December 1925) 19. See also *Birmingham Gazette* (15 December 1925) 6; *Birmingham Mail* (15 December 1925) 2. Press references are cited from <www.britishnewspaperarchive.co.uk>.

hidden choir and encouraging community participation by the singing of carols, in which the spectators were encouraged to join, and eventually did so with enthusiasm.

The devotional theology of the play has its own particular coherence, focused as it is on the figure of St Anne. She heads the group of three visitors to the new-born infant Christ, a feminised counterpart of the visit of the Magi, traditionally three, though not enumerated in Matthew's gospel. Through the Virgin Mary's account to her, the story of the birth and the traditional accounts of the visits of the Shepherds and Kings are mediated as elements in the action of the play. St Anne here fulfils the prophetic role enacted in other mystery plays by Old Testament figures such as Isaiah. This weighting of the Nativity story towards the figure of the Virgin Mary's mother will have had limited appeal in an early twentieth-century English ecclesiastical context where the cult of St Anne was no longer widespread or vibrant, and this is perhaps one reason why Aldington's play seems not to have attained general popularity. But at St Mary's Primrose Hill it found a timely and sympathetic niche in an ambience already favourable to drama. Not only did the focus of the play chime with the dedication of the church to St Mary the Virgin, but the figure of St Anne already had a place in the decoration of the building, in a window depicting St Anne teaching the Virgin Mary to read.[47]

An interesting little detail in the copy of the play obtained by the present writer from Amazon in February 2021 is an inscription showing that it was given as a Christmas gift from one 'Michael' to 'darling Elspeth' in 1943. So, people were still reading it then – or at least it was thought to be a suitable stocking filler in certain circles.

Cohen lists Aldington's translation in his own revised edition of 1953,[48] but there is no indication that he knew of the production at St Mary's. If he had done so he would likely have mentioned it, since he speaks with evident pleasure of other revivals since the publication of his original edition.[49]

King's College London

---

47 Window at the west end of the north aisle, in place by 1888 (Clayton & Bell), described and pictured in a leaflet compiled by Christopher Kitching, December 2020, available at St Mary's church.
48 *Nativités et moralités* xiv.
49 *Nativités et moralités* 165.

Acknowledgements

I wish to thank the Church of St Mary the Virgin, Primrose Hill for access to the parish archive and for permission to reproduce the images shown here as Figures 1 and 2, and I am particularly grateful to Dr Christopher Kitching, the Honorary Parish Archivist, for first drawing my attention to the production in question, and for generous help of various kinds in the preparation of this chapter. I am also grateful to Nicholas Huzan, Isobel Montgomery Campbell, Professor Max Saunders, Vivien Whelpton and the staff of the Reading Room of the University of Reading Special Collections for their advice and assistance.

'MORE MEDIEVAL MORALITY PLAY THAN 21ST CENTURY'
Spectacle and its Meaning at the Coronation of King Charles III

Aurélie Blanc

On 6 May 2023, as I sat down on my couch to watch King Charles III's coronation, I cannot say that I was especially excited about it. I am not from the United Kingdom and did not feel particularly engaged by an event that I perceived to be closely tied to that country and culture. However, I was curious enough to turn on the television that morning: the fashion would undoubtedly be interesting (would the hats be even more wonderful than those seen at royal weddings?) and it would be fun to spot our own Swiss president sitting in Westminster Abbey. As the ceremony started, my excitement rose and I found myself wanting to see the crown jewels, all the gold and the wealth on display, and museum pieces worn again. I was eager to listen to the music, some of which – like Handel's *Zadok the Priest* – I was aware had been composed for similar ceremonies in the past.[1] Spectacle (defined here as 'stage display or pageantry') was therefore the primary draw for me to watch King Charles III's coronation.[2] I was intrigued because the event was beautiful and unique, but also because I felt I was watching, in some ways, a recreation of a historical spectacle.

Yet, was the coronation not more than this spectacle? Was it even as 'historical', and perhaps medieval, as I felt it was when I was watching it? What was its meaning and how was it expressed through spectacle? Prompted by these questions, this article reflects on the meaning of this twenty-first century coronation and on its evolution over its 1,000-year history. It will do so by exploring the discourse around the coronation of King Charles III and by comparing the features of this royal event with those of its medieval antecedents. Both the perception of the coronation,

---

1 For more on the music, see 'Coronation Music' at <https://www.royal.uk/news-and-activity/2023-02-23/coronation-music-at-westminster-abbey>; 'New Music Commissions for the Coronation Service' at <https://www.royal.uk/coronation-music-commissions>.

2 Patrice Pavis *Dictionary of Theatre: Terms, Concepts, and Analysis* (University of Toronto Press, 1998) 346.

and the choices that were made during its organisation reflect the current – and the changing – view of kingship. I will first examine the meaning of the coronation as it was explained by those involved in planning and enacting it; I will then move on to consider the extent to which the intended meaning was understood, appreciated, or embraced by the recipients, the spectators of the event.

A Historic Event: The Coronation as Presented

The oldest description of a coronation in England is from the tenth century,[3] and although coronations have been adapted to accommodate changes in religion and the role of the monarch – most obviously at the Reformation[4] – their overall structure has remained similar over centuries: a central religious ceremony, accompanied by secular processions, celebrations, and military displays.[5] This was already the case in 973 for the coronation of King Edgar. According to the Vita S. Oswaldi, the event began with a procession involving 'everyone whom it is fitting to describe as the nobility of this wide and spacious realm', the 'glorious army of his realm'. A liturgical service then took place, followed by a 'day of celebration'.[6]

King Charles III's coronation was no exception. The central religious ceremony, with a rich and solemn liturgy, was celebrated at Westminster Abbey on 6 May. The king and queen travelled to this ceremony in a golden coach, accompanied by processions with music and, on the way back, by a large number of representatives of the armed forces.[7] Soldiers from the United Kingdom as well as from different parts of the Commonwealth

---

3 See P.L. Ward 'The Coronation Ceremony in Mediaeval England' *Speculum 14:2* (1939) 160–78, at 160.

4 See Alice Hunt 'The Bright Star of The North: James I and his English Coronation' *Medieval English Theatre 38* (2015) 22–37, at 27.

5 Alice Hunt 'The Tudor Coronation Ceremonies in History and Criticism' *Literature Compass 6:2* (2009) 362–72, at 367–8.

6 Byrhtferth of Ramsey '*Vita S. Oswaldi*: The Life of St Oswald (AD 997–1002): Part Four' in *Byrhtferth of Ramsey: The Lives of St Oswald and St Ecgwine* edited Michael Lapidge (Oxford UP, 2009; published online, 2019) 104–12, at 106–11. For more examples see Alice Hunt *The Drama of Coronation: Medieval Ceremony in Early Modern England* (Cambridge UP, 2008).

7 On the procession and coaches, see 'The Coronation Procession' at <https://www.royal.uk/news-and-activity/2023-04-17/the-coronation-procession>.

and the British Overseas Territories then presented a royal salute to the king and queen in the grounds of Buckingham Palace.[8] After this military display the royal family appeared on the balcony of Buckingham Palace, where they waved to the crowds who had assembled to see them, and watched a further display, this time from the Royal Airforce, including the Red Arrows aerobatic team. The coronation was widely marketed as a 'Coronation Weekend' and the celebrations continued on Sunday with a coronation concert at Windsor Castle in front of a crowd of 20,000 people.[9] Also on Sunday, members of the public were invited – through the Coronation Big Lunch initiative – to throw street parties with the aim of encouraging the 'whole country [in] sharing food, friendship and fun' during this 'right royal celebration'.[10] On Monday (8 May), members of the public were this time asked to take part in the Big Help Out, during which they could volunteer to help support their local area.[11]

The general structure of royal events, as exemplified by the coronation of Charles III, reflects and expresses – often through show and presentation – the aims of these events. The place given to liturgy both associates the monarch with an exemplary respect for religious traditions and promotes the idea of his unusual proximity to God. In the case of a coronation especially, the monarch is presented as chosen by God. The liturgy of the coronation thus asserts the legitimacy and the authority – secular and religious – of the monarch. This legitimacy is recognised by the guests attending the liturgical service. Through processions and celebrations, the monarch's legitimacy and authority are further displayed to the public. As for the military displays, they

---

8   The Sovereign's Bodyguard and Royal Watermen were also present. On the way to the Abbey, the king and queen were accompanied by the Sovereign's Escort of the Household Cavalry; 'The Coronation Procession'.

9   'Coronation Weekend plans' at <https://www.royal.uk/coronation-weekend-plans-announced>.

10 The Big Lunch was an idea started by the Eden Project in 2009, made possible by the National Lottery, and supported by patron the Duchess of Cornwall, now Queen Camilla, since 2013. See 'A royally good weekend!' in *Eden Project Communities* at <https://www.edenprojectcommunities.com/blog/a-royally-good-weekend>; 'The Duke of Edinburgh attends a Coronation Big Lunch' at <https://www.royal.uk/news-and-activity/2023-04-18/the-duke-of-edinburgh-attends-a-coronation-big-lunch-at-westminster>. See also <https://www.youtube.com/watch?v=75KvC_qCwok&t=11s>.

11 'Coronation Weekend plans announced.'

assert the temporal power of the monarch to all watching.[12] Finally, the coronation also aims to celebrate the nation itself, as represented by its Head of State. Its history, its unity, and its greatness are asserted through the secular and liturgical celebrations that are part of such an event.

I will consider in detail the Coronation service, which was – ostensibly at least – at the heart of the Coronation weekend. The significance of the service was explained in official publications in relation to two aspects: its religious nature, and its historical roots.

The royal website made the entire content of the coronation service available to the public. This text, which was presented to Abbey guests in a booklet on 6 May, contains most of the words spoken during the liturgy, as well as a description of its participants and their movements. It does not, however, assume that the liturgy will be immediately comprehensible to all, since it provides information about the meaning of objects, prayers, and gestures used during the service. From the start, it reminds readers of the religious nature of the coronation, opening with these lines: 'Today's service draws on that long tradition, set once again within the context of the Eucharist, which is the defining act of worship for the Church universal'. It then includes a statement by the Archbishop of Canterbury describing the purpose of this event. This purpose is in part the recognition of the king by the nation, but also for the congregation 'to offer worship and praise to Almighty God' and 'to witness with joy his anointing and crowning, his being set apart and consecrated for the service of his people'.[13]

Official press releases by the Palace described in further detail what would happen when the king was anointed during the liturgy in Westminster Abbey. He was first physically 'set apart' from the rest of the congregation before the anointing followed. This was 'a moment between the Sovereign and God, with a screen or canopy in place given

---

12   See Janos M. Bak 'Introduction: Coronation Studies – Past, Present, and Future' in *Coronations: Medieval and Early Modern Monarchic Ritual* edited Janos M. Bak (Berkeley: University of California Press, 1990) 1; Hunt *Drama* 3–4.

13   'The Coronation Service' at <https://www.royal.uk/news-and-activity/2023-05-06/the-coronation-service-order-of-service>; 'The Coronation Liturgy: "Called to Serve"' in *The Church of England* at <https://www.churchofengland.org/coronation/liturgy>; 'The Coronation Order of Service' at 3, 5–6, 21 at <https://www.royal.uk/sites/default/files/documents/2023-05/The%20Coronation%20Order%20of%20Service.pdf>.

the sanctity of the Anointing'.[14] It was a time of communion between the King and God, who had been called upon before the anointing: 'After the sermon, the ancient hymn *Veni, Creator Spiritus* is sung in languages from across the United Kingdom, calling on the Holy Spirit just before the most sacred part of the Coronation rite – the anointing with holy oil'.[15] The anointing is an ancient rite, marking a king – who has been chosen to reign by God – but also blessing and consecrating him. The blessing is meant to help the king govern and to confer God's grace onto him: 'that by the assistance of his heavenly grace you may govern and preserve the peoples committed to your charge in wealth, peace, and godliness'.[16] As for the consecration, it gives him a different, and more sacred, status; it sets him apart from his subjects 'for a holy purpose'.[17] This status also relates to his role as Head of the Church of England.[18]

The medieval perception of the anointing, this central moment of the coronation, is one aspect of the coronation ceremony that has undergone a change over time. In the Middle Ages, it was often believed to be the moment 'when the heir was anointed with holy oil and transformed into the king'.[19] This understanding of the king's anointing – although already debated in the medieval period – became even more disputed at the time of the Reformation because it was seen as akin to a 'sacramental change', antagonistic to Protestant belief. Did the king truly transform during the coronation service? Or was this service only an exterior expression of the fact that he was chosen by God? This question was still debated in the seventeenth century, but the second interpretation ultimately prevailed: while the sovereign is blessed and consecrated during the anointing,

---

14 'The Anointing Screen' at <https://www.royal.uk/news-and-activity/2023-04-29/the-anointing-screen>.
15 'The Coronation Order of Service' at 4.
16 'The Coronation Order of Service' at 31.
17 Jonah McKeown 'A guide to the Christian – and Catholic – symbolism in King Charles III's coronation' in *The Catholic News Agency* at <https://www.catholicnewsagency.com/news/254247/a-guide-to-the-christian-and-catholic-symbolism-in-king-charles-iii-s-coronation>.
18 Lauren Potts 'King Charles: Why does the monarch need a coronation?' in *BBC News* at <https://www.bbc.com/news/uk-65031625>.
19 Ward 'The Coronation Ceremony' at 162; Hunt *The Drama* 3, 6, 15–16, 28–9.

he is not transformed.[20] With the Reformation, the coronation thus lost some of its sacramental meaning and became closer to a show, a visual expression of the king's newfound status, power, and duties.[21]

The discourse around Charles's coronation, as that of a Protestant sovereign, has therefore been in line with what was established after the English Reformation. Palace commentary eschewed the idea of the coronation as itself sacramental, but nonetheless emphasised the event as a religious ritual. This might be because of the seriousness attached to the idea of liturgy. A ritual is perceived to have an important – and meaningful – effect: as scholars of liturgical ritual have suggested, it is a 'bridge between the human and wholly Other' and it allows its participants to be in the presence of God.[22] Official royal articles consistently use the word 'Service' when speaking of the part of the coronation that took place in Westminster Abbey, which refers to an explicitly religious event.[23] When presenting the anointing screen, they describe its design but also mention that it was blessed by the Sub-Dean and Domestic Chaplain to the King, Paul Wright, and emphasise its major role in the 'most sacred moment of the coronation'.[24] One article listing '100 Coronation Facts' tells readers that '[i]n the 18th and 19th centuries, public spectacle sometimes overshadowed religious significance'. Such significance, it is implied, should go first.[25]

The Royal Family website features a series of articles centred on the religious aspects of the event. One of them focuses on the Holy Coronation Oil and includes a prayer by the Archbishop of Canterbury, who asks for the King and Queen to be guided by the Holy Spirit.[26] Another details the Order of the Service to take place in Westminster Abbey. It begins by

---

20 Hunt 'Bright Star' at 28; McKeown 'A guide to the Christian – and Catholic – symbolism'; Hunt *Drama* 28.
21 Hunt 'Bright Star' at 30–2.
22 Penny Granger *The N-Town Play: Drama and Liturgy in Medieval East Anglia* (Cambridge: D.S. Brewer, 2009) 19; C. Clifford Flanigan '*Visitatio Sepulchri* as Paradigm' in *Medieval Liturgy and the Arts* edited Eva Louise Lillie and Nils Holger Petersen (Copenhagen: Museum Tusculanum Press, 1996) 9–35, at 10–12, 30.
23 See for instance 'Coronation Music at Westminster Abbey'.
24 'The Anointing Screen'.
25 '100 Coronation Facts' at <https://www.royal.uk/100-coronation-facts>.
26 'The consecration of the Coronation Oil' at <https://www.royal.uk/news-and-activity/2023-03-03/the-consecration-of-the-coronation-oil>.

asserting the religious nature of this service and the importance of God in the coronation and then adds that, '[r]eflecting the King's devotion to the traditional liturgy of the Church of England', there will be a consecration of bread and wine during the service. This emphasises the inclusion of the Eucharist, the act of Holy Communion, in the ceremony.[27]

The liturgy, as 'traditional', combines religion and history. Although the Anglican liturgy is a sixteenth-century creation, and in spite of Reformation changes to ideas of kingship, there were plenty of nods to medieval coronations at Charles's coronation. The precise similarities between medieval and modern, however, are not always easy to establish. Medieval sources for liturgical services are incomplete or lost, and surviving texts paint only a partial portrait of events. Various standard coronation ceremonies are recorded in pontificals (books prescribing rites), but it is not always clear when or whether these texts were used in practice, and if they were, whether they were used fully or partially.[28] As is often a problem for studies of medieval performative activities, manuscripts do not give information about all aspects of their performance. Costumes or vestments are not consistently described, nor are all the objects that the performers handled, or all the gestures that they made.[29] Even if the manuscripts do describe these, it is difficult to know whether the texts were performed exactly as written: they may have been composed after the performance to record what had been done, or they may have been written beforehand as a 'script' for the performers to follow; yet there are no guarantees that participants followed this script. They may have added words or movements; they may have

---

27 'The Coronation Service'.
28 Ward 'The Coronation Ceremony' at 160, 173-6; H.G. Richardson 'The Coronation in Medieval England: The Evolution of the Office and the Oath' *Traditio 16* (1960) 111-202, at 111-12, 126-8.
29 John J. McGavin and Greg Walker *Imagining Spectatorship: From the Mysteries to the Shakespearean Stage* (Oxford UP, 2016) 1; Gary Taylor *Moment by Moment by Shakespeare* (London: Macmillan, 1985) 2; Elisabeth Dutton 'A Manifesto for Performance Research' in *The Methuen Drama Handbook to Theatre History and Historiography* edited Claire Cochrane and Joanna Robinson (London: Bloomsbury, 2019) 249-60, at 252. See Clifford Davidson 'Improvisation in Medieval Drama' in *Improvisation in the Arts of the Middle Ages and Renaissance* edited Timothy J. McGee (Kalamazoo: Medieval Institute Publications, 2003) 193-221; Carol Symes 'The Medieval Archive and the History of Theatre' *Theatre Survey 52* (2011) 29-58, at 30, 33-6, 51; Carol Symes 'Liturgical Texts and Performance Practices' in *Understanding Medieval Liturgy* 239-67, at 239, 242-3.

forgotten their lines. Had the texts been performed exactly as written, each performance would still have been different: the performers, the spectators, and their expectations would have varied each time. All these variables must be considered when using texts as sources to understand medieval performances. In the case of coronations, in addition to the pontificals, there are extant sources such as ordinals that at times complement and at other times contradict each other.[30] Fortunately, the fourteenth-century Westminster *Liber Regalis*, which was compiled by someone who seems to have 'looked at every manuscript in the abbey which could furnish information on past custom', and which apparently influenced succeeding coronations, is perhaps a more stable source.[31]

Amid the difficulties created by the sources, there are, however, general elements that seem to occur – or to be expected to occur – consistently in medieval coronations. These general elements testify – perhaps surprisingly given the amount of time that has passed – to many parallels between the coronation of Charles and those of his medieval predecessors. Early coronations generally follow the same order of events, including the arrival of the king (often accompanied by the queen) at Westminster Abbey after a procession; the king and queen's processional entrance into the church in the company of significant members of the court; the recognition; the swearing of the oath by the king; the anointing of the king; the presentation to the king of the regalia during his investiture on St Edward's Chair; the homage by peers and clergy (for Charles, this was a homage performed by the Archbishop of Canterbury, the Prince of Wales, those present in the Abbey and, if they wished to do so, the public at home); and the conclusion of the service with a Eucharistic liturgy.[32]

Then, as now, the clergy, and especially the Archbishop of Canterbury, conducted the service.[33] The items of regalia also resemble the items used today – although the order in which they are given to the king, as well as their number, has varied over the centuries.[34] For instance, the regalia for the second coronation of Richard I, according to Gervase of

---

30 Richardson 'The Coronation in Medieval England' at 114, 118; Hunt *Drama* 21–2.
31 Richardson 'The Coronation in Medieval England' at 112, 146; Hunt *Drama* 19–20.
32 These elements are all, for instance, present in King Edgar's 973 coronation: Byrhtferth of Ramsey '*Vita S. Oswaldi*' at 104–12.
33 Hunt 'Bright Star' at 25–6.
34 Richardson 'The Coronation in Medieval England' at 117–19.

Canterbury, included: sandals, a tunic, a mantle (*pallium quadrangulum auro textum* ['a square cloak woven with gold']), coronation bracelets or armills (*armillae*), sword, spurs, a virge or rod of office (*baculum*), a sceptre, and a crown.[35] Charles's regalia also featured armills, swords, spurs, sceptres, and a crown. After the anointing, he was invested with the *Columbium Sindonis*, a 'shift-like tunic', the *Supertunica*, a 'coat', and the 'Imperial Mantle'.[36] According to Father Mark Vickers, a priest of the Diocese of Westminster and a historian and author: '[t]he imagery and the symbolism and much of the language [of King Charles's coronation] is that of the Catholic, medieval coronation service.'[37]

Was the 2023 coronation fundamentally a medieval ritual? We might consider this coronation as something akin to a modern performance of a medieval dramatic or liturgical text. Such modern performances consciously or unconsciously bring much of the modern to medieval sources.[38] It might be too extreme, however, to call the coronation of King Charles III 'medieval', especially given the adaptations made to coronations not only in 2023 but in previous centuries. In addition to the anointing, there are many things that a medieval king might have found strange had he attended Charles III's coronation: the language used during most of the liturgy was no longer Latin, a whole new audience (or congregation) now had access to the service in Westminster Abbey, much of the music was different as well.[39] Yet although change has occurred as various kings and queens have been crowned over the centuries, and although some of the meaning of the coronation has consequently changed, there remain, at the core of King Charles III's coronation, significant traces of the medieval.

---

35   Richardson 'The Coronation in Medieval England' at 119.

36   'Historic Coronation Vestments' at <https://www.royal.uk/news-and-activity/2023-05-01/historic-coronation-vestments-from-the-royal-collection-will-be-reused>. The term *Columbium Sindonis* was first introduced in 1273; Richardson 'The Coronation in Medieval England' at 142.

37   Quoted in McKeown 'A guide to the Christian – and Catholic – symbolism'.

38   For more, see Dutton 'A Manifesto'.

39   'The Coronation Service'. See also Charlotte Higgins 'Can monarchical drama really hold a modern audience's attention?' in *The Guardian* at <https://www.theguardian.com/uk-news/2023/may/07/modern-audience-the-drama-of-monarchy-coronation>; Hunt *Drama* 5–6.

The Palace seems to have tried to emphasise such connections with the past, laying special importance on the length of the historical tradition. On its official website, it repeatedly made mention of the ancient roots of the coronation liturgy and of some of its elements. When describing the regalia and the vestments, for example, royal articles consistently comment on their date of fabrication and name the king for which they were made.[40] About the coronation spoon, the royal website states:

> The silver-gilt Coronation Spoon is the oldest object in use at Coronations, having been first recorded in 1349 among St Edward's Regalia in Westminster Abbey, and is the only piece of Royal goldsmiths' work to survive from the twelfth century, having possibly been supplied to King Henry II (1133–1189) or King Richard I (1157–1199). It was used to anoint King James I in 1603, and at every subsequent Coronation. In 1649, the Spoon was sold to the Yeoman of King Charles I's Wardrobe, who returned it for King Charles II's Coronation in 1661, when small seed pearls were added to the decoration of the handle.

When discussing non-medieval objects, such as the spurs, royal articles remind readers of the medieval origin of their use: 'The Spurs were made in 1661 for King Charles II, but the use of spurs at Coronations dates back to King Richard I, the Lionheart, and his Coronation in 1189'. This is also the case for the armills, which are 'thought to relate to ancient symbols of knighthood and military leadership', for the staff of St Edward, and for the *ampulla*, which:

---

40   Many of these artefacts date from the seventeenth to the twentieth century (the *ampulla*, the spurs, the armills, the orb, the sceptres, the crown of St Edward and the staff (1661), the maces (1660 and 1695), the swords (seventeenth century and nineteenth century), the rings (1831), the queen's sceptre (1685), the Imperial State Crown and Queen Mary's crown (twentieth century)), but some were even older (the Coronation Spoon, the Coronation Chair (St Edward's Chair, 1296–1300) containing the Stone of Scone (a much older symbol of kingship, reportedly used in Scottish coronations for some centuries before being captured and brought to England by Edward I's forces in 1296), and the St Augustine's Gospel Book (sixth century)). 'The Coronation Regalia' at <https://www.royal.uk/coronation-regalia>; 'Historic chairs to be reused' at <https://www.royal.uk/news-and-activity/2023-05-01/historic-chairs-to-be-reused-for-the-coronation>; 'The Coronation Service'.

was supplied for the coronation of King Charles II in 1661 by the Crown Jeweller, Robert Vyner, and is based on an earlier, smaller vessel, which in turn was based on a fourteenth-century legend in which the Virgin Mary appeared to St Thomas à Becket.

Finally, St Edward's crown is said to have been:

> made for King Charles II in 1661, as a replacement for the medieval crown which had been melted down in 1649. The original was thought to date back to the eleventh-century royal saint, Edward the Confessor – the last Anglo-Saxon king of England.[41]

Some of the vestments worn by Charles are described in a similar way. The *Supertunica*, for instance, while dating from the twentieth century, 'has changed little [in its form] since medieval coronations'.[42]

Descriptions of the regalia and vestments thus focus and seem to put value on dates – emphasising the age of these objects and practices – and on their consistent use by different kings and queens – highlighting unbroken tradition. The words 'tradition' but also 'historic', 'historically', and 'traditionally' are repeatedly used in these royal articles, and they also occur in the Order of Service.[43] The Order opens with a short history of coronations at Westminster Abbey, beginning with William the Conqueror who started this 'long tradition', which has lasted 'almost a thousand years'.[44] The choice to place this history at the beginning of the Order, to make it the first thing that people read when they opened the booklet, shows its importance to the Palace. It wants this history known and remembered.

Similar ideas are brought to the fore in another publication on the Royal Family website, presenting '100 Coronation Facts'.[45] These facts continue to emphasise the ancient ('The earliest English coronation that is recorded in detail, although not the first, is the crowning of the Anglo-Saxon King Edgar in Bath in 953 [*sic*] CE'; 'The original 14th century order of service, Liber Regalis, was written in Latin and descends directly from that of King Edgar at Bath in 973 CE. The Liber Regalis has provided the

---

41 'The Coronation Regalia'.
42 'Historic Coronation Vestments'.
43 'The Coronation Regalia'.
44 'The Coronation Order of Service' at 3.
45 '100 Coronation Facts'.

basis for every Coronation since') and the continuous ('Westminster Abbey has been the setting for every Coronation since 1066'; 'The Earl Marshal is responsible for organising the Coronation. Since 1386, this position has been undertaken by The Duke of Norfolk'; 'The King will be crowned in St Edward's Chair, made in 1300 for Edward I and used at every Coronation since that time').[46]

The Palace not only emphasised the traditional and medieval elements of the coronation, but it also added more of the old and the traditional to it. The anointing screen, for instance, was partly built with contemporary techniques but it was also made using 'traditional ... embroidery practices'. Traditional crafts, in general, seem to have been especially important to King Charles III, who is, according to the Royal Family website, 'a keen advocate and supporter of the preservation of heritage craft skills'.[47] 'Traditional craft skills' were further used to make the wooden poles supporting the screen. These poles were carved from old wood, from a fallen oak planted in 1765 at Windsor by the Duke of Northumberland. The anointing screen therefore gestures towards the past through its construction, but also through its iconography. The design on the sides of the screen was inspired by the Cosmati pavement, the thirteenth-century pavement on which most of the coronation – and most previous coronations – took place. The front of the screen was embroidered with a quotation from the medieval anchoress Julian of Norwich (c.1342–1416): 'All shall be well and all manner of thing shall be well'. The design of this part of the screen – including the words – was inspired by the Sanctuary Window in the Chapel Royal of St James's Palace created for her Majesty Queen Elizabeth II on her Golden Jubilee. The royal article describing the screen does not, however, give a reason for including Julian of Norwich's quotation – apart from its presence on the Queen's window.[48] Reproducing this design for the screen may thus have been an homage to the king's mother rather than a nod to the Middle Ages – although in this year of the 650th anniversary of Julian's *Revelations*, it is possible that the quotation was meant to honour her more specifically. Whether intended or not, these words associate the most sacred and significant moment of the coronation with the previous sovereign, but – in conjunction with the Cosmati design – they also tie it

---

46   '100 Coronation Facts'.
47   'The Anointing Screen'. See also 'Historic chairs to be reused'.
48   'The Anointing Screen'.

to the Middle Ages, medieval literary production, medieval culture, and medieval coronations.

Such ties to the medieval were already visible in the invitation to the coronation, designed by Andrew Jamieson. The choice of the designer, described by the Royal Family website as a 'heraldic artist and manuscript illuminator whose work is inspired by the chivalric themes of Arthurian legend', shows a desire to reference the Middle Ages both aesthetically and by recalling famous medieval stories. The Arthurian legend is known all over the world and generally perceived positively as a fascinating mixture of stories and history. It is associated with heroic – if flawed – knights and kings, an association that the coronation may have wished to evoke. The invitation moreover included the figure of the Green Man, often found in medieval churches and described by a royal article as 'an ancient figure from British folklore'.[49] This description has been disputed by scholars, but it does again show the royal desire to attach the 2023 coronation to a medieval past – whether such a past is real or imagined.[50]

The liturgical service foregrounded a religious authority behind Charles's kingship; official Palace statements and press releases highlighted features of the coronation and explained their purposes and intended effects. The Palace displayed an attention to the spectacle of the coronation and its visual splendour, and recognised the public's interest in this feature of the event. It presented the clothes worn by the king and queen during the coronation, the flowers decorating Westminster Abbey, the coaches taking part in the processions, the chairs used by their Majesties in the church, the newly made anointing screen, the music, and the dazzling regalia.[51] However, there appeared to be a tension between wishing to depict this coronation as a continuation of the past, as a part

---

49 On the invitation, see 'The Coronation Invitation' at <https://www.royal.uk/news-and-activity/2023-04-04/the-coronation-invitation>.

50 It also ties in with Charles's interest in ecology. Molly Olmstead 'Is the Green Man British Enough?' at <https://slate.com/news-and-politics/2023/04/green-man-king-charles-coronation-invitation.html?via=rss_socialflow_twitter>.

51 'Flowers at the Coronation Service' at <https://www.royal.uk/news-and-activity/2023-05-04/flowers-at-the-coronation-service-of-the-king-and-the-queen-consort>; 'Historic Coronation Vestments'; 'Historic chairs to be reused'; 'A first glimpse' at <https://www.royal.uk/news-and-activity/2023-04-29/a-first-glimpse-at-their-majesties-coronation-robes>; 'The Anointing Screen'; 'The Coronation Procession'; 'The Coronation Regalia'; 'Coronation Music at Westminster Abbey'.

of a well-known and cherished history (as described above), and feeling the need to update this antiquated event to make it more modern and more palatable to the contemporary British public. The coronation was designed to impress with its spectacle, but the meaning of that spectacle was open to contest. Did the displays and presentations associated with the coronation of King Charles III communicate their intended meanings effectively? How were they perceived and discussed by those watching them?

The Coronation as Received

YouGov surveys show that the British public approached the coronation with mixed emotions. According to one of their polls, most Britons (64 per cent) showed little or no interest in the coronation. The same poll, however, when considered in more detail, reveals discrepancies depending on political affiliation (77 per cent of Labour voters but only 48 per cent of Conservative voters expressed this lack of interest) and age (75 per cent of those aged 18–24 versus 53 per cent of those aged 65+).[52] Older and more conservative people thus tended to care more about the coronation, and were more interested in watching it.[53] They also expressed the most ardent opposition to protests taking place in the vicinity of the coronation (although a general majority of respondents was not favourable to these either).[54] Such protests did occur before and on the day of the coronation, when a few hundred protesters chanting the slogan 'Not my King' mixed in with the crowd. These protests were widely reported.[55] Yet, in spite of the protests and of the public's partial

52 'How much do you care about the forthcoming coronation of King Charles?' in *YouGov* at <https://yougov.co.uk/topics/politics/survey-results/daily/2023/04/13/b7aff/1>.

53 'How likely are you to watch King Charles' coronation and/or take part in celebrations surrounding it?' in *YouGov* at <https://yougov.co.uk/topics/politics/survey-results/daily/2023/04/13/b7aff/2>.

54 'Do you think people should or should not be allowed to protest the coronation?' in *YouGov* at <https://yougov.co.uk/topics/politics/survey-results/daily/2023/05/03/09c56/2>.

55 Tim Adams '"Not my king", they chanted' in *The Guardian* at <https://www.theguardian.com/uk-news/2023/may/06/not-my-king-they-chanted-then-the-police-took-their-megaphones>; Niamh Kennedy, Christian Edwards, Lindsay Isaac, and Allegra Goodwin 'Something out of a police state' in *CNN* at <https://edition.cnn.com/2023/05/06/uk/king-charles-anti-monarchy-

lack of interest, YouGov polls show that a majority of Britons would not like the monarchy to be abolished: 52 per cent of responders said that they did not want a referendum on this issue.[56] Although the coronation was divisive, the monarchy thus remained, in the eyes of an albeit small majority, meaningful.

Newspapers presented similarly varied views of the event in their extensive coverage of it. While they cannot be said to be entirely representative of public opinion – they cater to their readership and to what they imagine this readership wants to read – they nevertheless offer some insights into the perception of the coronation in the United Kingdom. As might be expected after surveying the polls, left-wing newspapers tended to adopt more of a negative – and at times republican – stance on the coronation than right-wing newspapers did. *The Guardian*, for example, titled one of its articles rather grimly: 'The twilight king: why Charles's coronation does not feel like the start of a new era'.[57] An interest in gossip and fashion was more present in tabloids ('Kate looks regal in dazzling headpiece' wrote *The Sun*)[58] than in broadsheets (*The Times, The Telegraph, The Independent, The Guardian/The Observer*),

protest-arrests-ckc-gbr-intl/index.html>; Elly Blake, Shekhar Bhatia, et al. 'Not on our watch!' in the *Mail Online* at <https://www.dailymail.co.uk/news/article-12053517/Not-King-protesters-unfurl-flags-shout-anti-monarchy-slogans-Coronation-route.html?ico=topics_pagination_desktop>.

56   'Do you think there should or should not be a referendum on whether or not Britain should continue to have a monarchy?' in *YouGov* at <https://yougov.co.uk/topics/politics/survey-results/daily/2023/05/04/60f27/3>.

57   Jonathan Freedland 'The twilight king' in *The Guardian* at <https://www.theguardian.com/uk-news/2023/may/05/twilight-king-why-charles-coronation-does-not-feel-like-start-of-new-era>.

58   Tom Hussey 'Princess Kate looks regal' in *The Sun* at <https://www.thesun.co.uk/fabulous/22271888/kate-coronation-robe-tiara-diana/>; see also Becky Pemberton 'Princess Charlotte' in *The Sun* at <https://www.thesun.co.uk/fabulous/22270429/charles-coronation-princess-charlotte-twins-mum-kate-middleton-alexander-mcqueen-dresses/>; Gwyneth Rees and Gina Kalsi 'Here come the first ladies!' in the *Mail Online* at <https://www.dailymail.co.uk/femail/article-12053851/Here-come-ladies.html?ico=topics_pagination_desktop>; Harriet Johnston 'What was Kate smiling at in the Abbey?' in the *Mail Online* at <https://www.dailymail.co.uk/femail/article-12053981/What-Kate-smiling-Abbey-Princess-beams-performance-Kings-Coronation.html?ico=topics_pagination_desktop>.

which tended to provide deeper analyses both on the issues around the coronation and on its meanings.[59]

What emerges strikingly, however, from surveying the press's wide range of opinions, is its overwhelming interest in spectacle. It was spectacle that seemed to create excitement around the coronation. *The Sun*, for instance, praised the event as 'the greatest royal spectacle that most of us have ever seen', 'almost unchanged for 1,000 years – a blockbuster of historic richness unmatched anywhere else on earth'.[60] While more mixed in opinion, Rachel Cooke in *The Observer* qualified the coronation as both 'ludicrous' and 'magnificent' in its pomp and emotional impact.[61] Spectacle was also a point of focus in many articles published in *The Guardian*. Some of its journalists even compared and associated the coronation with drama, more specifically with medieval and early modern drama. Caroline Davies wrote that '[a]lmost every syllable bore the weight of history in this five-act drama with a script more medieval morality play than 21st century'.[62] The same newspaper even commissioned their well-known theatre critic Michael Billington to write a review of the coronation: he gave it four stars, calling it 'Shakespearean'.[63] Spectacle, and the historical nature of this spectacle,

---

59 See for example Potts 'King Charles: Why does the monarch need a coronation?' The BBC and *The Times* reproduced the liturgy of the coronation in full. Nonetheless, *The Guardian* did also include a long piece on the clothing <https://www.theguardian.com/uk-news/2023/may/06/coronation-fashion-royals-put-on-catwalk-show-to-launch-king-charles-britain>.

60 'King Charles's crowning was the greatest royal spectacle' in *The Sun* at <https://www.thesun.co.uk/news/22277155/king-charles-crowning-sun-says/>.

61 Rachel Cooke 'It was ludicrous but also magnificent' in *The Guardian* at <https://www.theguardian.com/uk-news/2023/may/06/it-was-ludicrous-but-also-magnificent-the-coronation-stirred-every-emotion>. Even a *Telegraph* article that complained about the lack of spectacle was first focused on the idea of 'spectacle': Judith Woods 'Why is penny-pinching Charles depriving us of the spectacle we all crave?' in *The Telegraph* at <https://www.telegraph.co.uk/columnists/2023/04/28/why-a-penny-pinching-coronation-is-a-mistake/>.

62 Caroline Davies 'Coronation of King Charles is a visual feast veiled in the mists of the past' in *The Guardian* at <https://www.theguardian.com/uk-news/2023/may/06/coronation-of-king-charles-is-a-visual-feast-veiled-in-the-mists-of-the-past>.

63 Michael Billington 'The Coronation review' in *The Guardian* at <https://www.theguardian.com/tv-and-radio/2023/may/07/the-coronation-review-immaculately-rehearsed-touching-and-shakespearean>.

thus seems to have been the main focus of the press when discussing the coronation of King Charles III.[64]

However, this spectacle does not always seem to have effectively communicated the intended generic meanings of the coronation. Some of the press associated it with emptiness and meaninglessness. *The Guardian* questioned the funding of what it called in various articles, 'a dated pageant that should be rethought', 'an empty conjuring trick', full of 'nothingness'.[65] In such articles, the meanings that the spectacle of the coronation was supposed to express were either not mentioned or, when mentioned, they were not recognised as true. That the spectacle was, for many, ineffective may have been the result – at least in part – of the current perception of Britain's economy and of its place in the world. Economic difficulties apparently incited members of the public to pay close attention to the cost of the royal celebration, especially when this celebration was funded partly by taxpayer money.[66] Such economic

64   See Tom Bower 'King Charles put on a brilliant, bewitching spectacle' in *The Sun* at <https://www.thesun.co.uk/fabulous/22276495/tom-bower-king-charles-spectacle/>; Davies 'Coronation ... veiled in the mists of the past'; Higgins 'Can monarchical drama'. See also Potts 'Why does the monarch need a coronation?'; Esther Addley 'How coronation of King Charles will revive some of oldest British rituals' in *The Guardian* at <https://www.theguardian.com/uk-news/2023/may/05/how-coronation-of-king-charles-revive-oldest-british-rituals-westminster-abbey>.

65   Editorial 'The Guardian view on the coronation of Charles III' in *The Guardian* at <https://www.theguardian.com/commentisfree/2023/may/04/the-guardian-view-on-the-coronation-of-charles-iii-a-dated-pageant-that-should-be-rethought>; Polly Toynbee 'Protesters in handcuffs' in *The Guardian* at <https://www.theguardian.com/commentisfree/2023/may/07/protesters-in-handcuffs-and-nonstop-bling-this-coronation-has-been-an-embarrassment>;   Higgins 'Can monarchical drama'.

66   'Do you think the coronation of King Charles should or should not be funded by the government?' in *YouGov* at <https://yougov.co.uk/topics/arts/survey-results/daily/2023/04/18/25178/3>. See also Norman Baker 'Now we know how fabulously wealthy Charles is' in *The Guardian* at <https://www.theguardian.com/uk-news/commentisfree/2023/apr/29/charles-coronation-pay-king-uk-taxpayers>; David Pegg 'Why we put royal wealth under the microscope' in *The Guardian* at <https://www.theguardian.com/uk-news/2023/may/04/why-we-put-royal-wealth-under-the-microscope-on-eve-of-coronation>; Laura Elston 'Multimillion pound coronation' in *The Independent* at <https://www.independent.co.uk/life-style/royal-family/how-much-coronation-cost-2023-b2335324.html>; Ariane Sohrabi-Shiraz 'Who is paying for King Charles III's Coronation?' in *The Mirror* at <https://www.mirror.co.uk/news/royals/who-paying-king-charles-iiis-29412292>.

issues combined with changes in the dominance of Britain on the world stage may have further led some British citizens to feel a lower sense of pride in their country than was the case in 1953, when the coronation of Elizabeth II took place. In contrast to the situation then, Britain is no longer the head of an empire that 'reached across the globe'. While Queen Elizabeth's coronation included 40,000 troops, as well as a naval review including 190 ships, Charles's coronation involved 6,000 members of the armed forces, reflecting the lesser military influence of Britain in the world today (the total number of British troops fell from 850,000 in 1953 to 150,000 in 2023).[67] The celebration of the greatness of Britain that had been such an important part of the previous coronation thus felt more muted in 2023 and, to some, still seemed out of place.

Although these factors offer reasons as to why a national celebration might feel meaningless in May 2023, they do not explain the lack of recognition by some of the press of the other generic aims of the coronation – an assertion of the king's power, legitimacy, and authority. Changes in the role of kingship have today severed the ancient ties between the monarch's effective power and the expression of this power. Although the king is the Head of the British Armed Forces in name, he is in effect removed from command.[68] This disjointed relationship between meaning and spectacle in the case of royal power may have led spectators to suspect or perceive a similar lack of meaning behind the whole of the coronation's spectacle.

The feeling of the meaninglessness of the spectacle and ceremonial seems to have been further exacerbated by modern ideas about hierarchy and meritocracy, which are incompatible, as Professor Anna Whitelock (director of the Centre for the Study of Modern Monarchy) states, with 'the idea that one man … by accident of birth, is being anointed and set above the rest of us; who is unelected, and doesn't represent Britain religiously or ethnically'.[69] The very idea of kingship may thus seem to many no longer relevant in modern Britain. Concerns were expressed in the press but also online about the fact that Britain had changed dramatically since the last coronation in 1953 and that the

---

67 Freedland 'The twilight king'; *The Guardian* view on the coronation of Charles III'; Jasmine Andersson 'King's coronation' in *BBC News* at <https://www.bbc.co.uk/news/uk-65286190>.
68 'The role of the Monarchy' at <https://www.royal.uk/role-monarchy>.
69 Potts 'Why does the monarch need a coronation?'

monarchy – led moreover by an older man – did not seem in tune with the modern world.[70]

What, moreover, has seemed difficult for many to agree with or even to recognise are the ties between kingship and religion, supporting the king's legitimacy and authority.[71] Historically, he is not king by 'accident of birth' only, but is supposed to be chosen by God. *The Guardian* pointed out that: '[p]ollsters found that 34% of 1950s Britons believed Elizabeth had been placed on the throne by the hand of God. Yet by 1992 a survey could find not a single respondent who was even aware, unbidden, that the monarchy had a religious dimension at all'.[72] The idea of a king chosen by God makes even less sense if one does not believe in God. Since 1953, there has been a significant decrease not only in the awareness of the ties between religion and the monarchy, but also in Christian faith in general in the United Kingdom.[73]

---

70   Freedland 'The twilight king'; Potts 'Why does the monarch need a coronation?'; Jane Corbin and Sean Coughlan 'Coronation: How popular is the monarchy?' in *BBC News* at <https://www.bbc.com/news/uk-65326467>; Higgins 'Can monarchical drama'; Diana Evans 'Can a monarchy sit easy?' in *The Guardian* at <https://www.theguardian.com/uk-news/2023/may/03/can-a-monarchy-sit-easy-in-modern-britain>.

71   For an example of someone who could not relate to the liturgy of the coronation religiously, see Barbara Ellen 'The coronation on TV' in *The Guardian* at <https://www.theguardian.com/uk-news/2023/may/06/the-coronation-latest-instalment-of-britains-longest-running-costume-drama-is-a-bit-of-a-damp-squib>.

72   Freedland 'The twilight king'. See also Higgins 'Can monarchical drama'; 'The Guardian view on the coronation of Charles III'; Toynbee 'Protesters in Handcuffs'.

73   According to the most recent census data, taken in 2021, 46.2 per cent of the English and Welsh population say they are Christian, a decline of 13.1 percentage points since the last census in 2011 <https://faithsurvey.co.uk/uk-christianity.html>. Christianity continues to be the most commonly identified religious identity, but it must also be acknowledged that many religious people in the United Kingdom are not of Christian faith. I have been unable to find their opinion on divine monarchy, but there seems to have been – at least in part – a positive reaction from these communities to the coronation and to its inclusion of representatives of various faiths. See for example Harriet Sherwood 'UK Jews "will be lining streets"' in *The Guardian* at <https://www.theguardian.com/uk-news/2023/may/03/uk-jews-will-be-lining-streets-on-coronation-day-says-chief-rabbi>; Cathy Newman 'Faith leaders discuss the significance of inclusivity' in *Channel 4 News* at <https://www.channel4.com/news/faith-leaders-discuss-the-significance-of-inclusivity-in-king-charles-coronation>.

In the case of the coronation of Charles III, this sense of distance from religion may have been further exacerbated by the fact that most people watched the royal event on a screen, away from the liturgical atmosphere of the church. They were not surrounded by the rest of the congregation, nor did they likely stand, sit, or speak with them. They remained, in many ways, removed from this ritual. This distance likely made it harder for them to be religiously invested in the coronation. Indeed, the participation of a congregation, which comes together in the presence of God, is a fundamental aspect of liturgy.[74] Experiencing the coronation on a screen diminished the ability of its religious spectacle to convey meaning, and probably had the same effect for other aspects of the coronation's spectacle. Whether it was military parades, salutes, or the general grandeur of the clothes or carriages on display, the weight of the spectacle was muted, made smaller and more distant, by the medium that simultaneously allowed this spectacle to reach so much of its audience.

The way in which the coronation of Charles III was experienced by its spectators, these spectators' opinions on Britain's economic and military status, as well as the changes in British faith and values, were all likely factors influencing the perception of this coronation by some as an empty spectacle. What further seems to have emerged in some of the media is an association between the very concept of spectacle and meaninglessness. As some journalists noted, the coronation would neither make Charles king, nor would it confer 'new power on him'.[75] Its aims were only to show. And because spectacle does not always have a tangible, immediately visible, or easily quantifiable effect, it can seem useless and futile. This appears to have been implied by SNP MP Mhairi Black when she appeared on ITV, stating that: 'Me personally, no I am not a fan of the monarchy. I think in the middle of a cost-of-living crisis the money could be much better spent than on what looks like a

---

74 On the participation of the congregation, see Matthew Cheung Salisbury *Worship in Medieval England* (Leeds: Arc Humanities Press, 2018) 43–65.

75 'The Guardian view on the coronation of Charles III'. Charles was already king from the moment his mother died. According to Dr George Gross (King's College, London), who leads a research project on coronations, the ceremony is 'a symbolic gesture that formalises the monarch's commitment to the role' but is not required by law. Addley 'How coronation of King Charles'; Potts 'Why does the monarch need a coronation?'

pantomime.'[76] In this interview, she mentions none of the meanings of the coronation, only its spectacle, which she qualifies as a 'pantomime' – evoking cheap and tacky entertainment and indicating her negative opinion of its value.

The idea of spectacle as meaningless entertainment is far from new. It underlies the long-standing philosophical and religious suspicion of theatre and dramatic performance as fictional and unreal.[77] Similar suspicions have recently been raised by modern scholars contrasting theatre with liturgy.[78] Yet both liturgy and drama are spectacular. In the case of liturgy, the use of spectacle is meant to help serve its primary goal: worship. For instance, according to Elizabeth Parker McLachlan, who dedicates an article to the ornate vessels and objects used during liturgical ceremonies, such objects are supposed to show the glory of God rather than the glory of man.[79] In his influential liturgical commentary *Rationale divinorum officiorum*, the thirteenth-century bishop Durandus describes liturgical vestments in similar terms: they must be worn to honour and glorify God.[80] Of copes – a type of vestment used by priests and bishops for processions and, in the Anglican church, Eucharistic

---

76 See also James Tapsfield 'It's like the Emperor's New Clothes' in the *Mail Online* at <https://www.dailymail.co.uk/news/article-12046969/Left-wing-MPs-rail-grotesque-costs-King-Charless-coronation.html?ico=topics_pagination_desktop>; Olivia Devereux-Evans 'We don't want pageantry ... we want affordable food and rent and bills' in the *Mail Online* at <https://www.dailymail.co.uk/tvshowbiz/article-12053595/Leigh-Anne-Pinnock-hits-Kings-Coronation-savage-message.html?ico=topics_pagination_desktop>.

77 This suspicion reaches back to Plato, who, in his *Republic*, argued that theatre is a lie, philosophically undesirable and bad for society; although other philosophers, notably Aristotle, defended theatre, anti-theatricalism continued, and thrived in the Middle Ages. See Jonas Barish *Antitheatrical Prejudice* (Berkeley: University of California Press, 1981).

78 Granger *The N-Town Play* 19; Flanigan '*Visitatio Sepulchri*' at 10–12, 30. According to Flanigan, ritual is a communal experience where imitation makes present in the community an event of the past. Drama is only imitation and defines a clear line between audience and actors. C. Clifford Flanigan 'The Fleury Playbook and the Traditions of Medieval Drama' *Comparative Drama 18* (1984) 348–72, at 351, 362, 361, 363–4, 369.

79 Elizabeth Parker McLachlan 'Liturgical Vessels and Implements' in *The Liturgy of the Medieval Church* 333–89, at 334–6.

80 Guillaume Durand *Rational ou manuel des divins offices* edited and translated Charles Barthélémy, 5 vols (Paris: Louis-Vivès, 1854) *1* 212–13.

services, and worn by many of the clergy participating in King Charles III's coronation – he says that they represent joy and perseverance, and that they show that eternal life is possible for those who live well. Vestments are thus meant to remind both priests and their congregation of the virtues that they should adopt and the behaviours that they should follow as good Christians: they are a way of communicating meaning.[81]

Yet spectacle does not communicate meaning only when used in liturgy, and a coronation includes both liturgical and secular instances of spectacle. Looking back to the Middle Ages when a coronation taking place in England is first described, spectacle was clearly used as a way of communicating ideas in many areas. It could help increase or direct spectators' devotion, teaching them about Scriptures or how to live a devout Christian life, but it could also appeal to their sense of civic duty. The great procession in Lille (Flanders) in honour of the Virgin Mary, for example, which took place each year on the octave of Trinity Sunday, celebrated the saint with liturgical ceremonies. It also, from the late fourteenth or early fifteenth century until 1565, saw neighbourhood youth groups and guilds stage both plays and pageants. From the fifteenth century onwards, this procession moreover involved 'all social groups and institutions of the city', uniting the city 'in a magnificent ritual of devotion and civic pride'.[82] Processions, much like coronations, could thus combine religious services with other spectacular and theatrical events, and with the celebration of the city in which they took place.[83]

Today, still, spectacle is used to convey meaning: it can be an expression of nationhood, of pride, of tradition. In my Swiss town of Fribourg, for example, the feast of St Nicholas – patron saint of the town – is celebrated widely. It features a long procession going from the *collège* St Michel to the cathedral. This elaborate procession is composed of the *collège*'s students dressed as the saint and his followers. At the end of the

---

81   Durand *Rational* 220–1.
82   Alan E. Knight 'Processional Theatre and the Rituals of Social Unity in Lille' in *Drama and Community: People and Plays in Medieval Europe* edited Alan Hindley (Turnhout: Brepols, 1994) 99–109, at 100–1.
83   The Feast of Corpus Christi was, in some English towns, the occasion of the staging of Mystery Plays: the civic and social dimensions of these stagings may have been, in some ways, as important as the religious: see M. James 'Ritual, Drama and the Social Body in the Late Medieval English Town' *Past and Present 98* (1983) 3–29; and Pamela King *The York Mystery Cycle and the Worship of the City* (Cambridge: D.S. Brewer, 2006).

procession, Nicholas speaks to the crowd, and a liturgy is then celebrated in the cathedral. This spectacular feast still bears a religious meaning for some of its attendees; moreover, it teaches people about the saint and his story. However, it also attracts spectators because it is a significant Fribourg tradition: students have been organising the procession since 1906 and many people have participated in the event in one way or another. The feast of St Nicholas unites generations and reminds them of the town's history: the spectacle thus has a civic dimension. The speech given by St Nicholas, which always provides a comedic commentary on the town and its inhabitants, only reinforces this dimension.

If spectacle has been and can still be so meaningful, why did some spectators watching the coronation of King Charles III take on board the meaning transmitted by its spectacle but others did not? An important factor seems to have been openness to belief. People who did not and could not believe in God and in his ties with royalty, in organised religion and Anglicanism, or in the greatness of their country, and the value of royalty, were more prone to perceive the spectacle of this event as an irrelevant waste of time and money. For those who did believe, however, the spectacle was meaningful.

This was the case with some of the journalists writing about the coronation. *The Sun*'s Tom Bower viewed this spectacle positively because, he argued, it showed the world a positive image of Britain and because it was also a reminder of the country's glorious history.[84] Spectacle thus displayed to all the greatness of this nation, but it also helped make the nation better. According to *The Sun*, the coronation and the monarchy brought British citizens together, emphasising a 'sense of unity and duty'.[85] *The Guardian*'s Michael Billington and Rachel Cooke, although mixed in their enthusiasm for the Crown, both found the spectacle of the coronation to be a point of national pride. While they were not happy with the state of the country, they expressed their pride in Britain organising such a momentous event and doing it so well.[86]

---

84 Bower 'King Charles … a brilliant, bewitching spectacle'.
85 'King Charles's crowning'. The idea of unity was also present in some letters addressed to *The Guardian*: Letters 'Coronation extravaganza sits badly in today's Britain' in *The Guardian* at <https://www.theguardian.com/uk-news/2023/may/05/coronation-extravaganza-sits-badly-in-todays-britain>.
86 Cooke 'It was ludicrous'; Billington 'Coronation Review'.

These journalists thus embraced the meaning of the national celebration associated with the coronation. As for the meanings tied more directly to the king, power was not discussed in the media – likely because the king does not wield any effective military power – but the question of his legitimacy and authority did feature in many articles. Several newspapers spoke of how the king was 'set apart' during his coronation; in this, they echoed official press releases.[87] In *The Guardian/The Observer*, Rachel Cooke said that the liturgical celebration – including the anointing – allowed her to 'think of him [King Charles III] differently' and, although she admitted to not being a royalist, she added, 'we have time for the king'. She mentioned the importance of spectacle in making her feel this way: the music, the faith on display, as well as, paradoxically, the perceived 'helplessness' of the king, convinced her – if for a limited time – of his special status. This sense of 'helplessness', which was also noticed by Billington, seems to have originated in the perception of the king as vulnerable, more specifically as he was being undressed just before the anointing. Cooke speaks of his 'plain linen shirt' and of the king's 'invalid quality',[88] while Billington says:

> there was still something incalculable in that moment that I found immensely touching. Seeing Charles shedding his golden robes and preparing to kneel before the archbishop in a white tunic, I was also reminded of the public solitude that is a feature of every crowned head in Shakespeare.[89]

For some observers, seeing the king divest himself of his symbols of power thus resulted in their sympathy for him and in their willingness to recognise him as king. He was a man, humble and simply dressed, yet ready to take on a task burdened with history and expectations, and even tied to the divine. The humanity of Charles made him more relatable and made this task seem more impressive. In that moment, it was not the flamboyance of the spectacle that was convincing, but its simplicity, which contrasted with the rest of the coronation. *The Sun* expressed a similar if more royalist view of the event, emphasising Charles's authority as well as his legitimacy. It described him as having been elevated: 'no

---

87 Cooke 'It was ludicrous'; Davies 'Coronation ... veiled in the mists of the past'. See also Bower 'King Charles ... a brilliant, bewitching spectacle'.
88 Cooke 'It was ludicrous'.
89 Billington 'Coronation review'.

longer a mere mortal, he would become the protector of the Church of England, the ultimate guardian of Britain's democracy.'[90]

Shaping the Coronation for 2023

The coronation was certainly shaped to address a modern spectatorship, and the concerns of modern Britain, intriguingly often through its use of history. The inclusion in King Charles III's coronation not only of objects and traditions connected to medieval coronations, but also of medieval craft skills, and of references to medieval literature and to medieval folklore, has the effect of emphasising tradition. On the one hand, this tradition relates to the monarchy. The message transmitted by the official royal publications is that the coronation, its function, and its meanings are not new; it is not something that has been instigated by Charles but it has existed for a long time, has been tied to many kings and queens, and it endures today. This discourse appeals to the pride and interest that British citizens may feel in their country's history. It encourages such pride further and attempts to associate it with the monarchy. The kings and queens mentioned in royal press releases are central to the way that British history is often taught and discussed: historical periods, for instance, are named after these figures ('Elizabethan', 'Victorian', etc.) and popular presentation of history regularly focuses on or includes them (see, for example, the countless books, television programmes, films, and even musicals about Henry VIII and his reign).[91] Royalty and British history are thus intertwined, and the pride that the British are encouraged to feel about their history can easily become tied to these famous royal names. This was the sentiment expressed by Edward Fitzalan-Howard, the Duke of Norfolk – the man overseeing the coronation – who explicitly associated the coronation of Charles with his own pride in his country's history: 'this [the coronation] is also a time to remind ourselves of the pride we have in our great country and our unwritten constitution which has served us so well for 1,000 years during

---

90 Bower 'King Charles ... a brilliant, bewitching spectacle'.
91 See, for instance, the musical *SIX*; the films *The Other Boleyn Girl* (2008), *Anne of a Thousand Days* (1969), *A Man for All Seasons* (1966), *The Private Life of Henry VIII* (1933); the TV series *The Tudors* (2007–2010), *The Spanish Princess* (2019), and *Wolf Hall* (2015). Many of these films and series are adapted from books and plays.

our long history.'[92] Despite her reservations about the monarchy, Cooke was also awed when seeing the history on display during the coronation of King Charles. She writes:

> Even the most ardent republican must find it astonishing, in its way, that the coronation chair, commissioned by Edward I, has been the centrepiece of this ceremony for 700 years; that the St Edward's crown was made for Charles II; that the imperial state crown (the second that the king wore) contains a ruby that Henry V is supposed to have worn at Agincourt.[93]

In a context in which the need for this coronation was debated, the repeated mention in royal articles of tradition, history, and of royal figures therefore seems, in some cases and to some people, to legitimise this need. They show the coronation's uninterrupted significance throughout the country's history and associate this coronation – and its meaning – with figures and times perceived as prestigious.[94] They also express one of the central meanings of the coronation: its celebration of the nation – including its history.

Furthermore, the inclusion in Charles's coronation of references to medieval literature, art, culture, folklore, and skills gestures further – if in a different way – towards British history. The kind of history evoked here, however, is vastly different from the one evoked above: this is not a history of kings, of the nobility and their glorious deeds, but it is the history of ordinary people living in Britain. Their beliefs, their work, as well as the broader culture of the Middle Ages, therefore become associated with the coronation of King Charles III, which thus embraces a more inclusive – and less royal – perspective on the history of Great Britain. The Palace's emphasis on history, while signalling the coronation's ties to the past, also shows its departure from tradition. The presence of the Green Man on the royal invitation was especially surprising to many. Royal invitations do not usually feature folkloric –

---

92 Rebecca English 'King Charles' Coronation "will make Britain proud"' in the *Mail Online* at <https://www.dailymail.co.uk/news/royals/article-12039595/King-Charles-Coronation-make-Britain-proud.html?ico=topics_pagination_desktop>.
93 Cooke 'It was ludicrous'.
94 Other kings and queens have emphasised tradition for the sake of legitimacy. See Hunt 'Bright Star' at 22.

'pagan' according to some – iconography such as this.[95] This idea of a departure from what had been done during previous coronations is emphasised in several official publications. For instance, a quotation by Lord Chartres, included in an article on the roles to be performed during the liturgy, states that '[t]he ceremonies of the Coronation are ancient but they have been freshly interpreted for our contemporary world'.[96] Royal press releases, moreover, consciously introduce and emphasise modern pre-occupations, repeatedly using the words 'diversity' and 'sustainability' to stress how different the 2023 coronation was.

The idea of sustainability was first expressed by scaling back attendance at the event: a reduced number of guests were invited to the ceremony in Westminster Abbey (only around 2,000 people versus 8,000 in 1953).[97] This meant a smaller infrastructure and less waste. Sustainability was further reflected in the materials chosen for the anointing screen: the website emphasised that the thread of the contemporary machine embroidery was made from 100 per cent lyocell and the fabric of the rest of the screen had been 'sourced sustainably from across the UK and other Commonwealth nations'.[98] Chairs used for previous coronations were re-used, once more in the interest of sustainability, and so were coronation vestments, which would usually have been commissioned anew.[99] The royal couple's interest in the natural world and its preservation was signalled by the new Robe of Estate created for the Queen, which featured plants and, for the first time on such a garment, insects.[100] The actual plants decorating Westminster Abbey were displayed without the use of any plastic and were donated to

---

95 For more on this, see 'King Charles in Paganism row' in *The Express* at <https://www.express.co.uk/news/royal/1755847/King-Charles-paganism-Green-Man-coronation-invite>.
96 'Roles to be performed' at <https://www.royal.uk/news-and-activity/2023-04-27/roles-to-be-performed-at-the-coronation-service-at-westminster-abbey>.
97 '50 Facts about the Queen's Coronation' at <https://www.royal.uk/50-facts-about-queens-coronation-0>; 'The Coronation Invitation'.
98 'The Anointing Screen'.
99 'Historic chairs to be reused'; 'Historic Coronation Vestments'.
100 'A first glimpse'.

a charity after the service.[101] Various other charities were also mentioned as partners in the organisation of the coronation.[102]

As for diversity, it was visible in the guest list, which was composed in part of deserving members of the public.[103] Insisting on meritocracy more than his predecessors had, Charles did not invite all the peers of the realm, and those who were invited were asked not to wear their distinctive robes. Instead of standing out as different from, and perhaps higher than, the rest of the crowd, they thus blended with them. Diversity was also seen in the number of women and non-white guests and participants in the service. Petty Officer Amy Taylor, for instance, was the first woman to carry the Jewelled Sword of Offering on such an occasion. In general, according to the Order of Service, the people presenting the regalia to the king were much more diverse in 2023 than they had been at the previous coronation, 'to reflect the diversity of the United Kingdom and its peoples'.[104]

New music had also been commissioned by the king with the goal of presenting 'a diverse and accessible musical programme'. This diverse programme included and gave space to the culture, language, and music of countries outside of England – whether these were part of the United Kingdom or the Commonwealth. Welsh was used – for the first time at a coronation – in Paul Mealor's *Coronation Kyrie*, sung by bass-baritone Sir Bryn Terfel and the Choir of Westminster Abbey. Later, the musical piece *Be Thou my Vision – Triptych for Orchestra* from Nigel Hess, Roderick Williams and Shirley J. Thompson responded musically to an Irish hymn. The tune *O Sing Praises* by Debbie Wiseman was performed by The

---

101 'Flowers at the Coronation Service'.
102 See for example the Eden Project involved in the Coronation Big Lunch. 'A royally good weekend!'
103 See 'British Empire Medal recipients' at <https://www.royal.uk/news-and-activity/2023-04-17/british-empire-medal-recipients-among-guests-at-the-coronation>; 'The Coronation Invitation'; 'The Congregation at Westminster Abbey for the Coronation Service' at <https://www.royal.uk/news-and-activity/2023-05-01/the-congregation-at-westminster-abbey-for-the-coronation-service>; Freedland 'The twilight king'.
104 'Roles to be performed'; 'The Coronation Order of Service' at 4. See also: 'The Coronation Service', 'The Gospel will then be read by the Bishop of London and Dean of His Majesty's Chapels Royal, the Rt Revd and Rt Hon Dame Sarah Mullally, marking the first active participation of female Church of England Bishops in a Coronation Service'.

Ascension Choir, the first gospel choir to sing at a coronation. Composer Tarik O'Regan, whose *Agnus Dei* was sung during the service, spoke of the influence of his Arab and Irish heritage, as well as that of Early Modern English composer Orlando Gibbons, on his composition. Finally, Iain Farrington's organ piece *Voices of the World* combined traditional tunes from the 'family of nations' that is the Commonwealth.[105] The importance of the Commonwealth was further emphasised by the design of the anointing screen, which was embroidered with the names of its fifty-six countries.[106] These fifty-six countries and their inhabitants are not of one faith and, although the coronation service was an Anglican one, King Charles recognised this diversity of faiths. Exiting the Abbey of Westminster at the end of the liturgy, he was 'greeted by five faith leaders, and Governors-General from the Realms'. This moment of recognition by the Head of the English Church is, according to the Order of Service, truly innovative: 'for the first time at a Coronation, The King prays publicly for grace to be "a blessing to all ... of every faith and belief"'.[107]

All these changes to the coronation, increasing its sustainability and diversity, were in line with Charles's well-known and long-standing interests. However, they were probably also made in response to expected criticism both about the expense of the celebration and about some of the values it promoted or displayed, which – as mentioned earlier – apparently did not feel relevant to a large portion of the contemporary British public. These changes did not alter the fundamental aims of the coronation: the event still showed the legitimacy, authority, and power of the king, and celebrated this king's nation. However, it attempted to communicate these meanings in ways that would accord more fully with the beliefs of its spectators. It was a modern Britain, rather than just an ancient one, that the coronation aimed to represent and celebrate. To the issue of faith, the palace responded by including in the liturgy representatives of diverse religions. It counteracted comments around waste by making the coronation smaller, less expensive, and more sustainable than it had been in 1953. To be in tune with modern beliefs around hierarchy and meritocracy, the palace presented a more 'popular', inclusive, history of Britain and modified the guest list. The most significant change was that relating to the function of the king. The

---

105 'New Music Commissions'.
106 'The Anointing Screen'.
107 'The Coronation Service'; 'The Coronation Order of Service' at 3.

coronation of Charles III communicated a very specific image of the king. Emphasis was put on his role of service.[108] The partnerships with diverse charities further reinforced this image: the king's 'power' was therefore no longer that of leading the nation in war and politics, but it was that of helping Britain, through his support of charities, through providing employment to those working for the coronation, and through raising his voice in favour of worthy causes – including the preservation of the country's nature.

The emphasis on change made by the royal discourse around the coronation seems in direct opposition with the emphasis on tradition discussed above. There is, therefore, a constant tension in royal communications between advocating for a new, modern coronation and setting this coronation within a long tradition. This tension likely arises from the difficulty of fitting an ancient ceremony to our modern times, while simultaneously maintaining what makes it important and – at least for some – necessary. Stripping the coronation of all its historical elements would remove much of its meaning, bringing its existence into question. It would also sever ties with previous monarchs, with the history of the nation, and therefore with what many people treasure about it: its historical significance and its historical spectacle. On the other hand, leaving it untouched might displease or make it irrelevant to a portion of the public who would fail to understand or agree with its historical meaning. It would also lose the opportunity to express King Charles's wishes and values. This tension was likely exacerbated by the knowledge that this service, and more generally the coronation weekend, would be watched by millions of people all over the world. It would be analysed in detail by a multitude of commentators and seen by many abroad as representing the United Kingdom. The choice of what to keep and what to replace in it was therefore crucial.

This choice between old and new seems to have ultimately favoured the old. While the changes made to the coronation were debated – some members of the aristocracy, for example, were interviewed about not

---

108 The idea of service was already important to Queen Elizabeth. See Danica Kirka 'King's pledge of service defines UK's modern monarchy' in *Associated Press* at <https://apnews.com/article/king-charles-iii-coronation-volunteers-service-cac7c3da4178a589a0e45b7e45bc8100>. The Order of Service began with an introduction describing the ceremony as 'centred around the liturgical theme of "Called to Serve" and The King's solemn vow and commitment to serve God, and the people of the nations and the realms'; 'The Coronation Service'.

having been invited – none of these changes were made to the core of the event.[109] Even Charles's unprecedented acknowledgement of other faiths did not alter the fact that the essential part of the service was of one faith, and he himself swore an oath to uphold the Church of England. The order of events, as well as the events themselves, remained close to what had been done in previous coronations. Changes were thus superficial rather than fundamental.[110] Moreover, some of the changes, while breaking with royal tradition, had the effect of making the coronation look more antiquated instead of more modern. For instance, the vestments worn by the king were not new: they had been made for the coronation of King George IV in 1821, King George V in 1911, King George VI in 1937, and Queen Elizabeth II in 1953.[111] Other items were re-used: the queen's crown (made for Queen Mary), the chairs on which the king and queen sat for much of the coronation (made for King George VI and for Queen Elizabeth II), and the gloves and belt (made for King George VI) worn by the king.[112] Usually, these items are made anew for each coronation. The gloves and belt are traditionally crafted and presented to the king by the Worshipful Company of Girdlers and by the Worshipful Company of Glovers, respectively. In this case, the companies adapted to the king's wishes and only re-presented (and at times helped conserve) these items.[113] By emphasising sustainability, Charles III modified the usual task of these corporations and thus moved away from tradition. However, this also meant that he and the queen were wearing and using a larger number of historical items than former monarchs had. This had the effect of visibly tying this coronation to previous ones and to the previous sovereigns whose items these were. By being more sustainable and 'modern', Charles and Camilla looked more traditional and 'historical'.

Historical traditions and new decisions were therefore combined, with the aim of expressing the meanings behind the coronation of Charles III. The mixed response to the coronation by the press and the public demonstrates that these meanings, if often understood, were not

---

109 See, for instance, Richard Eden and Iwan Stone 'One is not invited' in the *Mail Online* at <https://www.dailymail.co.uk/news/royals/article-12049103/One-not-invited-Not-grandchildren-Queen-Elizabeths-cousins-Coronation.html>.
110 Potts 'Why does the monarch need a coronation?'
111 'Historic Coronation Vestments'.
112 'Historic chairs to be reused'; 'Historic Coronation Vestments'.
113 'Historic Coronation Vestments'.

necessarily accepted or agreed upon by those receiving them. To some, the coronation was a powerful ritual and to others an empty spectacle. To some, it was a show of the power and glory of the United Kingdom and its monarchy, to others, a proof of its decay and misguidedness. To some, it was awe-inspiring, to others it was awful. It was too old or too modernised, not spectacular enough or too gaudy, too religious or not religious enough. The 2023 coronation shows the difficulty of tailoring a spectacle to its audience when this audience is divided on questions fundamental to the acceptance of what the spectacle communicates. The personal belief of spectators was thus essential in determining the efficacy of this spectacle. When the very fabric of the event is disputed, when the meanings that it wishes to communicate are divisive, it becomes extremely complicated to express such meanings in a convincing way. This coronation also demonstrates the significance of the connections between spectacle and meaning; changing one will undoubtedly alter the other. Attempts made to modify the spectacle of the coronation to please some of the audience thus ran the risk of rendering it meaningless. While the Palace tried, for instance, to bring the coronation in line with ideas around meritocracy, it could not fully embrace such ideas. An event stating that a man is chosen by God to rule is fundamentally not – and cannot be – about meritocracy. Other, more radical changes could have been made to the coronation, but they would have necessitated a more fundamental revaluation of its meanings and aims. On 6 May, traditional meanings mixed with some new expressions; yet, ultimately, the spectacle of the coronation remained, as it had to, rooted in the long history of royal events.

University of Fribourg

THE SEVEN SAGES OF SCOTLAND
The Scottish Storytelling Centre, Edinburgh, Saturday 22 July 2023

Sarah Carpenter

The Book of the Seven Sages of Rome seems on the face of it an unlikely text to interest those who work on medieval theatre. But this engaging performance raised a number of fascinating questions about the methods and purposes of theatrical presentation of medieval material to modern audiences. It also proved a stimulating demonstration of the inherent theatricality of expert storytelling and its ability to mediate complex points of view to live audiences.

The Middle English and Middle Scots versions of the work generally known as *The Seven Sages of Rome* have a profound temporal and geographical hinterland. The framed story collection derives from the East with versions of 100 or more tales included in Greek, Arabic, Hebrew, Latin, Persian, and Syriac re-tellings.[1] In the Middle Ages the work was translated and reworked in most of the languages of Europe, proving hugely popular. Its frame narrative tells the story of an Emperor, who on the death of his wife entrusts the education of his only son to seven Sages, away from the court. Some years later, the Emperor marries a second young wife who persuades him to bring the young man back to court where, when he rejects her advances, she falsely accuses him of rape and urges her husband to put him to death. This results in an extended storytelling contest: each day, one of the Sages tells a story, generally hinging on the untrustworthiness of women, that persuades the Emperor to doubt his wife and postpone the execution of his son; each night the Empress tells a counter tale that questions who and how one should believe, urging the young man's death. The situation is finally resolved when the son, who has remained silent throughout, finally tells a tale of his own that convinces the Emperor of his innocence, and the Empress is executed.

The blatant misogyny of many of the tales, along with the bare and undeveloped literary style of their re-tellings, have probably contributed to the lack of modern interest in the work. But this production, which

---

[1] Killis Campbell 'A Study of the Romance of the Seven Sages with Special Reference to the Middle English Versions' *PMLA 14:1* (1899) 1–107.

dovetails with a research project on the *Seven Sages* at the University of St Andrews, succeeded in developing a suggestive performance that engaged with the first, and looked beyond the second.[2] The project leaders who devised the event, Dr Jane Bonsall and Dr Caitlin Flynn, worked with the fifteenth-century Scots version of the *Seven Sages* included in the Asloan manuscript.[3] They approached the work as exploring 'pre-modern ideas of truth-telling, subjectivity, and the gendered interplay of power and vulnerability', while also aiming to convey how these ancient preoccupations, along with the uncomfortable scenarios outlined in the frame narrative and many of the tales, 'bear strange, even uncanny resemblance to our modern discourse'.[4] They designed a performance that invited its audience to recognise the imaginative complexity that the medieval form of a framed story collection could bring to intense and troubling questions of power, gender, and truth. At the same time, we were asked to consider these questions through the experiences and dilemmas current in contemporary society.

A key question was what performance, rather than written text, might bring to the communication of these ideas. The project leaders recruited a group of seven poets and storytellers, many of whom were also experienced performers of their own work. They shared with these performers a summary of the Asloan version of the work, selecting a reduced number of seven of the alternating tales, and assigning to each storyteller either the opening and closing frame narration or one, or occasionally two, of the tales. As their directors' notes show, they discussed with their cast what they hoped to bring out of the performance:

> How can we know the truth? What stories do we tell ourselves that shape who we believe, and what evidence we find convincing? ... This medieval narrative centres representations of sexual- and

---

[2] The performance was funded by the University of St Andrews' School of English via the Sloan Fund, which promotes Scots Language projects. It dovetails with an international project on the *Seven Sages* headed by Professor Bettina Bildhauer (St Andrews, School of Modern Languages) and Professor Dr Jutta Eming (Freie Universität Berlin).

[3] 'The Buke of the Sevyne Sagis' in *The Asloan Manuscript* edited W.A. Craigie *Scottish Text Society* 2 vols (Edinburgh: William Blackwood and Sons, 1923–1925) 2 1–88.

[4] Project leaders' notes for performers: 'Statement of Purpose'.

gender-based violence against vulnerable individuals. In response to this difficult story matter, this performance interrogates these representations and how narratives of culpability, blame, and innocence become crystallised in the popular imagination ... *The Seven Sages of Rome* is a narrative that both replicates and challenges popular (and contemporary) patterns of thinking about gendered power and abuse, and in our adaptive work, this performance attempts to highlight the longevity of those patterns, and to apply pressure to them. In practice, this means integrating reflection on interpretative instability into the telling of these tales, and dwelling on the way this narrative resists comfortable, easy 'truth'.[5]

Each performer/creator was then invited to develop a performance text from the story assigned to them. They were free to stick close to the original, simply finding expressive ways to perform it, or to adapt, or even entirely re-write the tale, casting it in modern form and addressing modern experiences.[6]

The staging of the performance was pared down, keeping it as openly and primarily a storytelling event rather than a dramatic embodiment of the text. The frame narrator and each tale-teller thus appeared on stage alone, addressing the audience directly and intimately, without props or costumes except for an occasional symbolic item. The frame narrator took centre stage, while tales told by the Sages began from stage right, and those by the Empress stage left. An empty chair represented the Emperor, and there was no attempt by the performers to embody the character of the teller – Sage, Empress, or Son. One performer was even assigned one tale from each side. Centre stage was a large pair of scales, and each teller concluded their tale by adding or removing weights from the scale pans.

The outline of aims shows the complexity of the task that the cast was set, with the multiplicity of material and the 'interpretative instability' they were asked to convey. One obvious challenge was to develop a performance that not only introduced an audience to the potentially problematic medieval material but deliberately engaged them with its

---

5   'Statement of Purpose'.
6   Some *METh* readers may remember the BBC television version of *The Canterbury Tales* (2003) that followed a strategy similar to this last option.

similarities to and differences from modern perspectives. This was a key foundation of the decision to encourage the performers to develop the tales in whatever way they chose. The resulting mix of modern and medieval tales, situations and attitudes the audience was presented with was compelling, if potentially somewhat disorienting.

Audience members with no knowledge of medieval traditions, or only the simplified images drawn from popular modern fantasy, might perhaps be at a certain disadvantage here. Given the nature of the original material, it would be easy for them to dismiss the medieval tales and the attitudes conveyed in them as simplistic if not offensive. Medievalists, although relatively few are likely to be familiar with the original work itself, are at least more likely to recognise the complex cultural and literary environment from which the original tales emerged. The production recognised this challenge, working to support the audience towards understanding the many-layered and open debate between medieval and modern. The ground was set by an introduction from the directors. They outlined the frame narrative and the popular history of the Seven Sages, to provide a stabilising sense of the overall scenario. Just as importantly, they pointed out how the original storytelling contest might be best understood as concerned with belief and persuasion, and the difficulty of perceiving the truth from the words of others. The spectators were invited to consider these issues, rather than focusing only on the overt attitudes to gender and sexual violence that they were likely to perceive (and quite possibly reject) in the original tales.

This introduction was richly reinforced by the opening narrator who invited us from the start to recognise the fictionality of the frame tale itself, and how we might best understand it. Harry Josephine Giles composed a subtle and absorbing introduction that not only set the scenario but opened up both the predicament of the Emperor and the role of the audience itself by a crucial shift of perspective. Having reported the original work's account of the Empress's false rape claim against the innocent son, the performer then renounced the role of omniscient narrator, reminding us that in truth only the two people in the Empress's bedroom at the time could have known what had happened. In an engaging, wise, and compassionately calm delivery, we were encouraged – since none of us had been present – to listen to the stories as critically engaged interpreters, evaluating what truths or advice they might contain, aware of the possible manipulations and biases of tellers, and even of our own prejudices and values. While this was a significant change from the reader-positioning of the original, it enabled a more involved and interpretative approach from the audience to both the medieval and the modern material.

Even with this support to be alert to nuance, it was not always easy to reflect on the implications of the tales – vivid and engaging as many of them were. The delivery of the opening guidance, and indeed of the tales themselves, did not leave much time to reflect beyond the immediate pleasure of their performance. It could sometimes be hard to remember or to work out which tales were supporting which side, or to figure out quite what light either the medieval or the modern stories might throw on the inter-relations of power and gender, or on the problems of trust and truth-telling. Nonetheless, this 'making strange' of the whole work certainly provoked us to recognise more fully the complexity of the problems raised, and to see how medieval and modern preoccupations might intertwine.

The juxtaposition of medieval and modern, original and re-written stories was another key feature. Both kinds of tale tended to be somewhat enigmatic in their relation to the frame situation and both usually presented problems of interpretation, though in rather different ways. Tales where performers had chosen to stick fairly closely to the original generally offered a form recognisable to medievalists: a fabular narrative that concludes with a 'moral' proposing an identification of the characters and action with the cast of the frame narrative, in a way that demonstrated advice to the Emperor. Shona Cowie's vividly enacted opening tale from the Empress thus identified the powerful marauding boar with the Emperor, while the poor herdsman who protects himself by lulling the boar with fruit before slaughtering it represents the Sages who flatter him with fair words. This might seem a comfortingly straightforward moral, if not a wholly expected interpretation – the emotional sympathies of the tale might well be thought to lie more with the poor herdsman than the aggressive boar. But medievalists familiar with the form are likely to have recognised the often partial nature of this type of medieval moralising, and the encouragement by scholars and poets to pursue differing possible levels of interpretation and multiple truths. Non-medievalists in the audience, who probably knew nothing of this tradition, had nonetheless been alerted to consider how interpretation may be inflected to suit the teller's purposes.

The more fully re-imagined tales, set in contemporary society, rarely presented such explicit morals for our consideration. They offered the audience much more immediately contemporary situations and language, drawing us in especially with comedy and in-references. There were some ingenious parallels to the more unfamiliar medieval settings – such as Dorothy Lawrenson's replacing of the original's (cheating) dream-prognosticators, claiming to discover gold beneath the gates of Rome, with (scam) metal-detectorists claiming to find a treasure trove of USB-sticks full of bitcoin in a popular Fringe festival venue. But the most thought-provoking of the modern re-tellings tended to offer parallels not to the action of the original tales, but to the wider problems that they explored – problems of assessing culpability, of gendered power, and of judgement, in twenty-first-century society. Laura Cameron-Lewis's performance of social media exchanges, and their distorting and judgemental effects, may not have had an obvious connection to the tale of Merlin and the manipulative advisers in 'The emprys tale of the sevyne sagis that dissauit the empriour be redyng of dremes' that it springboarded from. But it was obviously relevant to the issues around the coercive and misogynistic public judgement of women's behaviour raised both in the frame narrative and in many of the tales. Even if at times confusing, the mixture of tales was certainly successful in trailing a complex web of medieval and contemporary ideas – and technologies – around judgement and trust, power and gender.

But perhaps one of the most eye-opening aspects of the evening was the patent theatricality of the storytelling. Far from being a simple narration of tales, there were a number of compelling performances that included skilful physical evocation of scenarios, vividly expressive voices and accents, with direct address and engagement of the audience in events, emotions, and judgements. There was a poised, sometimes almost instantaneous, movement between funny, angry, poignant, and tragic moods. While engrossing for the audience, this also, oddly, enabled us to keep a kind of distance from the material, rather than being swept up into a single point of view. One might have expected that storytellers would act as omniscient narrators, reporting both the facts of the tale and the attitudes conveyed. But far from confining our perspective, the best tellers were able to convey through performance complex and often conflicting attitudes to their material, inviting us to question interpretation of the tales as the project had hoped.

The Sage's tale of the Faithful Hound was a particularly good example of how this worked in practice. In this story, a knight goes to joust leaving his new baby in its cradle in the care of his faithful greyhound. While he is gone, a snake enters the chamber and attacks the infant; the dog leaps to its defence, and in the struggle the cradle upends over the baby, who is safely hidden until the dog succeeds in tearing the snake to pieces. When the nursemaid and mother return they see no baby, but an overturned cradle and a dog covered in blood. The knight enters to find his wife screaming in distress and crying that the dog has killed their son, on which he draws his sword and kills his hound. Only then do they find the baby unharmed beneath the cradle. The knight swears he will never again take joy in arms, but will go on pilgrimage to the Holy Land, forever regretting that he drew his sword on his wife's word.

Read on the page of a manuscript, the tone of this tale seems one of unrelieved poignant misfortune, although the bare style of the narration of events does not encourage the emotive engagement of, for example, affective meditation. But in performance, Shona Cowie brought to life an emotionally moving sense of the tale's pathos, through expressive narration. Surprisingly, at the same time her acrobatically solo mimed action of what was happening invited laughter at the lurid events. This created for us in the audience a far more varied and complex response, drawing us in to the tragedy of the tale while simultaneously giving us a comic distance from its fictional scenario. All our reactions were intensified by the direct acknowledgement of and engagement with the audience and their surroundings, as is open to a live performer. We were thus challenged to see through multiple perspectives: the enclosed world of a long-ago fictional story and the physical space of our own here-and-now, the intense sorrow of supposed loss and terrible misunderstanding, and the laughter that asserts our common delight and gives us distance to reflect.

This complexity of viewpoint, made possible in performance, continued into the moral drawn from the tale. In the manuscript, the Sage-teller points out the sorrow that came to the knight for trusting his wife's word, and then explains to the Emperor how much more mischief 'sall cum to ye | Gif þat þou garris [*causes*] þi awne sone de [*die*] | for wordis of a fals woman'.⁷ In interpreting the tale to reflect the Emperor's situation, the Sage shifts its emphasis, to focus on the falsity of women. Although the distraught wife in the tale is not directly identified with the Empress, for a modern audience this moral, articulated in live performance, sits uneasily with the tale they have just heard. But

---

7   *Asloan Manuscript 2* 16 (lines 499–501).

without either changing or commenting on the words of the moral, the storyteller was able to acknowledge and convey that unease. The ironic tone in which we/the Emperor were advised not to trust 'a fals woman' challenged us to recognise a space between the Sage's moral and our own understanding of what might be taken from the tale. It brought home, yet again, the layers of meaning that performers can add to any text they deliver.

The performance as a whole effectively pursued its aim to alert us to difficulties of the interpretation of tales, to question judgements about who and what we should believe, and to point to problems concerning gender and power in both medieval and contemporary society. It did not, and did not try to, propose or invite any clear resolution either to the difficult questions and problems raised in the individual tales and the frame narrative, or to the events of the frame story itself. This clearly contrasts with the medieval original, which is decisively wrapped up in a reconciliation between the Emperor and his son, and execution of the Empress.[8] Although these problematic events were briefly touched on by the Frame Narrator, the sensitive and nuanced closing commentary focused primarily on assuring us that continued reflection, rather than conclusion, was the most positive response – both to the original work and to the performance. Given that a central emphasis of the project was to question our grounds for decisive judgements and to encourage us to experience the dangerously uncertain difficulties of interpretation, the decision not to address directly the outcome of the original text, but to maintain the performance in an unresolved space, seemed both necessary and inevitable.

It might be worth noting, however, the final tale told by the Son – which, as we had been told, though did not see, is ultimately decisive in persuading the Emperor. This tale, performed with engaging clarity and authority by Donald Smith, stuck close to the original. Interestingly, given the nature of the preceding tale-contest, it did not focus on whether the Empress (or women), or the Sages (or political/male advisers) should be most trusted. Instead, the tale took a familiar romance pattern: on a sea voyage, a rich man angrily casts overboard his young son who has

---

[8] The original conclusion also contains an episode, even more troubling to modern audiences, by which the Empress's guilt is decisively established not by challenging her evidence against the son but by uncovering a young man dressed as a woman among her attendant maids, thus 'proving' her promiscuity.

(correctly) interpreted the song of a nightingale to mean that his parents will one day kneel before him and wash his feet. After many adventures, including rescue, enslavement, and further interpretation of birdsong, leading to his marriage to the King's daughter, the son inherits the throne and rules wisely. Longing to see his mother again he visits his parents and reveals his identity after the predicted foot-washing scene. Begged for his forgiveness, 'he þaim rasit full tenderly' saying that it was folly for man to go against what God has willed.

This concluding tale thus steps away from the contested issues of human judgement that have played through the adversarial exchange of stories. Instead, it moves into romance mode to assert the over-riding acceptance of providence. Ending the performance with this tale rather than with the original's condemnation of the Empress seemed to support the implicit resolution of the performance as a whole. The audience, having been taken through the complicated and challenging interpretations of moral fables, were led into the space of imaginative fiction and the possibility of positive endings.

In all, this project posed some telling questions, not only about a problematic medieval text and how it might be encountered and understood today, but also about the theatrical power of performed storytelling to engage audiences in complex meaning. Live performance transformed the relatively bare texts of the original into a multi-layered and thought-provoking entertainment. It perhaps even threw a revealing light on the purpose of the regular payments recorded in the 1490s Scottish *Treasurer's Accounts* of James IV, which rewarded 'þe tale tellaris', Wallass, Widderspune, and Wattschod 'þat tald talis to þe king'.

University of Edinburgh

EDITORIAL BOARD (2023)

Executive Editor:
    Meg Twycross (Lancaster University)
General Editors:
    Sarah Carpenter (University of Edinburgh)
    Elisabeth Dutton (Université de Fribourg)
    Gordon Kipling (UCLA)
Advisory Board:
    Philip Butterworth (University of Leeds)
    Lucy Deacon (University of Edinburgh)
    Garrett Epp (University of Alberta, Université Catholique de Lille)
    Richard Hillman (Université de Tours)
    Pamela M. King (University of Glasgow)
    Sally-Beth MacLean (University of Toronto)
    James McBain (Green Templeton College, Oxford)
    John J. McGavin (University of Southampton)
    John McKinnell (University of Durham)
    Peter Meredith (University of Leeds)
    Tom Pettitt (University of Southern Denmark, Odense)
    Matthew Sergi (University of Toronto)
    Greg Walker (University of Edinburgh)
Latin Consultant:
    Alison Samuels (Oxford)
Subscriptions Editor:
    Clare Egan (Lancaster University)

SUBMISSION OF ARTICLES

Contributions for consideration should be sent to one of the editors:

Meg Twycross, Department of English and Creative Writing, Lancaster University, LANCASTER LA1 4YD, United Kingdom.
E-mail: <m.twycross@lancaster.ac.uk>

Sarah Carpenter, English Literature, School of Literatures, Languages and Cultures, University of Edinburgh, 50 George Square, EDINBURGH EH8 9LH, United Kingdom.
E-mail: <sarah.carpenter@ed.ac.uk>

Elisabeth Dutton, English Department, University of Fribourg, Ave. Europe 20, CH1700 FRIBOURG, Switzerland.
E-mail: <elisabeth.dutton@unifr.ch>

Articles should usually be sent as e-mail attachments, preferably in a recent version of Word. See website for further information: <http://www.medievalenglishtheatre.co.uk/submit.html>

Contributors are asked to follow the *METh* house-style (see website: address above). The language of the publication is usually English, and translations should be supplied for quotations from all other languages, including French and Latin.

Printed in the United States
by Baker & Taylor Publisher Services